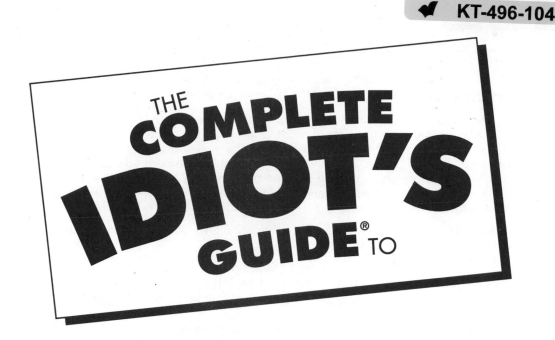

THE COMPLETE IDIOT'S GUIDE® TO

Playing Piano

Second Edition

by Brad Hill

ALPHA

A member of Penguin Group (USA) Inc.

International Standard Book Number: 0-02-864155-8
Library of Congress Catalog Card Number: 2001092310.

05 04   8 7 6

Interpretation of the printing code: The rightmost number of the first series of numbers is the year of the book's printing; the rightmost number of the second series of numbers is the number of the book's printing. For example, a printing code of 02-1 shows that the first printing occurred in 2002.

Printed in the United States of America

Publisher
Marie Butler-Knight

Product Manager
Phil Kitchel

Managing Editor
Jennifer Chisholm

Senior Acquisitions Editor
Renee Wilmeth

Development Editor
Joan D. Paterson

Production Editor
Billy Fields

Copy Editor
Cari Luna

Illustrator
Jody P. Schaeffer

Cover Designers
Mike Freeland
Kevin Spear

Book Designers
Scott Cook and Amy Adams of DesignLab

Layout/Proofreading
Angela Calvert
Mary Hunt
Kimberly Tucker

Contents at a Glance

Appendixes

Contents

Introduction

They say the first time is the best. I vividly remember my first childhood explorations of the piano: pressing the keys, combining notes, and on the second day, playing the complete piano sonatas of Beethoven. (Maybe it was the third day.)

My first piano experiments were unsupervised and without instruction. I can still recall the excitement of creating those pure piano tones by pressing the keys, and the thrill of putting notes together by playing two keys at once. But a time came when free experiments had to give way to organized learning or I would still be pressing keys at random today. I gradually learned how music works in general and how the piano works in particular. This book leads you along the same path and gives you a few gratuitous laughs along the way.

How to Use This Book

Learning any instrument requires a combination of *knowledge* and *practice*. Music knowledge is called *theory*, which sounds scientific, but in fact it's just notes, keys, scales, sharps, flats, and all the other elements that make music work. Music knowledge is all the technical stuff of music, just as grammar is the technical stuff of language. Practice, on the other hand, is the hands-on aspect of learning music. Music theory gives you something to practice, and the more you practice the more theory you're ready to learn.

This book is for beginners, and I don't assume that you know the first thing about the piano, keyboards, or reading music. Its parts and chapters feed you theory bit by bit, and give you plenty of exercises and easy pieces to practice. With a little effort, you can learn to:

➤ Understand and play written music notes

➤ Perform simple pieces smoothly and evenly

➤ Play a song from a lead sheet, music chart, or "fake book"

➤ Understand time signatures, key signatures, and scales

➤ Bungee jump off the Eiffel Tower (actually, I'll cover that in the third edition)

I've organized this book into big parts that, ingeniously, are called "parts." Here's what they cover:

Part 1, "Meeting Your Instrument," gets you started with some good reasons for choosing the piano (or electronic keyboard) as your instrument, plus some very basic knowledge about how pianos and keyboards work. This part teaches you a bit about the history of the grand old instrument, and if you've ever wondered what in the world a "harpsichord" is, this is where you find the answer. (If you have remained blissfully unencumbered by such weighty questions, all the more power to you.)

Part 2, "Give Yourself a Hand," shows you the notes played by the right hand. Along the way you learn how those notes appear in sheet music. While you're learning these notes, I also fill you in on certain *types* of notes, and how to count while playing music. (I assume you already know how to count when not playing music.)

Part 3, "Give Yourself Another Hand," broadens your musical horizons by adding the left-hand notes to the big picture. This is exciting stuff, but also challenging, and I give you several ways of practicing the coordination of two-handed playing. Furthermore, chords enter the picture in this part, as you begin to learn all kinds of ways for your left hand to make the right-hand melody sound good.

Part 4, "Master Class," deepens your understanding of how music is written, performed, and practiced. The chapters include more advanced details of music notation, how to use the piano pedals, tips for power practicing, how to "fake" a song arrangement, and advice about what piano music is worth learning and listening to. Part 4 even has a chapter on electronic home music studios.

Part 5, "Bringing It Home: Buying an Instrument," runs down the ins and outs, crucial questions, prices, and options when purchasing a piano or digital keyboard. An extra chapter explains how to maintain and repair a piano in your home.

Extras

A quick riffle through these pages reveals many shaded boxes containing assorted facts, anecdotes, quotes, and word definitions. I love these little boxes, and stuffed in as many as I could. Then I assigned clever (that's a matter of opinion) names to them so you could identify each box at a glance. This is what the shaded boxes boil down to:

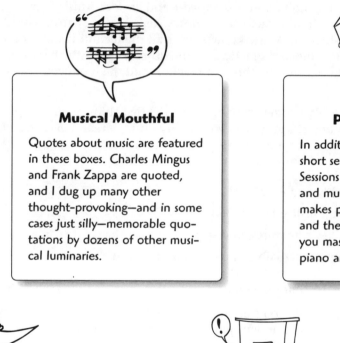

Musical Mouthful

Quotes about music are featured in these boxes. Charles Mingus and Frank Zappa are quoted, and I dug up many other thought-provoking—and in some cases just silly—memorable quotations by dozens of other musical luminaries.

Practice Sessions

In addition to the shaded boxes, short sections called Practice Sessions feature instructional text and music examples. Practice makes perfect, as the saying goes, and the Practice Sessions help you master the basic skills of piano and keyboard playing.

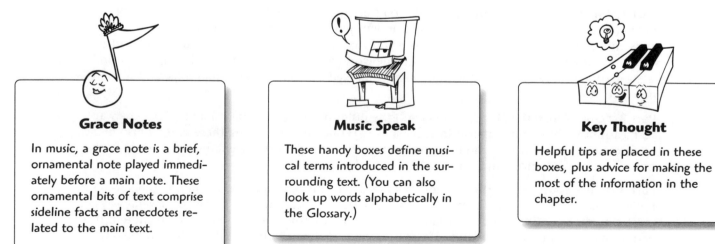

Grace Notes

In music, a grace note is a brief, ornamental note played immediately before a main note. These ornamental bits of text comprise sideline facts and anecdotes related to the main text.

Music Speak

These handy boxes define musical terms introduced in the surrounding text. (You can also look up words alphabetically in the Glossary.)

Key Thought

Helpful tips are placed in these boxes, plus advice for making the most of the information in the chapter.

Acknowledgments

Every book represents a collaboration of author and editor. Usually, the editors are unsung partners. You'll be happy to know I'm not going to break into song. (I have no trouble playing the piano in public, but singing is, for me, an activity that should be strictly limited to the shower.)

My thanks to Renee Wilmeth, who shepherded this project, and Joan Paterson, who read every word. (Joan may never fully recover.) And my gratitude goes to the truly unsung heroes of any book—the copy editors, proofreaders, and production experts who turn my typo-ridden text into published pages.

Trademarks

All terms mentioned in this book that are known to be or are suspected of being trademarks or service marks have been appropriately capitalized. Alpha Books and Penguin Group (USA) Inc. cannot attest to the accuracy of this information. Use of a term in this book should not be regarded as affecting the validity of any trademark or service mark.

Part 1
Meeting Your Instrument

Before beginning your study of the piano, you should know what you're getting into. Fortunately, you're getting into a long and glorious tradition of great music played on a noble instrument. Even if you aspire to play jazz standards or pound out Billy Joel tunes, you are participating in this enduring tradition.

The chapters in this part describe the history of pianos, the hammers and strings that actually produce sound, how the keyboard is designed, how to sit with good playing posture, and what the pedals do. Part 1 serves as a kind of overture to the next three parts, which are all about learning notes and playing pieces.

Why Play the Piano?

In This Chapter

➤ The unique qualities of the piano sound

➤ Dynamic range and pitch range of the piano

➤ Connecting music with inner creativity

➤ Why keyboard instruments are great for learning music

If you are reading this page (and something tells me you are), you may have recently decided to start playing the piano. You may have even bought a piano for that very purpose.

On the other hand it's possible that, although the idea of playing the piano may have crossed your mind, you haven't made any firm decision or acquired an instrument. Some doubts and hesitations may stick in your mind. Why not take up the Irish concertina instead, or the Bulgarian bagpipe? Or, more seriously, guitar or bass?

No instrument is better than another. I believe it is the music that has grandeur, nobility, and transcendence, and I cast a friendly eye over all its instruments. Still, as egalitarian as I am, the piano has some unique features that make it a wonderful choice for someone just learning about music. This chapter describes the characteristics of the piano and the unique values of learning music. In this chapter, I explain why the piano has so often been, since its invention, the home instrument of choice for adults and kids.

Soothing the Soul

One of the great delights of the piano is so obvious, it's easy to overlook. I'm talking about the sheer sound of the instrument. The tone of a piano strikes a perfect balance between different types of sonority. That is to say, the piano tone isn't too loud or too soft, too heavy or too light, too sharp or too blunted—or too much of anything that makes for tedious listening over a long period.

For many years I was a music producer, working primarily with electronic instruments that were able to mimic *acoustic* instruments. Part of my work involved creating new sounds within these digital instruments, and evaluating the sound creations of other people. The ideal was to create a tone that could be played effectively on an electronic keyboard, and that was pleasing to the ear through the whole course of a song. Many times during the labors of sound creation, I would wonder why I could never come close to formulating something as effective as the natural sound of a piano. During those times it seemed like the piano represented the perfect sound, never to be equaled even by the wonders of technology.

What makes the sound of a piano so great? Several factors go into the beauty and effectiveness of the piano tone, and most of the time we take them for granted. Here's what's really going on when we listen to piano music, and why our ears like it so much:

Music Speak

Acoustic instruments is a fancy way of referring to musical instruments that don't get plugged in. Every instrument in the orchestra is an acoustic instrument. Electronic guitars and keyboards, by contrast, require electrical power to make a sound.

➤ Pianos have incredible *dynamic* range. The dynamic range of an instrument is the difference in volume between its softest and loudest tones. Pianos can be played with remarkable softness, though it takes some practice to master the art of playing quietly. At the other end of the scale, pianos make quite a racket when played forcefully with both hands. This wide dynamic range makes the piano capable of great musical drama and excitement, as well as intimacy and peacefulness. Thanks to its tremendous dynamic range, the piano is an instrument of many moods.

➤ Pianos have the biggest *pitch* range in the music biz. What is a pitch range? No, it's not a big field for baseball hurlers to practice their pitching skills. An instrument's pitch range is defined by the lowest and highest notes it can play. With some instruments, the pitch range depends on the player—like the expert trumpeter who can squeeze out higher notes than other trumpeters. With the piano, the range is defined by the instrument's eighty-eight keys, and eighty-eight notes is a mighty pitch range. The piano can growl ferociously in the nether regions of its low range, while simultaneously tinkling ethereally among its highest keys.

Music Speak

Dynamics refer to the loudness of sound and music. Pianists talk about the dynamics of a piece, meaning that some passages are played loudly, and others softly. **Dynamic range** indicates the limits of loudness and softness contained in a piece, or capable of being played by an instrument. The piano has one of the largest dynamic ranges of any instrument.

➤ Pianos have an inexpressible expressiveness. (If that's not a confusing phrase, I don't know what is.) By that I mean the piano's tone is capable of great poetry, musical articulation, and emotional expressiveness, but in a way that's hard to describe. Tone is sometimes described in colors, and the piano offers a greater palette of tonal colors than most other instruments, especially under the hands of an expert player.

In short, many people say that piano music soothes the soul. When that is the case, it is partly due to the great music composed for the instrument. But just as important, it is the beautiful, fluid, dynamic, and lyrical tone of the piano that causes its listeners to melt.

Creativity and Other Mysteries

It isn't scientific, but I have to come right out and say it: Playing music is good for your soul. Of course, playing any instrument brings out innate musicality that may be lurking in your inner being, as well as creative impulses that you may not be in touch with through other means.

It has been said that music is the universal language. Though there are cultural differences among various types of music around the globe, music is generally and immediately understood by anyone. Music has a unique ability to reach directly into some inner portion of our selves, bypassing our brains. That's why listening to music—really listening, not just experiencing the ubiquitous background of pop-flavored musical formulas we are subjected to constantly—can be a shortcut to our emotions. Perhaps music even shortcuts to our very souls.

If just listening to music can be a transcendent experience, imagine how playing music may add another dimension. Two aspects of playing music make it uniquely valuable:

➤ Playing music, even somebody else's composition, is inherently creative. You are *making* the music happen, even if you didn't compose the piece. That particular expression of the piece would never happen if it weren't for you. When you play a piece, you are contributing a portion of beauty to the world, even if you're the only person listening. Like baking a cookie recipe or following a needlework pattern, playing a music piece gets the creative impulses flowing.

➤ The physical part of playing an instrument has its own satisfactions and rewards. When you engage your fingers and arms in the process of making music, the emotional and physical aspects of musical art come together in an almost addictive synergy. This phenomenon is especially true when playing the piano, which is more of a whole-body experience than many other instruments. The tactile component of pressing the keys and working the pedals, combined with the emotional component of hearing music issue forth from your efforts, adds up to a very gratifying experience.

You may or may not dabble in making up your own pieces on the piano, or creating musical compositions using the recording features of digital keyboards. But creativity in music establishes itself long before actually composing a piece. From the first time you sit in front of your instrument and begin experimentally pressing keys, you are involved in exploring your inherent creativity.

Music Speak

Pitch refers to the highness or lowness of a note. Women can sing higher pitches than men. (Except for men who don't mind sounding ridiculous.) **Pitch range** is defined by the highest and lowest possible note of an instrument, a human voice, or a piece of music. Tubas have a lower pitch range than piccolos. (They also make more noise when dropped out a fourth-story window.) Pianos have a larger pitch range than any nonkeyboard instrument.

Musical Mouthful

"When I hear music, I fear no danger. I am invulnerable. I see no foe. I am related to the earliest times, and to the latest."
—Henry David Thoreau, *Journal*

The Uniqueness of All Keyboard Instruments

The piano has been the instrument of choice in homes since it was first invented. Because the piano is admittedly not the easiest instrument in the world to learn, the question naturally arises: Why has it been so popular for so many years?

The piano, as well as other keyboard instruments, is uniquely versatile. First of all, keyboard instruments are the only instruments played with both hands. That is to say, with both hands producing notes. Most other instruments are *held* with both hands, but can only produce one note at a time. As long as we're on the subject, let me take you on a brief survey of other instrument types—seeing their limitations fosters an appreciation of the piano's adaptability.

➤ **Bowed string instruments.** Violins, violas, cellos, and contrabasses fall into this group. These instruments work by dragging a long bow (strung with thin filaments traditionally made of hair) across tuned strings, while pressing the points of the strings against the intrument's neck to produce different notes. Bowed strings usually produce one note at a time, but can play certain combinations of two simultaneous notes. They are basically melody instruments.

➤ **Strummed string instruments.** Other instruments like the guitar, banjo, ukelele, mandolin, bass guitar, and twelve-string guitar have tuned strings that are plucked and strummed with one hand. The other hand presses the strings against the neck to produce notes and chords. Because all the strings can be played at once, unlike bowed instruments, strummed instruments are good for playing chords. They are both melody and harmony instruments.

➤ **Wind instruments.** There are two basic types of wind instruments: brasses and woodwinds. Brasses include trumpets, trombones (all seventy-six of them), tubas, and French horns. Woodwinds include flutes (even though modern flutes are made of metal), piccolos (ditto), oboes, English horns, and bassoons. All these instruments operate by blowing air through the mouth to produce tones, and manipulating mechanical valves on the instrument's body to get specific notes. Wind instruments are restricted to single notes, and are for melody only.

➤ **Percussion instruments.** Any instrument that is hit belongs in the percussion family. Here's a surprise for you: the piano is a percussion instrument, because its strings are hit by internal hammers when you press keys. Most percussion instruments are drums, blocks of wood, bells, chimes, rattles (which are actually shaken more than hit), and cymbals. With the exception of tympani (tunable drums) and tuned blocks of wood (xylophones), percussion instruments don't create notes. They are primarily rhythmic, not melodic or harmonic.

Music Speak

Melody is a sequence of notes strung together into a tune. Melodies are often the most important part of a musical piece, certainly in popular music.

Music Speak

Harmony is the musical underpinning of a piece. Harmony is usually created by clusters of notes played together, called chords, that provide a context for the melody. You may not notice the harmony when you hear a song, or sing it in your mind. But without the tune's harmony, the melody would be harder to learn and remember.

Unlike all these instrument classes, pianos and keyboards merge all three aspects of music—melody, harmony, and rhythm. While the complexity of playing many notes with all ten fingers makes the piano a challenging instrument, the payoff is being able to play the full range of music. A guitar can play chords, a trumpet can make a melody, and a drum set can keep the beat. But only a piano can put it all together in one instrument. When you think about it, pianos put an amazing amount of musical power into your hands.

The Great Teacher

Playing music should be, above all, fun and emotionally rewarding. If you're taking up music as an adult, you probably don't yearn to relive the music classes from grammar school, or ancient, unwelcome piano lessons from your youth. Nevertheless, I must point out that the piano (and other keyboard instruments) is an incredible tool for learning about music generally.

Music theory—the notes, scales, keys, and other technical details of how music works—is rather on the abstract side. Music theory is book learning compared to the softer, more artistic side of actually playing an instrument. But the piano brings music theory right under your hands, because the keyboard layout makes learning about notes, scales, and keys a graphic and tactile experience. The arrangement of black and white keys makes it easier to perceive the *design* of music theory, and its logic.

Many times over the years, I've observed that piano players have an advantage in understanding music theory, which players of single-note or percussion instruments lack. So as you're enjoying the pure pleasure of playing a great instrument, you can have the satisfaction of gaining a foundation in a new language—the language of music theory.

Following the Footsteps of Immortality

Because the piano is such a great instrument in so many ways, it makes sense that most of the great classical composers were (and are) attracted to it. This is perhaps the finest reason to play the piano—there is so much great music written for it! Much of the classical *repertoire* is rather difficult to play, requiring skills that take time to develop, but there is also beginning-level music composed by Bach, Beethoven, and other masters. (See Chapter 18, "Power Practicing" for some recommendations.)

Even if you're not after classical music, the piano is the repository for the greatest compositions in many music genres, from jazz to new age. You can even play transcriptions of operas or symphonies—normally performed by orchestras.

All in all, the piano is a uniquely grand and flexible instrument.

Music Speak

Rhythm refers to the beat of music, and its movement through time. Quick rhythms create music that makes you tap your foot quickly, and slow rhythms are more langorous, used in ballads and torch songs.

Music Speak

Repertoire is the collected works for any instrument. The piano repertoire includes great music from most of the composers in classical and jazz traditions, as well as the work of modern composers who are not so easily categorized.

Key Thought

A good deal of the "piano" music we hear today was actually written for earlier keyboard instruments, such as the harpsichord or clavichord. Bach couldn't write for the piano because the instrument did not yet exist!

The Least You Need to Know

➤ The piano has unique characteristics that make it satisfying to play, and an excellent tool for learning the rules of music.

➤ Playing music is as much a creative enterprise as composing music.

➤ Keyboard instruments are unique because they allow you to play all three elements of music: melody, harmony, and rhythm.

➤ Most of the great classical composers wrote music for the piano.

Chapter 2

Hammers and Strings

In This Chapter

➤ A brief history of pianos

➤ Learning the five basic parts of a piano

➤ Keys, hammers, and strings

➤ Understanding the difference between grands and uprights

➤ Why the piano has a heavy keyboard

This chapter deals with the basics of how pianos work, and reviews how they evolved to this point. Don't worry: I won't get into overly complicated descriptions of the inner workings of pianos, and you won't be able to build a piano after reading this chapter. But you will have a general understanding of why you hear a note when you press a key. And the "back story" of the remarkable instrument might spark your amazement at this incredible musical invention.

On the outside, digital keyboards look much more complicated than pianos. They usually have a host of switches and dials that make them intimidating right from the start. Compared to the button-intensive complexity of electronic keyboards, the traditional piano appears to be a piece of cake. ("Piece of cake" is a figure of speech. Do not attempt to eat your piano, spread icing on it, or serve it with birthday candles.)

From the outside, a piano looks like a big hunk of wood with a keyboard attached. Of course, if you glance inside a piano, the big-hunk-of-wood theory is shot to pieces, but you don't need to know too much about how the complex inner mechanism works. If you suffer from the dreaded compulsion to know all about everything, please refer to the book, *The Complete Idiot's Guide to Knowing All About Tedious Subjects Like the Inner Mechanism of Pianos*.

Music Speak

The **keyboard** refers to a traditional arrangement of black and white keys that play musical notes. The keyboard may be attached to an acoustic piano or an electronic instrument. Electronic keyboard instruments are usually referred to simply as "keyboards," confusing things somewhat. A keyboard (an electronic keyboard instrument) contains a keyboard (an arrangement of keys), just as a piano does.

In the meantime, I'll tell you the fundamentals you need to know about how pianos create their dulcet tones.

Like a Harp, But Different

The basic idea of piano design comes from the harp, a much older instrument. Harps existed in ancient Greece, long before the birth of Christ. At some point, an enterprising young go-getter named Fred (maybe) conceived of a peculiar notion. Why not build a harp whose strings are not plucked with the fingers, but are plucked by a mechanical device? From this vision was born the idea of a harp operated by keys—the first primitive *keyboard*. (The strings in modern pianos are not plucked at all, but struck by little hammers. I'll get to that in a minute.)

The idea of fitting a keyboard to a strung harp was envisioned and sketched possibly in the fourteenth century, but certainly by the fifteenth century. (Which, coincidentally, is the last time the Cubs won the World Series.) Following that initial breakthrough, an interesting story of instrument design, innovation, and invention proceeded over the next five centuries.

Before the precursor to the modern piano was invented in the early 1700s, three instruments were used to play keyboard music:

Music Speak

Harpsichords were the predecessors of the piano. They had a metallic, unvarying sound. They could not be played loudly and softly as a piano can, and their strings were plucked by mechanical quills, not struck with small felt hammers as a piano's strings are. Oddly, the key colors were reversed on harpsichords, with the broad flat keys (white on pianos) being black, and the shorter, narrow keys (black today) being white.

➤ **Harpsichords.** If you're a fan of Baroque music of the seventeenth and early eighteenth century—Bach and his stodgy contemporaries—you may have heard the sound of a *harpsichord*. The instrument is very metallic sounding, with no variation in loudness from one note to another. The unvarying loudness and clanky tone gives harpsichords an almost robotic sound, well suited to the complex and ornate style of Baroque composition. The early harpsichords were small in scale, containing only as many keys (notes available for playing) as the smallest of today's home electronic keyboards—the kind you find in department stores. Harpsichords shared the same basic design as a modern piano, in that you pressed black and white keys to make notes. The keys were simple levers that forced a so-called plectrum to raise up and pluck a string with a small quill.

➤ **Clavichords.** Clavichords, likewise popular in the pre-Baroque and Baroque periods (though not as prevalent as harpsichords), operated a little differently. Like harpsichords, clavichords had standard keyboard arrangements, but the strings were struck, not plucked. Clavichords were very soft instruments, and you couldn't make them any louder no matter how hard you slammed down the keys. Their softness made clavichords inappropriate as performance instruments, and they were used primarily in the home for playing simple pieces, like heavy metal songs.

➤ **Organs.** Large and small organs have been around for centuries, primarily in churches where they accompany liturgical music. Organs do not operate on the harp principle, so they don't fit the model of harpsichords and clavichords and the instrument is not a precursor to the piano. Old organ music is not played on modern pianos as Baroque harpsichord compositions are. Still, organs are keyboard instruments.

Key Thought

If you want to hear Baroque music played on its most authentic instrument, the harpsichord, look up the recordings of Wanda Lendowski. Lendowski was this century's greatest performer of Baroque music on its original keyboard instrument, and the best-known harpsichordist of the modern era.

Early in the eighteenth century, something important happened. The first Starbucks opened in Venice. Besides that landmark event, a man named Christofori is credited with inventing and building the first piano. (You sometimes see Christofori's name spelled differently, but it should never be spelled "Schwartz.") Christofori's new instrument was called a *pianoforte*, which in Italian combines the words for soft (piano) and loud or strong (forte). The strange name, "softloud," emphasized the big difference between Christofori's invention and harpsichords: the pianoforte could play softly, loudly, and with many shades of volume in between. For a world accustomed to the unvarying volume of the harpsichord, the pianoforte was revolutionary.

Christofori accomplished his breakthrough with two advancements in keyboard design over harpsichords. First, the strings were struck by small hammers, not plucked by quills. The second innovation, which made the first innovation work, was (and still is) called an "escapement mechanism." The escapement mechanism caused the hammer to rebound off the string immediately after hitting it, getting the hammer out of the way and allowing the string to vibrate freely. These two developments distinguished pianofortes from both harpsichords and clavichords, which had a far more primitive and unworkable hammer action.

Music Speak

The first pianos were called **pianofortes**, which in Italian means "softloud." Pianofortes were the first keyboard instrument whose volume (loudness) could be altered by playing the keys more or less forcefully.

Christofori produced about twenty of his pianofortes, but they were not a big hit at first. The now-legendary instrument inventor went back to building harpsichords. But that didn't spell the end of the pianoforte by a long shot. New builders proliferated in Europe, then America. Composers (Haydn, Clementi, and Mozart in particular) wrote music especially for the new instrument. And the piano underwent refinements that improved its range, expressiveness, and power.

In modern times, piano-building in the European tradition has been continued by makers such as Steinway, Bosendorfer, and Baldwin. These companies have been somewhat affected by industrial-age factory methods and automated procedures, but still maintain an ethic that hand-crafting of important parts is essential. Japan has gotten into the act with high-quality pianos built largely by machines. Companies like Yamaha and Kawai have established reputations for their excellent instruments, whose strong points tend to be consistency and playability.

Parts of the Piano

Pianos consist of five basic parts:

➤ **Keys**, which you press to make notes

➤ **Hammers**, which hit the strings

➤ **Strings**, which vibrate when struck by the hammers

➤ The **soundboard**, which amplifies the sound of strings vibrating

➤ The **pedal mechanism**, which enables you to sustain or soften the sound

This section explains each of the five essential parts, boiled down to the basics you need to know for a general understanding.

Keys to the Piano

Piano *keys* are the things you push down to make sounds. As I explain in the previous section, they are arranged into a keyboard, which is identical among all pianos (and digital keyboards, too). The keys act as a sort of interface between you and the sound-producing mechanism of the piano.

Piano keys are actually levers. When you press one, a hammer smacks some strings. (Keep reading to learn more about hammers and strings.) However, a piano key is not as simple a lever as you may be imagining. Pressing it starts a series of small reactions in process, using a number of smaller levers, springs, and even a strip of leather. The series of actions that takes place when you press a piano key resembles a Rube Goldberg device that requires nineteen steps to get from here to there. The result is that a hammer hits a string, but a multitude of moving parts contributes to the effort. The entire mechanism, including the key, the intermediate moving parts, and the string-smacking hammer, is called the piano's *action*.

The piano action is the most complex and delicately calibrated part of the instrument. Some of the parts are fragile, and warp, crack, or break more easily than other parts of the piano construction. Piano tuners must know how the action works in order to make adjustments that affect how good the piano sounds and how easily it plays. When a note sticks, it's a problem with the action—one of its parts may be jammed or broken. If some keys seem harder to push down than others, the action needs to be regulated and evened.

Key Thought

None of the original pianofortes exist today, at least in playable condition. However, some instrument builders have recreated very early pianos, and some historically enthused performers have recorded eighteenth-century repertoire on those instruments.

Music Speak

The **action** of a piano is the entire mechanism that starts with pressing a **key** and ends with a hammer hitting the strings. Included in the piano action are many finely crafted wood, plastic, metal, and leather parts that work together, giving the piano its characteristic "feel" and sound. Piano technicians can remove the entire action from the piano case to adjust its parts.

Why is the piano action so complex? It didn't start out to be so complicated, but pianos didn't start out sounding as good as they do today, nor did they have such a smoothly responsive feel up and down the keyboard range. Imagine the simplest possible lever mechanism connecting the keys with the hammers that hit the strings. You would push the key down, forcing a hammer up against the strings. If you held the key down, the hammer would continue pressing against the string, stopping it from vibrating. Such a simple mechanism wouldn't work at all, so the first thing a piano action needs is an escape mechanism that lets the hammer rebound off the strings immediately, letting the strings vibrate freely. Other aspects of the action's complexity enable the player to have great control over the piano's loudness and softness, and maximize the speed and evenness with which the instrument can be played.

Hammering Home the Sound

At the opposite end of the piano action from the strings are the *hammers.* Hammers actually hit the strings and cause them to vibrate, creating the piano sound. Now, if you're picturing construction hammers in your mind, and imagining them slamming metallically against delicate piano strings, you may wonder why it doesn't sound terrible. In fact, piano hammers are fairly diminutive little strikers whose force is further minimized by a covering of felt. Each hammer is a small device consisting of a wood or plastic shaft topped with a felt-covered striker. If the felt were missing, leaving bare wood or plastic, the sound of the piano would be changed drastically—for the worse. Uncovered wood hammers would make a piano sound unbearably clangy and harsh.

Music Speak

Piano **hammers** are the last parts of the piano action, and perform the impactful assignment of striking the strings. When a hammer hits the piano strings, it immediately and automatically rebounds, letting the strings vibrate, which causes the piano to sound. Hammers are covered with felt—the perfect material for producing the sound of piano notes.

If you've ever seen a hammered dulcimer (a folk music instrument), you can understand piano hammers perfectly. Hammered dulcimer players hold a leather- or felt-covered hammer in each hand, using them to hit strings stretched over a soundboard. With a piano, you don't hold the hammers directly, but manipulate them by pressing the keys.

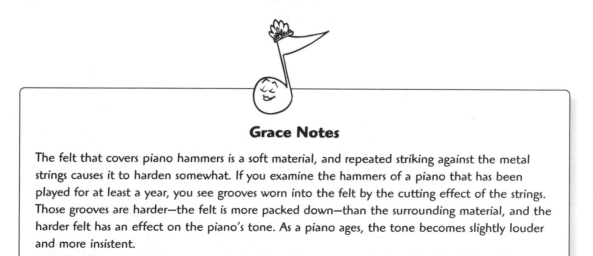

Grace Notes

The felt that covers piano hammers is a soft material, and repeated striking against the metal strings causes it to harden somewhat. If you examine the hammers of a piano that has been played for at least a year, you see grooves worn into the felt by the cutting effect of the strings. Those grooves are harder—the felt is more packed down—than the surrounding material, and the harder felt has an effect on the piano's tone. As a piano ages, the tone becomes slightly louder and more insistent.

V-V-Vibrating Strings

The whole point of the complicated piano action, which you use by pressing down keys, is to get those piano *strings* vibrating. The strings are attached to a metal frame, like a harp (in fact, the metal frame inside a piano is called the *harp*), positioned in relation to the action so the hammers can hit certain strings when keys are pressed.

One reason the piano sounds so rich and full is the number of strings it contains. You might suppose that each key causes a hammer to strike a single string, but in fact most piano notes are assigned three strings each. The hammer hits all three at once.

A basic fact about piano strings, and in fact vibrating strings in other instruments as well, is that thicker strings create lower notes. This is because thicker strings vibrate more slowly than thin strings, and it's a law of acoustics that slow vibrations create lower tones than fast vibrations. Accordingly, the low notes of a piano have thicker strings than the middle and upper notes. Because of the thickness, there is no room for three strings per note, so the lower piano notes are reduced to two strings, then just one string for the very lowest notes.

Piano strings are attached to the harp using pins. Pins are metal screws driven into a block of wood, and they can be tightened or loosened with a special piano-tuning tool. (The tool is called a tuning hammer, but you can forget I told you that.) Adjusting a pin causes a string to be more or less tautly strung on the harp, raising or lowering its note. Most notes must be tuned by adjusting the tension of three strings, by adjusting three pins.

Music Speak

Piano **strings** are thin metal cords stretched tautly around a frame called a **harp**. When struck by piano hammers, the strings vibrate, and it is the vibrating strings that create a piano's sound.

The All-Important Soundboard

Vibrating strings, by themselves, wouldn't be enough to make the piano into a musical instrument. At least, they wouldn't make it an instrument you could hear very easily. A string vibrating in the air barely makes enough noise to be heard without some sort of amplification. In acoustic instruments, amplification is created nonelectronically using wood. Violins and guitars employ wood to create a box over which the strings vibrate, making the sound more resonant and louder. Pianos use a crucial piece of crafted wood called the *soundboard*.

The soundboard is sometimes regarded as the most important part of a piano. In fact, the soundboard is no more important than the hammers, keys, or strings. But it is one of the most difficult parts to make. A soundboard's wood must be of a certain quality, and cured over time in a certain way. It must be of the proper thickness, and the entire soundboard is curved just slightly. The curvature, called the soundboard's crown, is crucial to amplifying the vibrating strings.

Music Speak

The **soundboard** is a large piece of wood placed just a couple of inches away from the strings inside a piano. When the strings are struck by hammers and caused to vibrate, the soundboard picks up the vibration and amplifies it to a volume that is easily heard.

The Solution to Bored Feet

Pianos are played with the fingers, but most pianos also have three pedals for the feet. (Some small pianos have only two pedals, leaving out the middle one.) Although the pedals' primary function is to taunt your feet while you're playing, they also have acoustic effects. Here's what the foot-teasers do:

➤ The right pedal is the *sustain pedal*, and it holds notes after you release the keys. Press any key, then push down the right pedal, and the note continues sounding if you lift the key up. This bit of wizardry works with any number of keys. If you want to really make a racket, use your palms to play every key while holding down the sustain pedal. Congratulations! You've composed your first piece of music. Let's give it an evocative title, like "Ear Meltdown."

➤ The left pedal is the *soft pedal*, named, astonishingly, because it makes the sound of the piano softer. Grand pianos accomplish this feat by shifting all the hammers, which hit the strings, ever so slightly to the side. Because most of the piano's notes have three strings assigned to them, shifting the hammers causes them to hit only two of those strings, lowering the volume of sound. Upright pianos use a different method, shifting all the hammers closer to the strings, so there is less distance between hammer and string, and therefore less striking power. In both grands and uprights, using the soft pedal also changes the instrument's tone, considerably in some cases.

➤ The middle pedal is the most exotic, and the least used. On grand pianos and some uprights, the middle pedal is a *sostenuto pedal*, and sustains whatever notes are being played when it is depressed. (Prozac for pedals!) The unique feature of the sostenuto pedal is that it does not sustain any subsequent notes.

Some upright pianos don't have a sostenuto pedal, but do have a middle pedal. What on earth is it there for? It is a *practice pedal* that makes the instrument drastically softer, much more than the soft pedal. You can use it when you don't want people in the next room to hear you practicing, and is great for apartments. The practice pedal works by lowering a piece of felt between the hammers and the strings, muffling the sound.

Grand and Less Than Grand

Pianos come in two basic styles. Grand pianos were invented first, and are horizontal instruments covered with lids that pivot upward to let the sound out. Grand pianos are awkward beasts, to be sure, because they take up too much real estate in many rooms. Upright pianos, the tallest of which are basically grand pianos tipped on edge with a keyboard sticking out the side, solve the space problem, and are cheaper to boot. (Actually, you can boot them for free, but doing so damages the wood.)

Grace Notes

One reason the piano is so difficult to tune is that most piano notes have three strings. The tuner has a daunting task—not only must each note be in tune with all the other notes, but each note must be in tune with itself. If one of the three strings goes out of tune, that note begins sounding sick.

Music Speak

The **sustain pedal** is the rightmost pedal of the piano, and the pedal used most often. The sustain pedal holds notes even after you release the keys.

Music Speak

The **soft pedal**, the left-most pedal of the piano, makes the whole instrument softer by affecting how the hammers hit the strings.

Grands and uprights are played identically, but sound different. Most grand pianos, even so-called baby grands, have longer strings than uprights. The long strings give grands sonic power, so their sound is louder and carries further. Imagine a large concert theater like Carnegie Hall in New York City, a vast chamber that seats thousands of people. A concert grand piano, which is nine feet long, effortlessly fills the entire hall with resplendent sound. An upright in the same situation would sound like a puppy whimpering in an airplane hangar.

Music Speak

The **practice pedal** takes the place of the middle sostenuto pedal on some pianos. Practice pedals cut the volume of the pianos drastically, making it almost inaudible in the next room. As such, it is a nice feature to have if you and your piano live in an apartment.

Whopping Big (and Heavy) Keyboard

Pianos have eighty-eight keys, which is a lot of keys compared to most electronic keyboards. One other significant quality of a piano's keyboard sets it apart from its digital cousins: the keys are heavier to push down. Now, this may not seem like a big deal, but it gives pianos a unique feeling when played, a responsiveness that takes more work to play—and is very unlike what an electronic keyboard feels like. People who have played only lightweight keyboards have trouble with the extra key weight of a piano, and it's no day at the beach for piano players trying to cope with unweighted electronic keyboards, either. The plastic keys are much harder to control for pianists, because they don't offer as much resistance.

The Least You Need to Know

➤ The harpsichord, probably invented in the fifteenth century, was the predecessor of the piano. The first piano was invented in 1709 by Christofori.

➤ You press keys to make notes, and keys force internal hammers to hit piano strings. When the strings are struck, they vibrate to make notes.

➤ The soundboard amplifies the vibration of struck strings, letting us hear the instrument's tones.

➤ The sustain pedal keeps notes sounding after you release the keys, and the soft pedal makes the piano subtly softer.

➤ Upright pianos are smaller and less powerful than grand pianos.

➤ Piano keys are heavier and harder to push down than electronic keyboard keys.

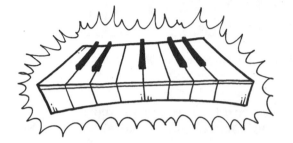

Chapter 3

The Keyboard in Black and White

In This Chapter

➤ Understanding the basics of the black and white key layout

➤ Learning about octaves and the range of a piano

➤ Discovering half steps and whole steps

It's time to approach the piano with the intent to play it. The previous chapters have given you some good reasons for playing the piano; a history of keyboard instruments; and a tour of the anatomy of the piano. So much for background information. Now it's time to put your hands on the keyboard and start exploring those black and white keys.

But wait. Before you approach the keyboard, stand back, squint your eyes, and gaze at it. All those gleaming white keys look a bit like teeth. Why, it's smiling at you—either that, or leering. Let's assume the friendlier of the two possibilities, and regard the keyboard as a welcoming instrument standing ready to deliver beautiful music through your fingers. With that encouraging thought, you can now approach it, confident in your (soon to be forthcoming) ability to tame a willing musical beast.

Key to the Keys

It's hard to believe that such an abstract device as a keyboard can make great music of all kinds. The violin, as an example, is more intuitive: you drag the bow across the strings while fingering the neck of the instrument. It makes sense that the violin would produce music, though it's usually not very musical when somebody tries it for the first time. The keyboard becomes more intuitive as you begin to experiment with it, and this section shows you how to begin.

Higher and Lower

The following figure illustrates a portion of a keyboard.

A 48-note keyboard, showing off the universal arrangement of black and white keys.

The illustration shows a small portion of the keyboard. The size of a keyboard is also called its *range*, because it determines how low and high, in pitch, the keyboard can play. The first thing to know about the keyboard is this:

➤ Keyboards play lower in pitch on the left end, and higher on the right.

There, you've learned something important already. Feel ready to jam with Keith Emerson, the legendary rock keyboard player, or show off a Beethoven concerto with the New York Philharmonic? Well, first things first. Let's begin examining how the keys are arranged, and leave Keith (and Ludwig) for a later day.

Practice Session

You can begin exploring the range of your keyboard right away in the easiest possible manner: just press keys randomly. Notice the lower pitch produced by keys toward the left end of the keyboard, and the higher tones of the right-hand notes. You can make a *glissando* by sliding your finger along all the white keys from left to right. (Glissandos are easier to do on electronic keyboards than on pianos.) Play keys far apart from each other and notice the extreme difference in pitch. Then play two notes right next to each other—try a black key and the white key next to it, one after the other—and hear how close they are in pitch. Now try playing two notes together, first far apart, then close. Try many combinations of two notes, letting your ear develop preferences for the results—some two-note combinations are harsh, and others harmonious. Two notes played together are called an *interval*.

Practice Session

Finding and playing octaves is a good way to start learning your way around the keyboard. It doesn't matter what note you start with, but to find an octave, you must pay attention to the pattern of black keys. If you select the white key immediately to the left of a group of two black keys, find the next white key (above or below) in the same proximity to the cluster of two black keys. The following figure gives you a couple of examples that you can try right away.

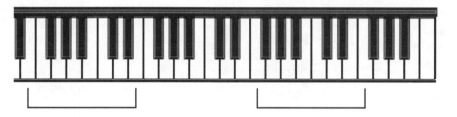

Octaves are a 12-note portion of the keyboard.

Don't worry about the names of the notes at this point; we'll get to that later. Just play the two keys, either together or one after the other, and notice the similarity of the tones. (If you play them together and they don't sound like the same note, you know you're hitting a wrong key!)

Now try finding black-note octaves. Finding the same black notes one octave apart is a bit easier than with white notes, because it's the black keys that form patterns on the keyboard. You can, for example, pick the lowest of any cluster of three black keys, then find and play the same key one octave up or down.

You can stretch this exercise by finding notes two or three octaves away from your chosen key. In fact, it's good to find *every* example of a given note. Choose the white key that lies between the cluster of two black keys, and find every one on the keyboard. Play them all, and notice how—though the pitch changes up and down—it is the same note.

Finally, try playing both notes of the octave with one hand (either hand will do). Don't strain to accomplish the stretch; if you have small hands it may prove difficult, but that's not important. If you can play the octave with a single hand, relax your wrist and forearm while holding both notes, then practice session little exercise:

1. Play a white-key octave with your right hand, using your thumb for the lower note and your pinky for the upper note.

2. After holding it for a few seconds and relaxing your wrist and arm, move your thumb up (to the right) to the next white key.

3. Likewise, move your pinky up (to the right) to the next white key. You are now playing a new octave, and will soon be ready to challenge Keith Jarrett to a jazz showdown.

Stretching Across the Octaves

Keyboard range is often expressed as a number of *octaves*. A single octave is the span from one note to a key twelve notes above or below it. If you play any note, then play the note twelve keys above or below it (be sure to count both black and white keys); you can hear that they sound very similar. In fact, they are the same basic note, existing in different octaves from each other. Play both notes at once (with one or both hands), and it almost sounds like a single note. A piano's range is a little over seven octaves. Plenty of room to stretch out with Rachmaninov or Oscar Peterson.

Music Speak

Intervals are the distances between notes on a keyboard. Play any two notes, and you're playing an interval. Intervals are named with ordinal numeral: thirds, sevenths, twelfths, fifteenths, and so on. The size of the interval is determined by how many keys lie between the two notes.

Black and White Keys

The first thing you notice when looking at a keyboard is that there are two types of keys; white keys and black ones. Having digested that crucial fact, you may also notice the pattern with which the black keys are arranged. (See the first figure of this chapter, or, if you're near a keyboard, look at that.) Black keys are clustered in alternating groups of two and three notes. This arrangement is important because it defines the keyboard's layout, making it possible to distinguish one note from another by sight.

Aside from giving the keyboard a recognizable pattern, the black keys do not function any differently than the white keys. Each key represents a note, regardless of its color. At the beginning it's easier to learn the white-key notes and play mostly on them, but more advanced playing uses the black keys just as much as the whites.

This brings us to the next earthshaking fact about the keyboard:

➤ The keys divide the keyboard into increments called *half steps*.

Music Speak

A **half step** is defined as the distance between one key and its neighbor.

Why in the world are they called half steps, you may ask. Because they are half of whole steps, I would unhelpfully answer. Actually, there's no good reason why the smallest increment of keyboard notes should be half of anything, but that is simply the way it is. The difference in pitch between any note and the very next note (up or down) is called a half step. Play the two neighboring keys at the same time, and you're playing a half step, the smallest interval possible on the keyboard. The following illustration gives you a few examples of half steps on the keyboard.

Examples of half steps on the keyboard. A half step is the smallest interval that can be played on a keyboard.

Grace Notes

Grand pianos and upright pianos have the same number of keys: eighty-eight in both cases. Grand pianos may be very much grander in other respects, such as the ability to dominate a small room so you have to crawl under it to get to the hallway, but they don't have any edge over their smaller cousins in the keyboard range department. Some older uprights—very small models called *spinets*—are missing a few keys at the top and bottom of the range.

Where there are halfs, there are wholes (that's an ancient Irish proverb). If two contiguous keys on a keyboard make up a half step, then logically, adding one more step makes a whole step. Fortunately for logicians, that's exactly how it works on keyboards. Pick any note, and count up (or down) to the second key away, and that's one whole step.

The keyboard can be thought of as an arrangement of half and whole steps, but half steps are the most basic increment. The value of distinguishing half and whole steps becomes clearer when we discuss scales later on. For now, one good thing to remember is that an octave consists of twelve half steps. Accordingly, you can find octave notes in one of two ways:

Music Speak

A **whole step** is found by moving two keys up or down the keyboard.

➤ Look at the arrangement of black keys to orient yourself, as described in the previous sidebar.

➤ Pick any note and count twelve half steps in either direction.

The following figure shows a few examples of whole steps on the keyboard.

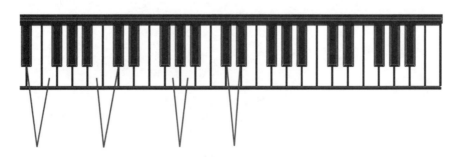

Examples of whole steps on the keyboard. A whole step consists of two half steps.

Music Speak

An **octave** is the keyboard distance between any note and the next (higher or lower) same note. The two notes that form an octave are said to be an octave apart from each other.

The Least You Need to Know

➤ All keyboards play lower notes toward the left of the keyboard, and higher notes toward the right.

➤ White keys and black keys divide the keyboard into increments called half steps.

➤ An octave is the distance on the keyboard from any one note to a note twelve half steps away. The two notes of an octave are actually the same note, but one is higher in pitch.

➤ The piano's range is a little over seven octaves.

Chapter 4

Sitting on the Bench

In This Chapter

➤ The three types of piano benches

➤ The essentials of good piano posture

➤ Positioning the bench

➤ Using the pedals comfortably

➤ Deciding where to place a home keyboard

When it comes to sitting on a piano bench, you'd think a simple instruction like "Sit on the bench" would be sufficient. That would be the end of the chapter, and we could move on to more interesting subjects, like how to baste an eggplant. But n-o-o-o. I have to go and complicate a simple issue by devoting an entire chapter to sitting down.

In fact there is a right and wrong way of sitting at the piano, and I'm determined to spell it out. This chapter explores and explains such crucial topics as posture, positioning yourself to use the pedals, finding the right placement for a home keyboard, and what kinds of piano benches are available. It's not the longest chapter in the book, but if you just don't have the patience for it now, you can always come back later.

A Hundred Ways to Make a Piano Stool

If there are actually a hundred ways of making a piano stool, I don't know them all. But there probably are that many different kinds.

Traditional piano stools are rare these days. I'm referring to the circular wooden stools that spin around, raising and lowering depending on the direction of the spin. You can still find them in used piano stores and, perhaps, old-style saloons.

The problem with those old stools is that they did indeed spin around, making them less than ideally stable for playing the piano. Fun, though.

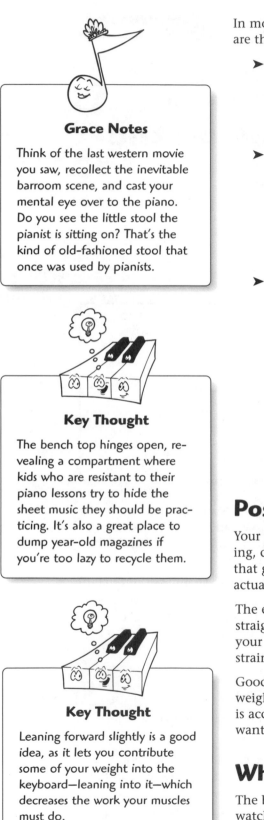

Grace Notes

Think of the last western movie you saw, recollect the inevitable barroom scene, and cast your mental eye over to the piano. Do you see the little stool the pianist is sitting on? That's the kind of old-fashioned stool that once was used by pianists.

Key Thought

The bench top hinges open, revealing a compartment where kids who are resistant to their piano lessons try to hide the sheet music they should be practicing. It's also a great place to dump year-old magazines if you're too lazy to recycle them.

Key Thought

Leaning forward slightly is a good idea, as it lets you contribute some of your weight into the keyboard—leaning into it—which decreases the work your muscles must do.

In modern times, stools have been replaced by benches, of which there are three major types:

➤ **Regular old benches.** By far the most common piano seat, the basic bench is basically ... a bench. Completely utilitarian, the common piano bench is a rectangular, unpadded, bottom-bruising construction of wood. These benches cannot be adjusted in height.

➤ **Concert benches.** The Mercedes of piano seats, concert benches are luxuriously (but firmly) padded affairs with circular knobs on each side of the seat. Turning the knobs raises or lowers the sitting surface. These benches are heavy! As a result, they are also very solid, stable, and durable. Not to mention expensive. Normally, concert benches are not included in the cost of a piano—you must buy them separately.

➤ **Piano chairs.** Some people prefer a curious seat made out of wood, that has a small back on it. The sitting surface is pitched slightly forward, encouraging you to topple onto the keyboard face first. Actually, the slightly tilted sitting surface helps you maintain good playing posture, which is slightly forward-leaning. What then is the chair back for? I told you these things are curious. I have never found it a good idea to lean back in one of those chairs while playing, but it is rather reassuring to wedge the bottom of your spine against the back, bracing yourself. Like concert benches, piano chairs are usually not standard equipment, and must be purchased separately.

Posture Has a Bearing

Your posture has a bearing on good playing. Say, if posture has a bearing, do bears have good posture? Never mind. The important point is that good piano posture makes it easier to play well. Bad posture can actually create tension problems in your hands and arms.

The essence of good posture is comfort, but no slouching. A reasonably straight back is key. You want your torso to be straight and stable, so your arms hang naturally, and your hands rest on the keys with no strain.

Good playing technique is as much a matter of distributing your weight effectively as muscle agility. In particular, loud, forceful playing is accomplished through weight, not muscle. As much as possible, you want your hand, arm, shoulder, and back muscles to remain relaxed.

Where to Sit

The big question is: How far from the piano should you sit? If you watch a lot of pianists, you see a lot of variation in how close the bench is drawn up to the instrument. Some players like to be right on top of the keys, while others push way back and must reach for the keyboard, with their legs lunging forward to the pedals.

Here is the best way to start:

➤ Put the bench a moderate distance away from the piano.

➤ Sit on the bench. Let the forward edge of the bench reach to the halfway point from your bottom to your knee. In other words, looking down, you should the edge of the bench about halfway along your thighs.

➤ Place your hand on the keyboard. Your upper arms should be pointing straight down to the floor, with your elbow forming a ninety-degree angle. If you must reach forward for the keyboard, you're too far back. If the keyboard seems to be in your lap, and you must scrunch your arms back to place your hands on the keys, you're sitting too far forward.

➤ Adjust the bench—not your position on the bench—until that ninety-degree angle of your elbow is acheived.

Playing Footsie with the Pedals

The comfort of your feet is important to the whole question of posture and how to position the bench. In normal playing, the right foot is almost always resting on the right-hand piano pedal. (If you have a home keyboard, there is probably just one pedal. Your right foot is near it, sometimes resting on it. I'll talk more about positioning home keyboards later in this chapter.) If your piano is normal, you can rest the front part of your right foot on the pedal lightly, without pushing it down, with your heel anchored on the floor. That position shouldn't cause much stress to your leg or foot muscles.

Some pianos have unusually high pedals that make the standard resting position uncomfortable. With those pianos, you must angle your foot upward too much, and it's tiring. In those cases, pushing the bench backward helps. If you do end up pushing the bench backward to accommodate high pedals, you need to develop a posture that leans forward more.

Grace Notes

Pianist Glenn Gould would never remove his gloves while playing, because his hands were cold. Instead, he cut out the fingertips so he could keep his hands warm and still have a good touch.

Key Thought

As time goes on and you gain some playing experience, it is natural to make adjustments and experiment with your ideal sitting position. An aggressive posture puts you more on the edge of the bench, with the bench pushed back a bit, so you're leaning forward considerably. A more relaxed position is achieved by pushing the bench forward somewhat, and sitting farther back on the bench's surface.

Key Thought

If a piano has unusually high pedals, you might also try placing a thin book (but not a valuable one) under your heel. A piece of carpeting also works, and doesn't slip around as much as a book does.

What to do with the left foot? Well, there is a pedal for that foot (grand pianos and some uprights even have two other pedals), and you may choose to rest your left foot on the other pedal, which isn't used as much. I like slipping my left foot *under* the pedal. Another option is to bend the left leg so that the foot rests on the floor, behind the right foot's pedal position. That is the standard classical virtuoso position.

Key Thought

If there is one supremely important thing to keep in mind when finding your posture at the keyboard, it is to remember *to relax*. Hands, wrists, arms, shoulders, back, thighs, knees, shins, ankles, feet—the whole chain of movement from top to bottom should ideally be stable, comfortable, and stress-free.

Musical Mouthful

"Give me a laundry list and I will set it to music."
—attributed to Gioacchino Rossini, Gioacchino

Placing a Home Keyboard

Fiddling with your posture is complicated if you're using a home keyboard, because the instrument itself is so adjustable. If you put it on a kitchen counter, you're likely to sit with a different posture than if you place the keyboard on the floor. (Lying on your stomach is definitely not good playing posture.)

Digital pianos are built with their own cabinets, like upright pianos, so you can't change a digital piano's altitude. Use the above recommendations for sitting in front of your digital instrument, just as if it were a real piano.

Home keyboards, the light and portable little devils, can be placed just about anywhere. Here are some suggestions:

➤ On a table. (I know, I know—if I keep giving out such great advice I'll win some kind of prize.)

➤ Your desk. Small keyboards fit on large desks without disrupting things too much, and this is a viable alternative if you're thinking of hooking your keyboard up to your computer.

➤ The big problem with tables and desks is that they are a little too tall. Piano keyboards are slung rather low, almost touching your lap when you sit in front of them. Tables and desks are considerably higher, and force you to angle your forearms upward to place your hands on the keys. This position may not seem problematic at first, but it will strain you in the long run, believe me. You can't advance to more difficult keyboard music with that posture.

➤ The best keyboard alternative is a keyboard stand, conveniently sold at the same store (most likely) at which you got the keyboard. Stands put the keyboard at a good height, and furthermore, are usually adjustable.

Key Thought

The famous drawback to keyboard stands is that they are not exactly rock-steady. Some of them shake around like a hyperactive chihuahua on caffeine every time you touch a note. Audition the stand at the store before buying it, and get the most stable one you can find—any extra expense is worth it.

The Least You Need to Know

➤ There are three types of piano benches: unpadded wood benches (commonplace), padded concert benches (luxurious and expensive), and angled piano chairs (funny-looking but useful).

➤ Start by sitting so that your arms form a ninety-degree angle, and your back is fairly straight.

➤ Rest your right foot on the right-hand pedal, with your heel on the floor. The left foot can stay back, or rest on the left-hand pedal.

➤ Home keyboards can be placed on tables and desks, but they are too tall for long-term use. Keyboard stands are shaky, but place the keyboard at the correct height.

Part 2

Give Yourself a Hand

Part 2 shows you the basics of music and how music is notated, step-by-step. To simplify matters, this part concentrates on playing just with the right hand.

Starting at the beginning, Chapter 5 introduces the right-hand notes, learning how to find "Middle C" and surrounding keys. Chapter 6 covers "accidentals," the flats and sharps that occur in some scales and throughout notated music. Chapter 7 introduces the concept of rhythm and basic note values, which is further broadened in a discussion of bars, time signatures, and rests in Chapter 8. Finally, Chapter 9 introduces the world of scales and related keys.

Chapter 5

Learning the Right-Hand Notes

In This Chapter

➤ Learning the notes from A to G

➤ Finding middle C

➤ How notes are placed on the music staff

➤ Learning how sharps and flats work

This chapter is all about music notes: how to find them, what they're called, how they relate to each other, and how to begin playing them in a musical way. A note is a musical tone, representing a certain *pitch*. I could be very technical about how a pitch is determined by soundwave frequencies, but you'll be relieved to know I won't describe all that. The important thing to know about pitch is that it is how high or low a note is.

I believe in starting simple, so in this chapter I present only the right-hand notes. In fact, all the chapters in this part are restricted to right-hand notes throughout the examples and instructions. Don't worry about whether you're starting with the hand that is naturally dominant. Right-handed and left-handed folks play the piano exactly the same way. Learning to play a keyboard is such a specialized skill that "handedness" becomes quickly irrelevant. So for now, perhaps you can bake cookies with your left hand while your right hand starts learning music.

Knowing the Letters

Music notes are named by letters of the alphabet. But don't worry: you don't have to learn twenty-six different notes. There are only seven basic notes, which get expanded to twelve notes when you add *sharps* and *flats*. I describe how sharps and flats work in Chapter 6, "Sharps, Flats, and Fingerings;" this section teaches you the first seven basic notes.

Because there are seven notes, it stands to reason that you only need to know seven letters of the alphabet. Conveniently, it's the first seven letters you need to know: A through G. Each letter is a note, and there are no notes beyond G (H, M, or S, for example).

You may wonder how this can be, because any keyboard has many more than seven keys. Good question! The answer is that the letters are used over and over. An octave is the distance between two notes twelve keys apart (counting white and black keys). Every octave uses the same seven notes, plus the sharps and flats (but don't worry about the sharps and flats yet).

This brings us to the first important thing to know about keyboard notes:

➤ Every note exists several times across the keyboard.

What distinguishes the repeated keyboard notes is their pitch. If you play a D note, for example, low on the keyboard, then play another D note up high (toward the right), you hear the same basic note but higher in pitch. Read on to discover how to do this for yourself.

Music Speak

Pitch is defined two ways: as relative or absolute. *Relative pitch* indicates the relation of a note (higher or lower) as compared with another note. *Absolute pitch* is defined as the fixed position of a note within the entire range of all possible notes.

Key Thought

Throughout this chapter, you'll simultaneously discover where notes are located on the keyboard and in written music.

Finding C on the Keyboard

The best way to start identifying notes on the keyboard is to learn a single note, and become adept at finding all the examples of that note on the keyboard. You might think you should start at the beginning of the alphabet, with the A note, but it's easier in the long run to start with C. C is the most basic keyboard note for reasons that become clearer in later chapters. In this chapter, I show you that, on the printed page, learning C first helps you learn how to read all the other notes.

The following figure illustrates how to find C on the keyboard—in fact, how to find all the Cs. As you can see (no shabby pun intended), C is played with the white key directly to the left of the cluster of two black keys. Don't confuse it with the white key directly to the left of the cluster of *three* black keys—it's an easy and common mistake.

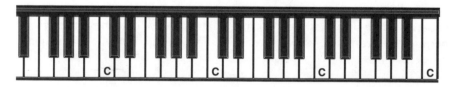

On the keyboard, C is played on the white key immediately to the left of each cluster of two black keys.

Practice Session

With the help of the previous illustration, find and play any C on the keyboard. Find the C that lies above and below the first C. Identify the surrounding Cs by recognizing their proximity to the clusters of two black keys. Now try playing two adjacent Cs with one hand, using your thumb and pinky—you're playing an octave! While playing all these Cs, notice the tones, and how similar they are. You are actually playing the same note, but in different octaves. This may be a tricky concept to understand mentally, but it's intuitive to the ear. Listen to the differently pitched C tones, and let your ear soak in their similarity.

Lines and Spaces

Now that you know where C is on the keyboard, the next step is to identify it as written music. And the first step in learning what C looks like on the page, is learning the basics of how music is printed. First of all, it's time to learn a word. Printed music is called *music notation*. (OK, so you had to learn two words. Stop complaining.) Music notation consists of four basic items, as I describe in the following sections.

The Staff

The music staff is the group of five parallel, horizontal lines on which notes are drawn (see the following figure). Piano music is written on two connected staffs, one for each hand. Other types of keyboard music sometimes uses just one staff.

Music Speak

Music notation, often called just notation, is the written form of music. Notation is what music looks like on the printed page, in sheet music and music books. For the most part, notation consists of round notes placed on the lines and spaces of a music staff, but even guitar chord symbols are music notation. In short, notation is anything written down that tells you what to play on an instrument.

The music staff consists of five lines on which symbols for notes are drawn.

Music Speak

Clefs are used at the beginning of staffs to indicate which hand should play that staff. The **treble clef** is for the right hand, and the **bass clef** is for the left hand. Actually, in intermediate and advanced piano music, the right hand sometimes plays bass clef notes, and the left hand sometimes strays into treble clef territory. But mostly, each hand stays in its own clef.

Clefs

Clefs are symbols placed at the far left of every staff, indicating whether that staff contains notes for the lower or upper portion of the keyboard. Although there are several clefs, piano and keyboard music uses just two: the *treble clef* and the *bass clef* (see the following figure). The treble clef is for upper-keyboard playing with the right hand, and the bass clef is for lower-keyboard playing with the left hand. This chapter shows examples of notes on the treble clef.

Treble Clef

Bass Clef

Treble and bass clefs indicate which hand should play the notes.

The Notes

Keyboard notes are represented by circular symbols placed on the staff. The notes are placed on either a line, or in the space between two lines (take a look at the following figure).

Each line and each space represents a different note on the keyboard. Knowing about the lines and spaces, and looking at the five-line staff, it's immediately obvious that there are more keys on the keyboard than lines and spaces on the staff, even if you include both treble and bass clefs. The solution to that dilemma is a system of *leger lines* that extend the music staff up and down. Leger lines are small extra lines added above or below the staff as needed. You can see what leger lines look like in the following examples.

Written notes are circular symbols placed on the music staff.

Leger lines show notes that lie above or below the range of the music staff.

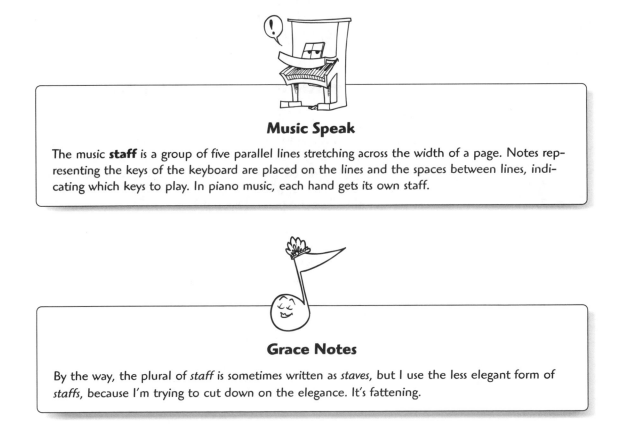

Music Speak

The music **staff** is a group of five parallel lines stretching across the width of a page. Notes representing the keys of the keyboard are placed on the lines and the spaces between lines, indicating which keys to play. In piano music, each hand gets its own staff.

Grace Notes

By the way, the plural of *staff* is sometimes written as *staves*, but I use the less elegant form of *staffs*, because I'm trying to cut down on the elegance. It's fattening.

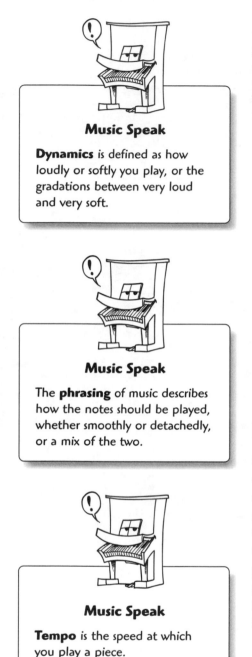

Music Speak

Dynamics is defined as how loudly or softly you play, or the gradations between very loud and very soft.

Music Speak

The **phrasing** of music describes how the notes should be played, whether smoothly or detachedly, or a mix of the two.

Music Speak

Tempo is the speed at which you play a piece.

Middle C appears like this in music notation.

Expression Marks

In addition to the notes and clefs on the staff, written music is filled with various lines, symbols, and abbreviations that indicate *how* the notes should be played. All the variations that give music its character can be indicated on the printed page. Here's a quick rundown of the basic types of expression marks:

➤ **Dynamics.** Some expression marks tell you whether to play loudly, softly, or some gradation of loudness. Furthermore, there are notation symbols that tell you to gradually get louder or softer.

➤ **Phrasing.** Other expression markings indicate how a portion of music should be "phrased," just as if you were talking. When describing something in words, you may speak slowly and haltingly, or smoothly without any pauses. Likewise, when playing the piano, you may articulate the notes sharply and detachedly, or smoothly and connectedly.

➤ **Tempo.** Tempo is speed, or pace. Tempo marks suggest the proper speed to play a piece. The pace of playing my accelerate or decelerate during the piece (the piece pace?), and there are other tempo markings to indicate speed fluctuations.

Finding Middle C When Reading Music

This is where you begin to put it all together. You know where all the Cs are on the keyboard. Each one of those Cs has its own spot on the music staff. For now, it's important to learn just one, which is traditionally called *middle C*. Middle C is, as you might surmise, the C closest to the middle of the piano keyboard.

In music notation, middle C hangs just beneath the treble clef staff on a single leger line. (The following figure shows you what middle C looks like.) Remember that written note refers only to middle C, not any of the other Cs on the keyboard. I'll get to the other Cs later.

Grace Notes

Piano and keyboard music uses treble and bass clefs to notate right-hand and left-hand notes, but other instruments sometimes use different clefs. Viola music, for example, is notated using the *alto clef*, the most common "alternative" clef. Alto clef notes lie between the ranges of the treble and bass clefs, and you never see it in a piano score.

Finding Other Notes

Fortunately, the details of music are fairly logical, at least when it comes to how notes are laid out on the keyboard. Here is what you now know:

➤ You know how to find any C on the keyboard.

➤ You know that all the white keys are named after letters of the alphabet.

As the alphabet has a certain order, so do the notes of the piano, moving from left to right up the keyboard. It's logical that the white key to the *right* of any C would be the next letter of the alphabet, which is D. And the white key to the *left* of any C would be the previous letter of the alphabet, which is B.

The following figure shows you how the Bs and Ds of the keyboard are placed in relation to the Cs of the keyboard.

Key Thought

Actually, there's no law against playing bass clef notes with the right hand or treble clef notes with the left hand, but generally each hand stays with its own clef.

Once you know where C is, you can find the adjacent notes—B and D—very easily. As always, you can find notes either by their relationship to other keys, or by their proximity to clusters of black keys.

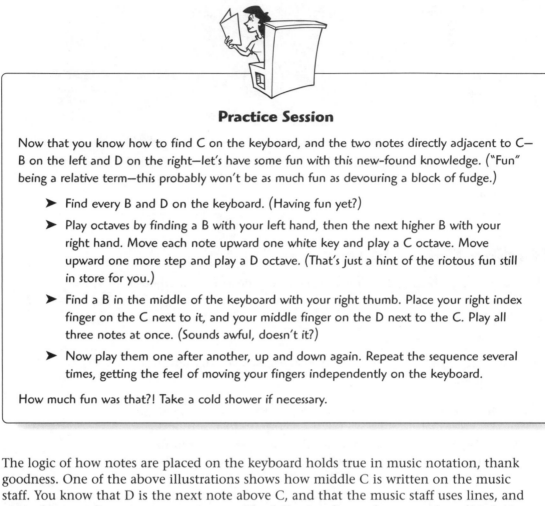

Practice Session

Now that you know how to find C on the keyboard, and the two notes directly adjacent to C—B on the left and D on the right—let's have some fun with this new-found knowledge. ("Fun" being a relative term—this probably won't be as much fun as devouring a block of fudge.)

➤ Find every B and D on the keyboard. (Having fun yet?)

➤ Play octaves by finding a B with your left hand, then the next higher B with your right hand. Move each note upward one white key and play a C octave. Move upward one more step and play a D octave. (That's just a hint of the riotous fun still in store for you.)

➤ Find a B in the middle of the keyboard with your right thumb. Place your right index finger on the C next to it, and your middle finger on the D next to the C. Play all three notes at once. (Sounds awful, doesn't it?)

➤ Now play them one after another, up and down again. Repeat the sequence several times, getting the feel of moving your fingers independently on the keyboard.

How much fun was that?! Take a cold shower if necessary.

The logic of how notes are placed on the keyboard holds true in music notation, thank goodness. One of the above illustrations shows how middle C is written on the music staff. You know that D is the next note above C, and that the music staff uses lines, and spaces between lines, to represent notes. The following figure shows you how this logic plays out in finding the D above middle C on the music staff. Notice that D rests in the space between the lowest line of the treble clef staff and the leger line used to indicate middle C.

The D above middle C lies in the space above the leger line that C is on.

Returning to the keyboard, you can use the same principle of note placement to determine all the seven basic notes that are played by the white keys (see the following figure). I've kept C as the starting key, and gone upward from there to the next C, showing all the white-key notes of a C octave. You could continue upward (or downward) to the next octave in exactly the same way, repeating the letters of the notes.

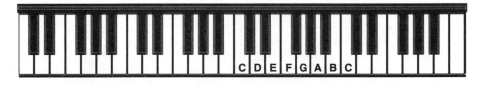

All seven basic notes, as shown on the keyboard from C to C.

Music Speak

Middle C is the C closest to the middle of the piano's keyboard, or the fourth C from the bottom left-hand side of an eighty-eight-key piano.

Now back to the written music, so you can see how those keys correspond to written notes. Again starting with middle C, the following figure illustrates what the entire octave to the next higher C looks like on paper.

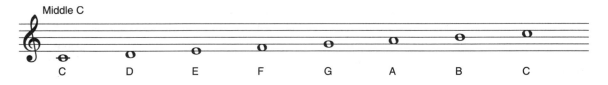

The seven white keys from middle C to the next higher C, as written on the music staff.

Key Thought

Middle C is the fourth C up (to the right) from the bottom (most left-hand) note of the piano keyboard.

Practice Session

You now know how to find all seven basic notes of the keyboard. Your task now is to experiment with this new knowledge until it becomes second nature. Your goal is to learn the note placements so well that you never have to think about where a note is—you just *know*. It's especially important to be fluent in this regard if you read music, which this book can teach you to do, but even if you don't go the music-reading route, knowing instinctively where the notes are located helps you play better by ear. Here are a few suggestions:

➤ Taking one note at a time, study and recognize its relationship to the pattern of black keys. The F note, for example, is directly to the left of the cluster of three black keys, and this is true for every F key on every keyboard in the world. It never varies.

➤ With each of the seven notes, find every example of that note on the entire keyboard.

➤ Take any five adjacent notes, placing your thumb on the bottom key. Start with this group: C–D–E–F–G. Place your thumb on C, your index finger on D, middle finger on E, ring finger on F, and pinky on G. (Who invented the word "pinky" for that finger, anyway?) Play them in sequence, bottom to top, then back down. Go slowly, and as you play each note, say its name out loud. Notice each note's proximity to the pattern of black keys around it. Now move to different groups of five adjacent keys and repeat the process.

Making Music

Here's the first piece of music for you to play in this book. Congratulations on getting this far! There's a lot missing from this musical example—for one thing, there are no timing or rhythmic indications, which I introduce in the next chapter. But why wait for rhythm to begin making music? No reason at all.

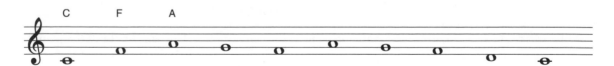

A simplified version of the first line of a famous song.

Here are a few things to keep in mind as you play the above little piece:

➤ Go slowly. Take all the time you need to figure out the notes.

➤ Use any fingers of your right hand to play the notes. Use just one finger if you want.

➤ Play the piece several times, until you feel yourself getting more comfortable with it, recognizing and finding the notes more quickly.

➤ Try to figure out what the song is. A hint: If a friend named Grace happens to be in the room, you can turn to her and say, "It's amazing!"

Here is another piece for you to try. As with the above tune, no rhythmic indications are present, so just pick out the notes at your own speed. What is this melody? It's commonly called "Ode to Joy," and is a melody from Beethoven's Ninth Symphony. (Beethoven contacted me from the spirit world, asking to be included in this book. How could I refuse?)

Key Thought

Notice that the notes proceed alternately on lines and spaces up the staff, and could continue beyond the upper C, extending into leger lines above the staff to notate the entire upper portion of the keyboard.

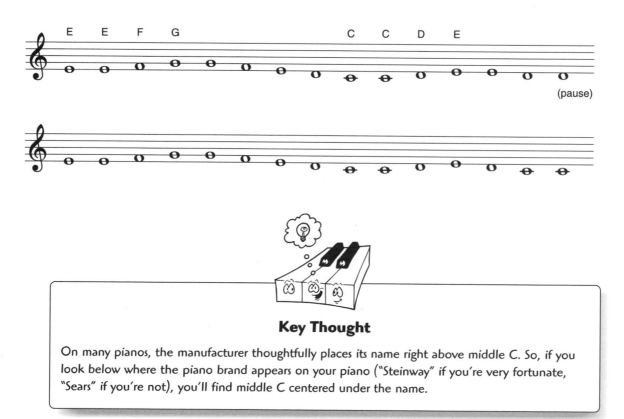

Key Thought

On many pianos, the manufacturer thoughtfully places its name right above middle C. So, if you look below where the piano brand appears on your piano ("Steinway" if you're very fortunate, "Sears" if you're not), you'll find middle C centered under the name.

The Least You Need to Know

➤ There are seven basic notes, which become twelve notes when you add sharps and flats.

➤ Printed music is called music notation, or just notation.

➤ Notes are written on the music staff, which consists of five parallel, horizontal lines. The notes are placed on the lines and in the spaces between lines.

➤ Clefs are placed at the beginning of staffs to indicate which hand should play the notes. The treble clef is for the right hand, and the bass clef is for the left hand.

➤ Notes are named by the letters of the alphabet, from A through G.

Chapter 6

Sharps, Flats, and Fingerings

In This Chapter

➤ An introduction to accidentals—sharps and flats

➤ Sharps and flats in music notation

➤ How sharps can be flats, and vice versa

➤ Unusual sharps and flats

➤ How fingerings work

Oh, if only music were played with just seven notes. Things would be a lot easier. Music would also be a lot more boring! None of the songs we like, or the classical masterpieces that have resonated through history could have been composed with only seven notes. (Well, maybe a few of the songs.)

The basic seven notes introduced in Chapter 5, "Learning the Right-Hand Notes." are expanded to twelve basic notes with the help of sharps and flats, called *accidentals*. Those new notes, and their notation symbols, are the focus of this chapter. Read on to see how it all works.

Accidentals Are No Accident

You may have heard of *sharps* and *flats* in music. "That singer is always flat," a friend in a local choir might complain. Classical music enthusiasts are accustomed to referring to pieces by names that may include sharps or flats, such as Schumann's Symphony in B-flat.

Here are the two big facts about sharps and flats, as they relate to pianos and keyboards:

➤ On the keyboard, the black keys are referred to as either sharps or flats.

➤ In written music, sharps and flats are symbols that indicate the black keys of the keyboard, and these symbols are called *accidentals*.

The following sections show you how accidentals work, and how sharps and flats fit in with the basic seven notes (the keyboard's white keys) that you already know.

Whole and Half Steps Revisited

In Chapter 3, called "The Keyboard in Black and White," I introduce the concept of whole steps and half steps. Here is a brief review:

➤ The keyboard is divided into half steps.

➤ A half step is the distance between two keys that are right next to each other, whether black or white.

➤ A whole step is the distance between a key and the second key above or below it, whether black or white.

The following figure is an illustration of whole steps and half steps. Whole and half steps are important when it comes to sharps and flats, because sharps and flats are inserted between whole steps to make half steps.

Music Speak

Accidentals are a general name for the notation symbols that indicate sharps and flats in sheet music. Nobody knows how accidentals got their name, so it should just be considered, well, an accident.

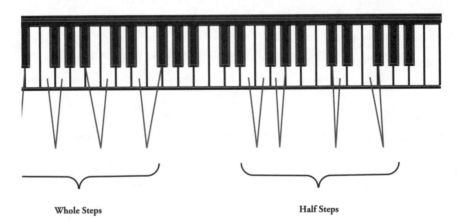

Whole Steps   Half Steps

Whole steps and half steps on the keyboard.

Pinching 'em Upward

Sharps raise any white key one half step upward (to the right). You know, for example, that C and D are two adjacent white keys on the keyboard. They represent a whole step. Looking at them, you can also see that a black key lies between them, dividing the whole step into a half step. That key is called C-sharp (see the following figure).

In exactly the same way as with C and C-sharp, you can name the other black keys on the keyboard. All the black keys lie directly to the right (upward one half step) of a white key. Because you know the names of all the white keys, it's a simple matter to slap a "sharp" after the white key's name, and you have that black key's name.

Music Speak

Sharps are alterations to music notes that raise any individual note upward by one half step.

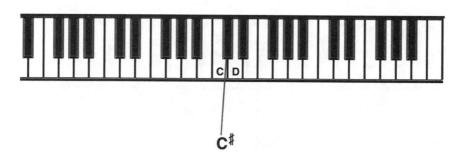

On the keyboard, C# is C raised one half step.

If that explanation is too convoluted, the following figure shows you an illustration of all the black keys, named as sharps of the white keys to their left.

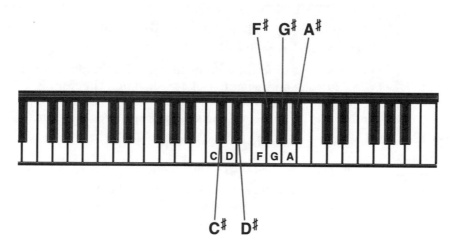

All the black keys on the keyboard can be named as sharps of the white keys to their left.

Here is a summary of how sharps work:

➤ Sharps raise a note by one half step.

➤ Any black key on the keyboard can be named as the sharp of the white key one half step down (to its left).

Pushing 'em Downward

Just as sharps move notes upward by a half step, flats move notes downward by a half step. The symbol for a flat is "♭." The following figure identifies E-flat as the black key one half step downward (to the left) from E.

But wait a minute! Isn't that the same key, in the above illustration, that you've aready learned to call D-sharp? Yes, and this brings up a crucial fact of musical notation:

➤ Black keys can be called sharp *or* flat. A single black key is either the sharp of the white key one half step below, or the flat of the white key one half step above.

> **Music Speak**
>
> **Flats** are alterations to music notes that lower any individual note downward by one half step.

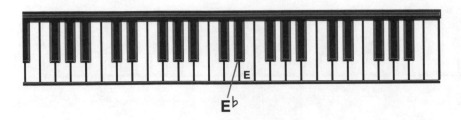

On the keyboard, E-flat is E lowered one half step.

Key Thought

I'll tell you a lot more about how to know whether to call a note D-sharp or E-flat in Chapter 9, called "Unlocking Keys and Scales," in which I introduce keys and key signatures.

How can one key have two different names? The answer is a matter of spelling—musical spelling. In English, there are words that sound the same but are spelled differently, such as *night* and *knight*. In the same way, D-sharp and E-flat sound the same, and are played with the same key—they are just spelled differently when notated in different keys.

The following figure illustrates the two possible "spellings" for each black key on the keyboard.

With all these different note spellings, the question naturally arises: How do you know what to call a black note? The truth is, the spelling depends on the musical meaning, just as with English words like *night* and *knight*. Musical meaning and note spellings are related to keys.

Here is a summary of how flats work:

➤ Flats lower a note by one half step.

➤ Any black key on the keyboard can be named as the flat of a white key one half step up (to the right).

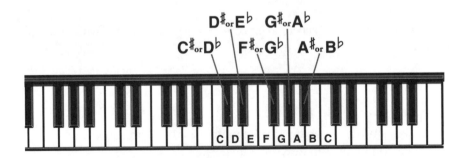

Each black key on the keyboard can be either a sharp or a flat.

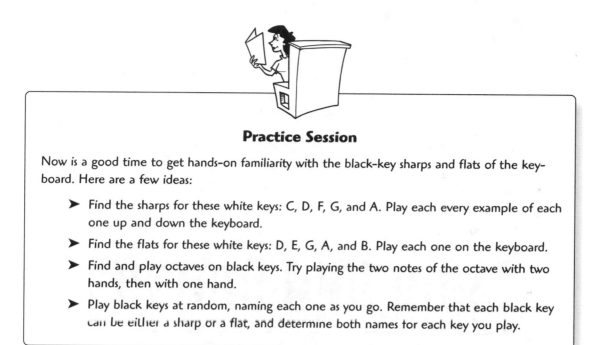

Practice Session

Now is a good time to get hands-on familiarity with the black-key sharps and flats of the keyboard. Here are a few ideas:

➤ Find the sharps for these white keys: C, D, F, G, and A. Play each every example of each one up and down the keyboard.

➤ Find the flats for these white keys: D, E, G, A, and B. Play each one on the keyboard.

➤ Find and play octaves on black keys. Try playing the two notes of the octave with two hands, then with one hand.

➤ Play black keys at random, naming each one as you go. Remember that each black key can be either a sharp or a flat, and determine both names for each key you play.

Sharps and Flats in Written Music

On the music staff, sharps and flats are indicated by symbols placed immediately in front (to the left) of any single note. An additional wrinkle concerning accidentals is provided by *key signatures*, which place certain sharps or flats at the beginning of each music staff.

For now, it's best to learn the sharp symbol and the flat symbol, and how they look when placed before a note. The following figure illustrates the symbols and their placement.

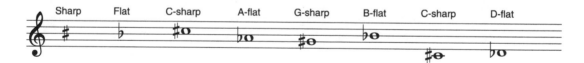

Sharps and flats are placed before notes to be raised and lowered.

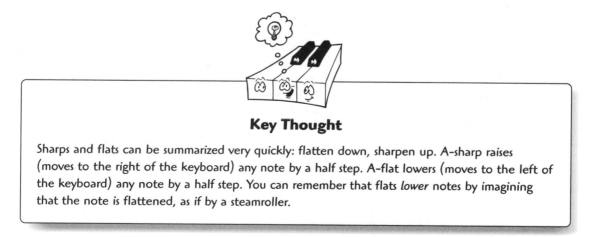

Key Thought

Sharps and flats can be summarized very quickly: flatten down, sharpen up. A-sharp raises (moves to the right of the keyboard) any note by a half step. A-flat lowers (moves to the left of the keyboard) any note by a half step. You can remember that flats *lower* notes by imagining that the note is flattened, as if by a steamroller.

The Black Sheep of Accidentals

In exploring sharps and flats, you may have noticed that I left out a few notes. Specifically, the following four notes are missing: E-sharp, F-flat, B-sharp, and C-flat. I left them out to avoid confusion, but I'm putting them in now for the sake of completeness. Those four notes are unusual because—even though they are accidentals—they are played by white keys on the keyboard.

Sharps and flats can be white keys? It makes sense when you apply the logic of accidentals. Remember that sharps and flats raise and lower a note by one half step. That rule cannot change, so the four notes listed above all fall on white notes between the gaps of the black-key clusters.

The following figure clarifies how the white key accidentals are possible.

Some accidentals fall on white keys, but those keys are rarely "spelled" with sharps or flats.

Music Speak

Fingerings are choices of using certain fingers to play certain notes of a piano piece. Music notation sometimes labels notes with numbers that indicate which finger should play which note.

The accidentals that fall on white keys are very rare. That's not to say those particular keys aren't played as much as any other keys—they are. But the keys that fall in the gaps between the black-key clusters are rarely *spelled* with accidentals. Nevertheless, it's good to know that the possibility exists, even though you may never encounter such an accidental unless you study advanced classical piano music. Though such spellings may seem to create unnecessary confusion, they preserve the rigorous logic of music notation, without which reading music would be an exercise in chaos.

As if accidentals weren't complicated enough, you'll be delighted to know that *double-flats* and *double-sharps* actually exist. These esoteric accidentals are so rare that it's not worth showing the symbols for them. I'm only mentioning them to uphold my reputation as a pain in the neck. Double-sharps raise any note *two* half steps, and double-flats lower notes by two half steps. Doubled accidentals are used only by emotionally troubled composers who kick cats and are mean to dogs.

Key Thought

Playing the piano with correct *fingering* is a little like rock climbing, where you must plan each foot placement several steps ahead. Without such careful planning, you can find youself in a position where you can't proceed any further, and must retrace your steps. In the same way, playing a piece with bad fingering can leave your hands in a tangle that brings the music to a fumbling halt. Fortunately, when playing the piano, falling off a cliff to a horrible death is extremely unlikely.

Using the Right Fingers

Look at your hands. You've got ten choices when it comes to using a finger on a note. It may not seem like an important decision now, while you're exploring relatively simple pieces. But later it becomes very important, especially with classical music. Playing a certain note with the right finger makes it possible to play subsequent notes without disrupting the piece's rhythm. More importantly, playing a note with the *wrong* finger can make it difficult to proceed with the piece. Suggestions about which finger to use are marked in music notation with numbers called *fingerings*.

Some printed music suggests which fingers to use on certain notes, and those markings are called fingerings. Fingerings use a simple system that assigns a number to each of your five fingers—the same number system for each hand. Here's how it works:

The thumb (of both hands):	1
Index finger:	2
Middle finger:	3
Ring finger:	4
Little finger:	5

Here's Beethoven's *Ode to Joy*, with right-hand fingerings added.

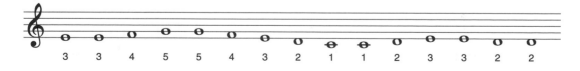

Fingering numbers suggest which fingers to use, making the piece a bit easier to play.

Making Music

Accidentals make it possible to play tunes in different keys, without altering their melodies. In this section we revisit two melodies presented in Chapter 5, written this time in keys that require sharps or flats. As in Chapter 5, I have written these out without bar lines, in whole notes, so there are no rhythmic indications at all. Still, you'll recognize the melodies, and once you get the notes under your fingers you can add the correct timing by ear if you choose.

First, "Amazing Grace":

Now try this version of Beethoven's "Ode to Joy," a melody from Ludwig's Ninth symphony.

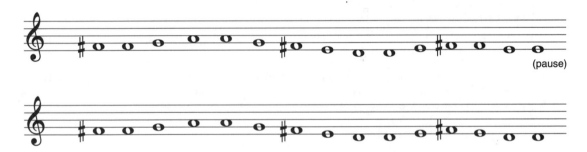

Finally, wrap your fingers around the time-honored beginner's classic, "Mary Had a Little Lamb." (I know, I know, but it makes a good illustration of this chapter's purpose.)

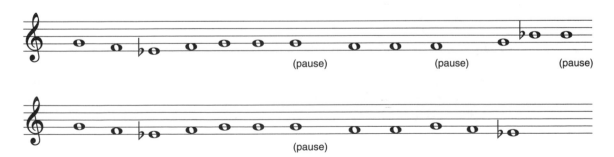

The Least You Need to Know

➤ Accidentals consist of sharps, flats, and naturals.

➤ Sharps raise any note by one half step, and flats lower any note by one half step. Naturals neutralize the effect of sharps and flats.

➤ On the keyboard, a note may be named either a sharp or a flat, depending on the musical spelling.

➤ Every finger has a number, and these fingering numbers are used to suggest the best way to play notes.

Whole Notes and Their Offspring

Music is not just notes—it consists of notes played at a certain time, in a certain rhythm. Every note you play lasts for a certain length of time, relative to other notes and the overall speed of the piece. In written music, every note on the music staff has a *time value*, indicating how long you should hold it. (This is very helpful, or you'd be holding down notes through the night.)

Every piece you play proceeds at a certain speed, called the *tempo*. A piece's tempo may be defined precisely by written instructions on the sheet music, or it may be vaguely defined with leeway for interpretation on your part. However fast or slowly you play a piece, the time value of the notes determines how long each note is held in comparison to other notes.

This chapter spells out how to understand rhythms and the timings of notes as written on the music staff. Chapter 5, "Learning the Right-Hand Notes," explained the notes themselves, including how to name them and where they appear on the staff and the keyboard. (You're only coping with right-hand notes for now.) So that chapter dealt with the *where* of notes, and this chapter deals with the *when* of notes.

Counting in Music

In Chapter 5 you can see several illustrations of the music staff with notes on it. There are even a couple of well-known melodies for you to play with your new-found understanding of notes, written music, and the keyboard. However, none of those illustrations is complete, because there are no rhythmic or timing indications. In those earlier illustrations, the notes are placed on the staff in a steady stream, with no instructions for how long each note should be held. (Same for Chapter 6, "Sharps, Flats, and Fingerings.")

Grace Notes

You're probably beginning to notice that some words I use in this book, like *tempo*, aren't English words. I'm sure you didn't expect to be learning a new language in addition to a new instrument! For reasons known only to certain ascetic monks living in the Himalayan foothills, Italian has for centuries been the traditional language of classical music notation.

Music Speak

Tempo is the speed of music. It's mostly classical music that refers to fast tempos and slow tempos, but it's also a general term for all kinds of music, and the speed with which it's played.

Key Thought

For the beat-a-holics in the crowd, there is a handy instrument called a *metronome* that mechanically keeps a rigid, perfect beat. The metronome can help tell you when you've strayed too far away from the central beat or pulse of the music.

The duration of notes is measured in *beats*. Here are a few crucial facts about beats:

➤ A note may last a certain number of beats, or a certain fraction of a single beat.

➤ The speed of beats in any piece is determined by the piece's tempo. A piece with a slow tempo has a leisurely pace of beats: One … two … three … four. A piece with a quick tempo has faster beats: One-two-three-four!

➤ Whether fast or slow, beats are always regular. Beats tick by at a completely even pace.

Learning to count beats evenly is an important part of playing music with a good sense of rhythm. Fortunately, foot-tapping is a universal skill. In fact, tapping a foot while playing was considered good form when ragtime was developed in the urban south of early twentieth century America. The idea was that the quirky rhythms and jazzy note values of ragtime could be played better by keeping a beat clock going with the foot throughout the piece. In fact, tapping was allowed, but foot-*stamping* was considered even better.

When you tap your foot you may notice that the beat is not absolutely even or perfect. No one can keep tapping a mechanical, perfect beat forever! A little variety is actually desirable; the flow of music should not be like the steady drill of a sledgehammer. On the other hand, wandering too far off the beat is not recommended.

Note Values

When I speak of *note values*, I'm referring to the time value of a note—in other words, how long you hold it down or play it. The note value is always measured in beats and fractions of beats.

Here are the three crucial facts that will send you sure-footedly down the path of understanding note values and rhythm in music:

➤ The largest note value is a *whole note*. Makes sense, right? After all, what could be larger than a whole? Every other type of note is a fraction of the whole. There are half notes, quarter notes, and on down to very small fractions of that original whole note.

➤ Whole notes are worth four beats. It doesn't matter for now how fast those beats are—that depends on the tempo of the piece. No matter whether a piece is fast or slow, every whole note in the piece is held for four beats.

➤ Every other type of note—half note, quarter note, and others—is worth less than a whole note. No other note type can be worth a full four beats, so every other note value is worth either fewer beats or a fraction of one beat.

Music Speak

A **metronome** keeps you "on tempo" by clicking audible beats while you play a piece. By setting the metronome to a faster or slower tempo, you can keep up the pace or stop yourself from rushing the pace. Metronomes come in mechanical and electronic models.

Whole notes look like plain circles in written music. Placed on lines or spaces in the music staff, they are round, unfilled circles—as shown in the following figure.

This is what whole notes look like on the music staff. Whole notes are counted with four beats.

Wholes, Halves, and Quarters

You've learned that a whole note has the largest note value of four beats. Now let's start dividing it up. This is where basic arithmetic comes in handy, but only temporarily. You don't need to perform mental calculations to play music, rest assured. Once you learn note values well enough, and can identify them instantly when you see them in written music, playing with good rhythm becomes instinctive.

The first division of the fat and regal whole note cuts it in half, and the result is two half notes. (See the following figure.)

The total beat count of the two half notes must equal four beats (the value of a whole note), so each half note naturally gets two beats. Just as with whole notes (and every other type of note), it doesn't matter how fast or slow the piece is—every half note gets counted with two beats.

Practice Session

Time to begin counting! Now, don't be self-conscious. The best way to learn counting is to do it out loud. Under your breath is fine if you're nervous about eavesdroppers (though once an eavesdropper realizes what a tedious exercise you're practicing, that person will drop eaves no longer). The following figure shows the most boring piece of music ever written. (Thank you very much, but no autographs, please.)

A good piece for insomniacs. Boring maybe, but a good exercise. Count four beats for each note.

Yes, as you can see, the above masterpiece is one whole note repeated several times. Forget about its mind-numbing musical quality and go for the educational value. Play this "piece" with any finger, counting four beats for each note: "one-two-three-four, one-two-three-four, one-two-three-four," and so on. The first count ("one") comes exactly when you press down the key. It doesn't matter how quickly or slowly you count. What *does* matter is that you count evenly, like a clock. If tapping your foot helps, tap away. Feel free to repeat this exercise with a different note—the immortal qualities of the music won't be diminished, much.

Now try the counting exercise a little differently. I'm about to ask you to do something a little subtle, but important. As you play each note, count four beats as before. This time, emphasize the first beat like this: "ONE-two-three-four, ONE-two-three-four." If you're muttering the counts aloud, mutter louder on the first beat. If you're tapping a foot, tap hard on the first beat, or use your heel on that beat. Try to really *feel* the emphasis on the first beat. Feel the other beats flowing out of the first beat. Let the first beat be the anchor for the whole note.

Once you get the hang of counting through the notes of that simple non-piece, move on to the following composition.

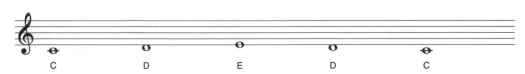

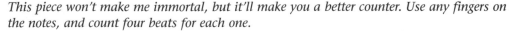

This piece won't make me immortal, but it'll make you a better counter. Use any fingers on the notes, and count four beats for each one.

The above piece isn't heading for the Smithsonian as an example of great American composition, but it's slightly more diverting than the first exercise. The goals are the same as before. Play the notes with any finger (or fingers), counting four beats for each note. Count evenly. Then try the piece with a strongly emphasized first beat.

Congratulations—you're counting!

Whole Note = 2 Half Notes
4 beats = 2 beats each

One whole note, equal to four beats, is evenly divided into two half notes, worth two beats each.

Grace Notes

I know, I know—this is beginning to sound like a math lesson. Truthfully, music and mathematics are related, but you don't have to be good in math to play music, that's for sure. I'd be sunk if an aptitude for math were a requirement for playing the piano. Playing with good rhythm is a musical ability, not a mathematical ability. But learning about how music works requires understanding note values, beats, and fractions of beats. Once you understand how it works, your musical intuition takes over and makes the whole experience much less mathematical.

The next figure illustrates what half notes look like on the music staff. Notice that they resemble whole notes in that they use unfilled circles, but the *stem* sticking up (or down) gives them away as half notes.

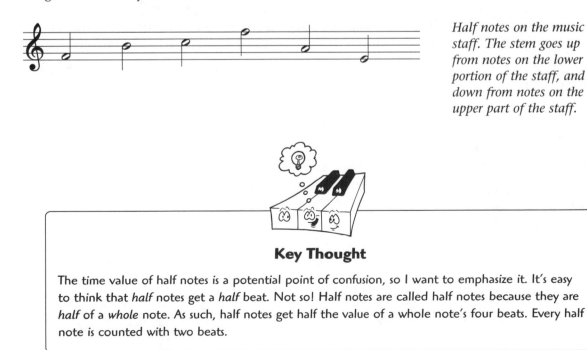

Half notes on the music staff. The stem goes up from notes on the lower portion of the staff, and down from notes on the upper part of the staff.

Key Thought

The time value of half notes is a potential point of confusion, so I want to emphasize it. It's easy to think that *half* notes get a *half* beat. Not so! Half notes are called half notes because they are *half* of a *whole* note. As such, half notes get half the value of a whole note's four beats. Every half note is counted with two beats.

Key Thought

Just as with half notes, quarter notes present possible confusion. The name *quarter* suggests that perhaps quarter notes are worth only one quarter of a beat. Resist that assumption! Quarter notes are worth exactly one beat each.

Time to divide again, like cell mytosis you learned about in biology class. (Are you sorry now you slept through it?) Take the half note, worth two beats, and divide it in half, and what do you have? Two notes that are half of a half—quarter notes! Yes, we're delving deeply into fractions now. Quarter notes are counted with half the time value of half notes, so naturally they get one beat each.

The following illustration shows the value of quarter notes.

Quarter notes are worth half the time value of half notes.

Half Note = 2 Quarter Notes
2 beats = 1 beat each

Music Speak

The **stem** of a note is the stick-like line that extends upward or downward from the circle of the note. Whole notes are the only type of note that doesn't have a stem.

The next figure illustrates what quarter notes look like on the music staff. They look like half notes, except the circles are filled in.

Here are a couple of ways to think about how the whole notes, half notes, and quarter notes are divided:

➤ Two quarter notes add up to one half note, and two half notes add up to one whole note.

➤ You can play two quarter notes while holding down one half note. You can play four quarter notes while holding down one whole note. You can play two half notes while holding down one whole note.

This is what quarter notes look like on the music staff.

Practice Session

As a further exercise in our grand project in counting (next week we'll learn all about colors), please look at the following figure.

This counting exercise contains half notes and whole notes. Count evenly and use any finger to play the notes.

I'm not headed for the Grammy awards for the above little piece, but it'll help you develop counting skills. As you can see, the staff contains both half notes and whole notes. Your mission, should you decide to accept it (and you'd better), is to play the notes with any finger, counting steadily and evenly. Remember to hold the whole notes (no stems) for four beats, and the half notes (stems) for only two beats, as you count to four. Count as quickly or as slowly as you like, but keep it even. Tap your foot, unless you have hypersensitive and grouchy downstairs neighbors.

Once you've played the above exercise a few times, move on to the next one, below.

Count evenly while playing this sequence of half notes and quarter notes.

In the above piece, as you can see to your chagrin, half notes share the staff with quarter notes. Again, use any finger to play the notes, and count evenly. It's a good idea to count a little slower this time, because the notes don't get held as long (shorter time values, don't you know), so they go by quicker. As always, the important thing is to count *evenly*, no matter how slowly.

And now the pièce de resistance—the coup de grace—the ultimate thrill—the ... well, you get the picture. Take a gander at the following figure, and revel in the sight of whole notes, half notes, and quarter notes coexisting on the same staff.

Here you have whole notes, half notes, and quarter notes.

You know what you must do with the above exercise. Count slowly and evenly. Use any finger, and play the notes in their proper rhythm: whole notes get four beats, half notes get two beats, and quarter notes get one beat.

Making Music

Now that you know a few note values (whole notes, half notes, and quarter notes), you're a much more empowered musician than you were just a short chapter ago. Understanding note values lets you play pieces that depend on rhythm as much as melody, and it gives your playing recognizability. I'm giving you two pieces here that you can play to amaze your friends (and yourself).

The following piece, a written version of "Jingle Bells," should obviously be played in the holiday spirit—if you're reading this in July, some imagination may be required.

Happy Holidays!

The next piece is a melody composed by Mozart, which is now commonly known as "Twinkle, Twinkle, Little Star." (Mozart's original title was "I Think I See a UFO," demonstrating that Wolfgang was way ahead of his time.)

This familiar melody was originally composed by Mozart, specifically for this book. The man had great foresight, and great wigs.

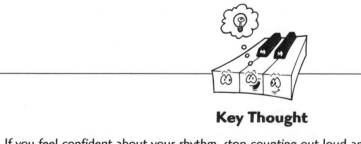

Key Thought

If you feel confident about your rhythm, stop counting out loud and do it in your head. Even better, forget about counting numbers and just tap your foot. Eventually, you want to drop the number-counting exercise when you play, and rely on your inner sense of rhythm. Foot-tapping is always allowed.

In playing both of the above pieces, here are a few things to keep in mind:

➤ Don't worry about which fingers to use on which notes. For now, just concern yourself with hitting the right notes.

➤ Play the correct note values. Counting is important, and you should do it just the way you did earlier in this chapter. Go slowly and keep the counting even. The count should go up to four, then start over: "One—two—three—four, one—two—three—four."

Key Thought

The division of notes and their resulting time values is perhaps the most confusing part of learning music. Consider: an eighth note equals a half beat?! I realize how bizarre it seems at first. There's nothing to do but grin and bear it. Believe me, it does become intuitive after a while, so hang in there. Grumbling inconsolably helps.

Dividing the Quarter

You can play a lot of music with just whole notes, half notes, and quarter notes. But it's useful to understand how quarter notes are divided—don't worry, it works exactly the same way as you've already learned, just with smaller fractions.

You know that a quarter note equals one beat. If you divide it in half, you get something called an *eighth note*. An eighth note is worth half of a quarter note's one beat, which means an eighth note equals one-half beat. (Are you flashing back to grammar school math class yet?)

The following figure is an illustration of how eighth notes relate to quarter notes.

Quarter Note = 2 Eighth Notes
1 beat = 1/2 beat each

One quarter note is equal to two eighth notes.

Please notice what eighth notes look like; they appear just like quarter notes, except for the little flag-like squiggle at the end of the stem. Good news: There are two ways to write eighth notes. Twice as much for you to learn! (Sarcasm provided at no extra charge.) The next illustration shows you the alternate way of writing eighth notes, with a horizontal line connecting the stems instead of the flag on each stem. The horizontal line is usually used when consecutive eighth notes appear. The flag is usually used when a single eighth note stands alone, surrounded by other note types.

Eighth notes can be written in either of two ways.

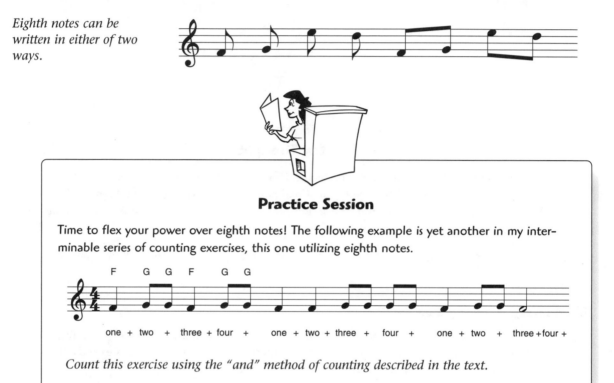

Practice Session

Time to flex your power over eighth notes! The following example is yet another in my interminable series of counting exercises, this one utilizing eighth notes.

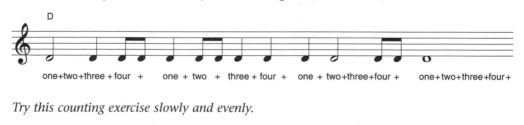

Count this exercise using the "and" method of counting described in the text.

Playing eighth notes while counting is a little tricky, because two eighth notes (each worth a half beat) fit into one count. In other words, you're counting in quarter-note time values, so eighth notes go by quicker than you're counting. This may not be a problem, but I want to tell you about a counting technique that helps. Simply put, say "and" between each count, like this: "One-and-two-and-three-and-four-and, one-and-two-and-three-and-four-and." Keep the counting perfectly even. Now you're counting off in eighth-note increments, which makes it easier to time the playing of eighth notes. I've written out the count underneath the notes in the above illustration, but don't count on seeing such hints in regular printed music!

After you've worked with the above example for a while, go on to the following illustration, which mixes in all the types of notes you've learned. In both exercises, you are viewing a music staff with a time signature of 4/4, so you're counting to four in each measure.

Try this counting exercise slowly and evenly.

Dotted Notes

I want to introduce one more note type, and then we're through with note values for this chapter. (Whew) You may have noticed something missing in the note types you've played so far. Whole notes equal four beats, half notes equal two beats, quarter notes equal one beat, and eighth notes equal a half beat. Isn't there a note that equals three beats? Yes there is, but it's created with the help of a peculiar little thing that can be applied to any type of note. Read on to see how it works.

Dotted notes are notes with dots placed immediately after them. The following figure shows what a dotted note looks like on the music staff.

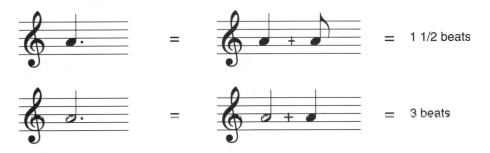

$= 1\ 1/2$ beats

$= 3$ beats

Dotted notes add one half the value of the undotted note.

A dot extends the value of a note by one half its inherent value. I know that sounds uncomfortably like a mathematical formula, but you'll quickly begin recognizing dotted notes, and their time values, without having to compute them. Dotted half notes are the easiest example. You know that a half note is worth two beats. If the dot adds half of the note's usual value (half of two beats is one beat), the dot adds one beat to the time value of the half note. One beat added to a half note's two beats adds up to three beats. You would hold down a dotted half note for the same amount of time it takes to play three quarter notes. And there you have a note with three beats! Of course, it's easier to simply learn that a dotted half note equals three beats than to calculate the formula anew each time you see one.

Now try adding a dot to quarter notes. You know that a quarter note equals one beat. If a dot adds one half of the quarter note's inherent value (one half of one beat is a half beat), then a dotted quarter note equals one and a half beats. You would hold down a dotted quarter note for the same amount of time it takes to play three eighth notes. (The above example illustrates how dotted quarter notes work.)

You can find dots after all kinds of notes, but dotted half notes and dotted quarter notes are, by far, the most common types of dotted notes. Your best bet is to treat them each as a specific type of note in its own right, forgetting that the dot is an added feature. A dotted half note simply equals three quarter notes, and a dotted quarter note simply equals three eighth notes.

Music Speak

Dotted notes are regular notes (whole, half, quarter, and eighth notes) with small dots after them. The dot extends the time value of the note by one half its original value. A dotted half note equals three beats, and a dotted quarter note equals one and a half beats.

Practice Session

Do you detect a pattern? I introduce a new type of note, then torture you mercilessly by forcing you to into a counting exercise. Of course, you could close the book, but it would only jump up and chase you around the house. You might as well just come to grips with the following figure, which is a little fragment of musical sublimity using dotted half notes.

one two three one   two three one two three   one   two   three   one two three   one two three

Count this one in three, not four.

As with previous insufferable counting exercises, be sure to keep your counting even, and go as slowly as you like. But there is one big change: Now you are counting to three, not four! So your counting now sounds like this: "one-two-three, one-two-three." Try counting to three a few times before you start playing, to get your mind in the rhythm of three.

The following figure uses dotted quarter notes. When counting through this exquisite piece of music, use the "and" method of counting, like this: "one-and-two-and-three-and; one-and-two-and-three-and." That way, the eighth notes fall on a count, either a numbered beat or one of the "ands" between the main beats. Eventually, if you get comfortable enough with it after a several repetitions (it's one of those pieces you love more and more each time you hear it), you can eliminate the "ands," or even do away with counting out loud entirely.

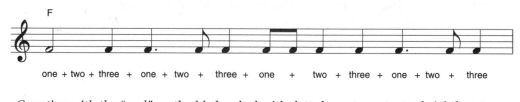

one + two + three + one + two + three + one + two + three + one + two + three

Counting with the "and" method helps deal with dotted quarter notes and eighth notes.

Making Music

Now that you know how to count whole notes, half notes, quarter notes, eighth notes, and dotted notes, your playing can sound more musically realistic. Instead of reading (and playing) nothing but whole notes, you can decipher and articulate notes of varying durations. Remember to count! Even advanced players count inwardly, and sometimes aloud when practicing. (Not when performing, of course.)

The three pieces in this section are written out for the right hand, using varying note values including a few dotted notes. Rhythm really starts making sense in the next chapter, which introduces bar lines and measures. For now, just count the notes out as written and the pieces will sound pretty good.

Start with this notation of "Happy Birthday." If it actually *is* your birthday, thank your lucky birthday stars for the happy coincidence. Go easy on the cake.

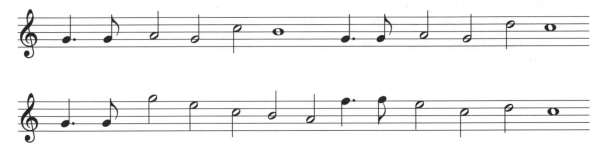

You probably won't recognize this next piece, a traditional melody called "The River" which is not often heard. I'm including it here because it offers a good practice opportunity for playing quarter notes and half notes. And, more important, because it's a lovely tune.

As a cross-cultural exercise, try playing the traditional French folk song "Frere Jacques," which can be loosely translated as "Jack ate the fries." This piece throws some consecutive eighth notes at you, so don't start out too fast. It's always better to play slowly and evenly, than to start quickly and be forced to slow down.

The Least You Need to Know

➤ Every note lasts a certain number of beats.

➤ Whole notes are worth four beats; half notes are worth two beats; quarter notes are worth one beat; and eighth notes are worth a half beat.

➤ Dotted notes are worth half again as much as the original note.

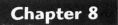

Chapter 8

Bars, Time Signatures, and Rests

In This Chapter

➤ Dividing the music staff into measures with bar lines

➤ Letting time signatures determine the number of beats per measure

➤ Taking a breather with rests

Until now in this book, all the musical examples have had a couple of things missing. The previous chapters in this part introduce you to the notes for the right hand; sharps and flats; fingerings; and the different note values.

A couple of things are missing from the musical examples of earlier chapters. The most important is *bar lines*, which organize the music staff into segments. You also need to know about *time signatures*, which tell you how to count a piece. Read on to discover these two important aspects of music notation. Later in the chapter I introduce the concept of *rests*, which tell you when (and for how long) *not* to play.

Organizing the Music Staff

Writing out music without bar lines works up to a point. With simple melodies, you can convey the notes and their time values, indicating how to play the melody. But if the music were to get any more complicated, the staff would be a mess. Smaller note values, indicating quicker notes, would clutter up the staff and it would become very difficult to understand how the piece should be counted. At that point, the staff would need to be organized in some way, bringing order to the chaos.

Up to this point in the book, I've left out the organizing elements of the music staff for the sake of simplicity. But the fact is, all written music, no matter how rudimentary, contains those organizing features, and this section is where you learn about them. I'm talking about *bar lines* and *time signatures*. I know, it seems like a lot to learn, but this new information actually makes the printed music page more coherent, and easier to understand at a glance.

Bar lines and time signatures take some of the work out of counting. So read on, and you're playing will actually get a bit easier. (Boy, is that a flagrant sales pitch, or what?)

Where's the Bar?

You've probably noticed that we're always counting to four, then starting over. In earlier chapters I never asked you to count to five, or three, or (heaven forbid) to eleven. It makes sense to count to four, because the basic note value—the whole note—always lasts for four beats. Furthermore, every type of note you've learned divides evenly into four: half notes (two beats each) and quarter notes (one beat each).

Wouldn't it be convenient and helpful if written music gave you some indication of when in the piece it was time to start your counting over? In other words, a mark on the page that tells you, "If you're counting correctly, you should be at four right HERE, and should start your count over." Well, there *is* such an indication, and it's called the *bar line*. (Not to be confused with a queue of thirsty people waiting for a frosty cool one.) Bar lines are vertical lines that divide the music staff into sections, each of which equals a certain number of beats. (Four beats for now, but later I show you how the sections can equal different numbers of beats.) The portion of the staff between bar lines is called a *measure* or a *bar*.

The following figure illustrates bar lines and the measures they define.

Measures lie between the bar lines. In this example, the measures equal four beats, and all the note values in each measure add up to exactly four beats.

Grace Notes

Measures (also called bars, because they lie between *bar lines*) are the fundamental bite-size chunks of written music. In classical music notation, the measures are often numbered, especially in chamber music (composed for two to eight instruments) and orchestral pieces. When rehearsing, the leader of the orchestra or chamber group can instruct the other players to "take it from measure 38," pinpointing where in the piece they should all start playing.

Grace Notes

The time signature is sometimes referred to as the *meter*. Like a parking meter that ticks off how much time remains before a cop slams the dreaded summons on your windshield, the meter indicates how to tick off the beats of each measure in your mind. *Meter* and *time signature* are musical synonyms.

As you can see, there are several measures on any given staff. Here are the important facts about measures:

➤ There is no theoretical limit on how many or how few measures can exist on a staff, but space limitations and the nature of most musical pieces usually dictates about five to eight measures per staff.

➤ The end of a staff (at the far right) is always the end of a measure, and concludes with a bar line.

➤ The beginning of a staff is always the beginning of a measure.

➤ There can be any number of notes in a measure, but all the note values must add up to exactly the number of beats assigned to the measures. (We are assuming for now that every measure equals four beats. Differently valued measures are introduced a bit further in this chapter.)

Music Speak

Time signatures are placed at the beginning (far left end) of the music staff, and tell you how many beats are in every measure.

Sign of the Times

This is where another crucial element of the music staff is introduced, that lets you understand measures completely. Until now I've diabolically let you assume that measures are always worth four beats, as if four were the cosmic essence of all rhythm. Four is a good number to use for examples, because a whole note equals four beats. But the fact is that the measures of a piece can be assigned any number of beats. The part of the staff that assigns the value of measures is called the *time signature*. The time signature is placed at the beginning of the staff, way over toward the left (see the following figure). The time signature appears only on the first staff of a piece, not on every staff throughout the piece.

This time signature indicates that each measure contains four quarter-note beats.

As you can see in the above figure, time signatures consist of two numbers, one perched oddly on top of the other. Here's what they mean:

Grace Notes

Time signatures can get pretty crazy, especially in twentieth-century piano music. A signature like 11/16, indicating that each measure contains eleven sixteenth notes (or the equivalent time value of other note types) is much harder to count than a simple 4/4 meter. Fortunately, exotic meters (time signatures) are just about as rare as a mocha cappucino with the perfect sprinkling of nutmeg. And considerably less tasty.

➤ The top number of the time signature indicates how many notes exist in each measure.

➤ The bottom number of the time signature indicates what type of note is referred to by the top number.

Looking at the example illustrated in the previous figure, the top number is 4. That top number indicates that each measure can hold four notes. But what kind of notes? Whole notes, with four beats each? (That would mean each measure contains sixteen beats.) Half notes, with two beats each? (That would mean each measure contains eight beats.) Actually, the bottom number, which is 4, means quarter notes, indicating that the top number is referring to four quarter notes in each measure. (That means that each measure, in fact, contains four beats, because quarter notes are worth one beat each.)

The top number on any time signature refers to the number of notes in every measure, and the bottom number clues you in to what kind of note. When 4 is the bottom number, it means quarter notes. We are sticking with that bottom number for now, because it is the most common and easiest to work with. When the top number is three, it means that every measure holds three quarter notes. When the top number is two, it means that every measure holds two quarter notes. (See the next figure for an illustration of what these time signatures, and measures, look like.)

Three different time signatures, as they would appear at the beginning of three different pieces.

When the time signature is 4/4, 3/4, or 2/4, don't make the mistake of thinking that only quarter notes are allowed in the measures! The time signature represents the total *note value* allowed to be in any measure. It doesn't matter whether that note value is filled in with quarter, half, or whole notes, or even other note types I haven't discussed yet. Look at the following two figures to see different note types filling in the measures.

Here is "Jingle Bells" with a time signature and bar lines.

This is what "Twinkle, Twinkle, Little Star" looks like with a time signature and bar lines.

Taking a Rest

There's no rest for the weary—but there are rests in music! You've got one more important thing to learn about music notation before this chapter is over. Fortunately, it builds easily on the note values described in this chapter. Music has two items of time value: notes, and *rests*. You know what a note is: it's a key on the keyboard that lasts for a certain number of beats. Rests also last for a certain number of beats, but they mark where you *shouldn't* play a note. Rests are used to indicate the absence of notes.

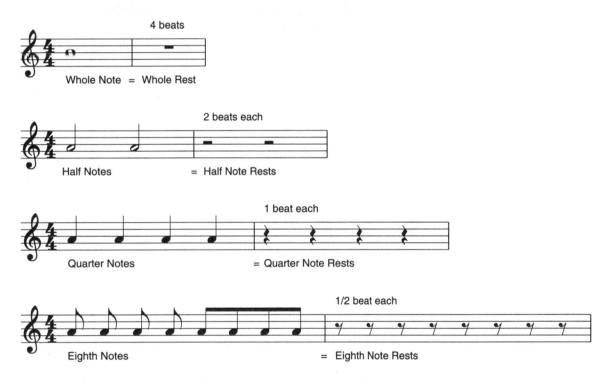

This is what the basic rests look like, and how they correspond to note values.

Rests are a big help when you're playing a piece from music. Without these silent markers, it would be harder to count your way through any measure that isn't filled with notes. Rests keep track of the beat even when nothing is sounding, and if you know the rest values you can keep counting through the silence.

You may wonder why rests are necessary. If there are no notes, just don't put any notes on the staff, right? What's the point of any other indicator? The answer is that written music is compulsive in its accounting. Everything needs to add up perfectly. If there are four beats per measure, each staff of the music has to add up to four beats whether there are notes for all the beats or not.

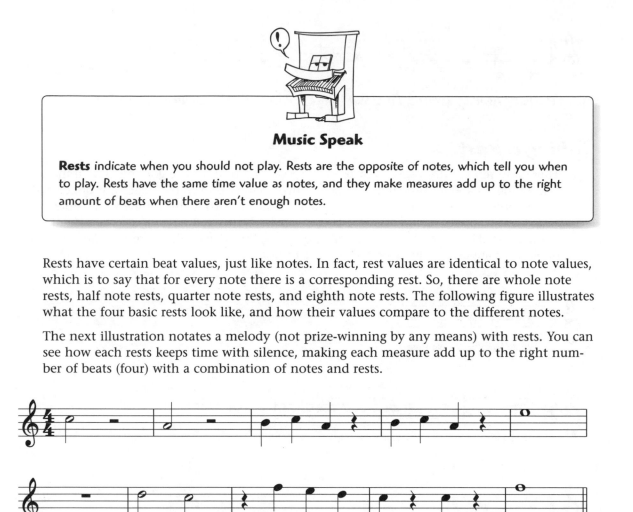

Music Speak

Rests indicate when you should not play. Rests are the opposite of notes, which tell you when to play. Rests have the same time value as notes, and they make measures add up to the right amount of beats when there aren't enough notes.

Rests have certain beat values, just like notes. In fact, rest values are identical to note values, which is to say that for every note there is a corresponding rest. So, there are whole note rests, half note rests, quarter note rests, and eighth note rests. The following figure illustrates what the four basic rests look like, and how their values compare to the different notes.

The next illustration notates a melody (not prize-winning by any means) with rests. You can see how each rests keeps time with silence, making each measure add up to the right number of beats (four) with a combination of notes and rests.

Notes and rests make each measure add up to the correct number of beats.

Making Music

With the staff divided into measures, written music makes rhythmic sense for the first time. Now when you see a piece spelled out you know how many beats are in each measure, and therefore how you should count the piece. Combined with your knowledge of note values (Chapter 7, "Whole Notes and Their Offspring"), you're quickly becoming an empowered musician.

The pieces in this section are written out without any of the compromises of musical examples in earlier chapters. This is what music notation looks like in the real world. Start with "Frere Jacques," which you encountered in the previous chapter. This time, I've written it in a different key, and with bar lines that organize the piece rhythmically.

This next piece, "When the Saints Go Marching In," is also in 4/4 time, with four beats to every measure. Notice that the first measure is a little different; it's incomplete, and contains only three eighth notes, totaling up just 1.5 beats. Pieces often begin in this fashion, and these orphaned notes are called the *upbeat*.

Now try a piece in 3/4 time, also known as waltz time, or simply "in three." This traditional Irish song, "Molly Malone," can be played slowly and with a melancholy spirit. Remember to count in groups of three: "one-two-three, one-two-three."

The Least You Need to Know

➤ Bar lines divide the staff into measures, and each measure contains the same number of beats.

➤ Time signatures appear at the beginning of the piece, and determine how many beats are in each measure.

➤ Rests correspond to note values, and tell you how many beats *not* to play.

Unlocking Keys and Scales

In This Chapter

➤ Understanding keys and tonics

➤ Learning about major and minor scales

➤ Introducing key signatures

➤ A brief summary of modes

Music is a highly organized art form. There's plenty of room for experimentation and improvising, but the technical parts of music—how its rhythms, melodies, and harmonies are constructed—is as fastidious as an accountant's checkbook. Chapter 5, "Learning the Right-Hand Notes," introduced the music staff and written notes, showing that every key on the keyboard has a precise spot on the written music page; each hand even has its own staff. Other chapters in this part reveal note types, rests, rhythms, tempos, and measures, showing that written music accounts for every beat in a piece. This chapter affirms the disciplined quality of music's underpinnings by discussing scales, keys, and key signatures.

What Keys Do

Music keys don't unlock anything, but they do affect how listeners hear music, and how players play music. At one time or another you've probably seen a singer who tells her band to play the song up or down a few notes, or who says, "Play it in G, boys." Such an instruction is referring to a key. In music, the key refers to the main note of the piece. The main note can be thought of as a kind of home base, around which the whole piece gravitates. That main note is important enough, in fact, to have its own name: tonic. Sounds like it should go in your drink, but a piece's tonic is its key note. (This is a good time to mention that drinking while playing your keyboard, while possibly fun, can result in lots of bad music.)

How do you tell one key from another? Good question; I'm glad I asked. Keys are identified by key signatures, which are the number of sharps or flats used to play music in that key. Stay with this chapter for a discussion of key signatures a bit later.

A piece's key is not just a theoretical distinction. In most cases, you can actually hear that the tonic note is special, and important to the piece sounding good to your ear. The following figure shows a portion of "The Star Spangled Banner," which you can either play or just look at for the time being. (For once this isn't one of my confounded exercises!)

Music Speak

In music, the **key** indicates the main note of the piece, and which sharps or flats are needed to play the piece around that central note. The main note is called the *tonic*. Every key has a scale, which is a sequence of notes starting with the tonic note.

Try humming the above piece to yourself while following the music with your eyes. The point is to see how important the tonic notes are to the piece—each tonic is marked in the music. The piece, as I've written it out in this example, is in the key of C, which means that C is the tonic note. (Every C on the keyboard is equally the tonic.)

As you look at the previous piece and either play it or hum it, notice not only the visual placement of the tonic notes, but also how your ear and your musical sense respond to them. The tonic, C, anchors the piece and gives it a musical home base that sounds right—it feels right. When a tonic falls on the first beat of a measure, it is an especially grounding experience, because the key is driven home all the more strongly.

Transposing music from one key to another is not a skill you need, most likely, which is fortunate because it's quite hard. I'm certainly not going to ask you to do it in this book, unless you spill coffee on the pages, in which case you must transpose "Flight of the Bumblebee" into the key of BZZZZZ. So be careful.

This version of the American national anthem is a good example of how tonic notes have an anchoring effect on a piece's sound.

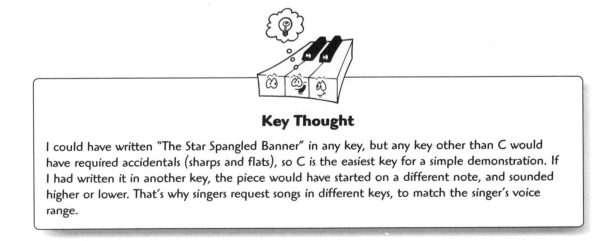

Key Thought

I could have written "The Star Spangled Banner" in any key, but any key other than C would have required accidentals (sharps and flats), so C is the easiest key for a simple demonstration. If I had written it in another key, the piece would have started on a different note, and sounded higher or lower. That's why singers request songs in different keys, to match the singer's voice range.

Climbing a Hill of Scales

Keys and scales form a perfect relationship: In order to understand keys, it's helpful to know scales, and in order to understand scales, you have to know about keys. You know that a piece's key is defined by its tonic note. A *scale* is a sequence of notes that goes from one tonic note to the next tonic note above it. In the key of C, for example, the scale runs from any C on the keyboard to the next higher C.

The following figure shows a C scale, going from middle C on up to the next C. Notice that the scale has seven notes, with the top note, C, being either number eight or number one. Because the upper C is essentially the same note as the bottom C (they are both the tonic), scales are considered to have seven notes.

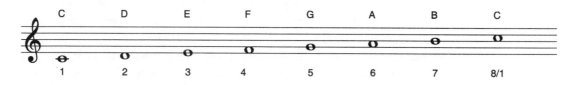

The scale of C. All scales consist of seven notes, with the eighth note being the tonic, just like the first note.

Practice Session

Using the following figure for reference, play a C scale on the keyboard.

The ascending and descending C scale, written in quarter notes with fingerings.

The first part of the above illustration shows the ascending scale (going up), and the second staff shows the descending scale (going down). I've put in fingerings for you to follow. Keep in mind that your thumb is finger 1, index finger is 2, middle finger is 3, ring finger is 4, and little finger is 5.

77

Try this exercise in three steps:

1. First, just pick out the notes on the keyboard and get used to what the scale sounds like. Notice how the two tonic notes—at the top and bottom of the scale—really sound like the main note. Going up, the C at the top seems to resolve a question posed by the B preceding it. Going down, the last C sounds like the logical, inevitable conclusion to the scale.

2. Second, forget about rhythm and counting. Just work on the fingerings. Pick out the notes using the correct right-hand fingers, as marked.

    It would be easy to play a scale if we had seven fingers; unfortunately, God wasn't thinking too clearly, and gave us only five. For this reason, we have to make a slight accommodation to play a scale smoothly. The tricky part lies between the third and fourth notes of the first measure, where you go from an E with the third finger to an F with the first finger (thumb). Lift your wrist a bit when playing the E, and slip your thumb underneath to play the F. On the descending scale, you have the same situation in reverse: You must play the descending F with the thumb, and the following E with your third finger. Cross your middle finger over your thumb to play the E.

    Both going up and coming down, try to hold down each key until the very moment that you play the next note, resulting in a smooth sound without any gaps of silence between the notes. Keep working on the fingerings until you're pretty comfortable with the scales.

3. Third, play the scales, up and down, with the correct fingerings and in the correct rhythm. There is nothing fancy about the rhythm—it's just a sequence of quarter notes. I've written the scales with a 4/4 time signature, so your counting should be up to four. Go slowly and keep the rhythm even. If you have trouble with the fingerings, try again with a slower count, because it's more important to play with the right fingers than to play fast. With practice, you can build up a little speed.

Music Speak

Changing a piece from one key to another is called **transposing** the piece. Transposing a piece from C to D, for example, moves it up one whole step. Transposing a piece from G to F moves it down one whole step. You can transpose any piece to any key, and the process moves every note of the piece up or down the same number of whole or half steps.

Major and Minor Scales

You know now that scales have seven notes, and they are the sequence of notes between two tonic notes an octave apart on the keyboard. But which seven notes make up the scale?

In the case of the C scale it's easy: The scale consists of the seven white keys between any two consecutive Cs. But it doesn't work that way for any other note besides C. If you play the seven white keys between D and D, for example, or F and F, you get a scale that doesn't quite sound right. You're still playing seven notes, but it doesn't have the same natural sound as the C scale. (Don't take my word for it; try it yourself. Just pick out the notes without regard to fingering or rhythm.)

The truth is, there are two important types of music scales, and several other less important ones. (Hey, don't shoot the messenger; I didn't invent this sytem.) The only two scale types you need to know about in this book are major and minor scales. Despite what the names sound like, the major scale is not more important or larger than the minor scale. They each have seven notes, and they each are constructed in a certain way; it is the difference in how they are constructed that distinguishes them. I'll get to the minor scale a bit later in this chapter. For now, the major scale is your focus, because it is the C-major scale that you've been playing in this chapter.

Music Speak

A **scale** is a sequence of notes starting with the tonic note of a key, and going up or down to the next tonic note. Every key has its own scale.

What makes a scale a major scale? Aside from natty clothes and a sunny disposition, a major scale is made from a certain sequence of half steps and whole steps. The concept is difficult to convey in words, so cast your gaze over the following figure, which illustrates a C-major scale broken down into its steps.

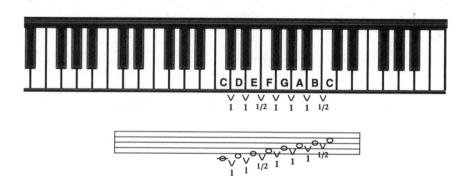

The C-major scale, showing whole steps (1) and half steps (¹/₂) Every major scale has the same sequence of whole and half steps.

Every step of the major scale (the distance from one note to the next) is either a whole step or a half step. To be precise, just two of the steps in the C-major scale (and any major scale) are half steps. The table below shows where the half steps lie in any major scale:

Between notes 1 and 2	Whole step
Between notes 2 and 3	Whole step
Between notes 3 and 4	Half step
Between notes 4 and 5	Whole step
Between notes 5 and 6	Whole step
Between notes 6 and 7	Whole step
Between notes 7 and 8	Half step

Now you know one way to determine a major scale. Just start with any note on the keyboard, and step your way upward using this sequence of whole steps and half steps, playing both white keys and black keys. As I mentioned before, the C-major scale is the only major scale that is played on white keys only.

Practice Session

You now know enough to construct major scales beginning on any key of the keyboard. You can try it by referring to the major-scale table, and counting up whole steps and half steps. Start with G, and proceed up the keyboard with this sequence: whole, whole, half, whole, whole, whole, half. (Those are whole steps and half steps.) If all goes well, you are playing a scale with one black key, which is the key of the seventh note, just before the upper G. That note is F-sharp.

Now try one more, this time starting on F. As with the G-major scale in the previous paragraph, play up the keyboard with whole steps and half steps in the major scale sequence. This time, you'll play one black key at a different point of the scale—it's the fourth note, which is B-flat.

Scales and Key Signatures

There is another way to determine a major scale besides counting whole steps and half steps, which requires less work but more memorization. This section shows you how, using key signatures.

Music Speak

Key signatures determine the key of a piece by showing which sharps or flats are necessary to play a scale in that key. Key signatures make their appearance at the beginning of every staff in a piece, and look like a cluster of sharp or flat symbols.

You know that scales are closely related to keys. The C scale, for example, is the scale of the key of C. Major and minor fit into the scale/key relationship too. The C-major scale is the scale of the key of C major. This leads to an important fact, worthy of spotlighting:

➤ Every key is either major or minor, and every major and minor key has a scale.

Major keys are still our focus right now, and it's time to move beyond C major to some other major key and its scale. Trying out another major scale brings accidentals (sharps or flats) into play, and leads you right to key signatures. The following figure shows you the F-major scale. As you can see, the scale contains one accidental, which is B-flat on the fourth note. Because the F-major scale is associated with the key of F major, and because the scale always has one flat (B-flat), the key signature of F major is one flat, or B-flat.

The F-major scale, which has a key signature of one flat.

Here's a handy list of things to know about major keys and their key signatures:

➤ Key signatures are defined by the number of sharps or flats in the scale of that key.

➤ Every major key has a unique key signature, not shared by any other major key.

➤ Key signatures have either sharps or flats, but never a mixture of sharps and flats.

Key Thought

The sharps and flats of key signatures are always added in a certain sequence. The key signature of D major, for example, is two sharps—F-sharp and C-sharp. Those two sharps must be included in the key signatures of every key with more than two sharps. Accordingly, the key signature of A major, which is three sharps, contains F-sharp, C-sharp, and G-sharp. Flatted key signatures work the same way, although the order is different.

Key Signatures in Written Music

Generally speaking, every piece is written in a key. Every key has a signature number of sharps or flats that are needed to make a major scale in that key. Imagine if you wrote a piece in a key that has three sharps: F-sharp, C-sharp, and G-sharp. If you wrote the piece out, you'd have to write in a sharp before every F, C, and G in the piece. Not exactly hard labor in a salt mine, I admit, but still on the inconvenient side. Key signatures show you at a glance how many sharps or flats are in the piece, and which notes the sharps or flats apply to. Key signatures are placed at the beginning of every staff in the piece, and they keep the notes less cluttered with accidentals.

The following figure shows a key signature of two flats: B-flat and E-flat. This particular key signature indicates that every B and E in the piece is automatically flatted to B-flat and E-flat. The two-flat sign at the beginning of the staff constitutes the key signature, and applies not only to the specific B and E notes on those particular lines and spaces, but to every B and E, anywhere on the keyboard, through the whole piece. The key signature flats are placed at the beginning of every staff to remind you which notes are flatted by default.

Musical Mouthful

"You make me feel like a natural woman."
—Aretha Franklin

81

A key signature of two flats, namely B-flat and E-flat. Key signatures appear at the beginning of every staff in a piece.

A Natural Thing

So what happens when a piece with a key signature of two flats (B-flat and E-flat) has a non-flat B or non-flat E as part of its melody? After all, there is no rule that a melody must use one note instead of another—and believe me, most pieces break their key signatures many times.

In music notation, a certain symbol can be placed before any automatic sharp or flat to override that sharp or flat, returning the note to its natural state. Accordingly, the symbol is called a natural. When a note that is normally a flat or sharp (because of the key signature) is made natural, it is called B-natural (if B is the note). Naturals are accidentals just like sharps and flats.

The top staff has a key signature of B-flat and E-flat, and shows how natural sign can neutralize the flats. The bottom staff is a similar illustration using the key signature of F-sharp, C-sharp, and G-sharp.

Music Speak

Naturals neutralize previously established sharps and flats. The natural sign is an accidental just like a sharp sign or flat sign. Naturals lower sharped notes by a half step, and raise flatted notes by a half step.

Following are a few miscellaneous but important facts about key signatures and accidentals:

➤ The key signature of a piece can change during the piece, although this happens mostly in intermediate and advanced classical piano music. When a key signature changes, the new assortment of sharps or flats is inserted at the change, even if it happen in mid-staff. Then, the new key signature is placed at the beginning of every subsequent staff. No matter what, there is always a key signature at the beginning of every staff.

➤ No sharps and no flats is a key signature, too. It is the signature of the key of C major. It means, as we have seen earlier in this chapter, that if you play all the white notes (no accidentals) from C to C on the keyboard, the result is a major scale.

➤ Each key has a unique signature. The uniqueness of key signatures means that only one major key has a signature of three sharps, for example, or two flats. There is no such thing as another key that uses a different set of three sharps or two flats. As an example, remember that F major has a key signature of one flat (B-flat). It is impossible to have a key signature of one flat, using another flatted note, like E-flat or G-flat. A key signature of one flat automatically means B-flat is the flatted note, and it automatically means F major is the key. This means that when musicians refer to the key signature as "one flat," everyone knows it must mean the key of F major, with all Bs flatted.

➤ When an accidental is written before a note (and is therefore not included in the key signature), it lasts for the remainder of the measure before it loses its effect. Take a glance at the following figure for an example of how accidentals last through a measure. After the measure ends, if a composer wants the sharped, flatted, or naturalized note to be played again, the accidental is rewritten.

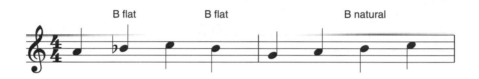

When an accidental is written before a note, as with the B-flat in this example, the accidental lasts through the measure on that note. After that measure, the note automatically reverts to its natural state.

Practice Session

The trickiest aspect of key signatures is remembering which notes are sharped or flatted throughout the whole piece. Because accidentals aren't used to indicate sharps or flats of the notes in the key signature, you must burn the key signature into your brain's circuitry before starting the piece. Once you get familiar with the handful of basic keys, playing the correct sharps and flats becomes second nature (well, maybe third or fourth nature). For now, it takes more effort to remember the key signature, and effort takes practice, and practice requires ... exercises! (I know how happy exercises make you.)

The purpose of each of this little bit of torment is to give you practice remembering a key signature. The figure below illustrates the relatively easy key signature of F major—one flat (B-flat). It's a touching piece, so don't be ashamed if it brings tears to your eyes. Don't be surprised if it doesn't, too. When playing the piece, remember that all Bs are flatted unless they have a natural sign in front of them.

With a key signature of one flat, all Bs are automatically flatted in this piece, except when the flat is neutralized by a natural.

Key Thought

Other minor scales use different sequences of whole and half steps, and are called harmonic minor and melodic minor scales. I mention these other two scales just for the sake of completeness, but now that I've mentioned them, feel free to forget them.

A Little Less Major

Most of this chapter deals with major keys, their scales, and their key signatures. But I can't end this discussion without introducing the siblings of major keys: minor keys. Minor keys work similarly to major keys in a couple of important ways:

➤ Minor keys, like major keys, have key signatures.

➤ Minor keys also have scales, called—naturally enough—minor scales.

The main difference between a major key and a minor key lies in the scales. Refer to the previous table in this chapter to refresh your memory of how major scales are constructed from whole steps and half steps. Minor scales are likewise built from whole and half steps, but they are ordered differently. The following figure illustrates the A minor scale, which is the one minor scale (like C major) that doesn't use accidentals. You can see that half steps lie between the second and third notes of the scale, and between the fifth and sixth notes. The following table spells out how to construct a minor scale by counting whole and half steps on the keyboard.

Music Speak

Relative minor and **relative major keys** share the same key signature. The major key with a key signature of two sharps (D major) is the relative major of the minor key with a key signature of two sharps (B minor). By the same token, B minor is called the relative minor of D major.

Between notes 1 and 2	Whole step
Between notes 2 and 3	Half step
Between notes 3 and 4	Whole step
Between notes 4 and 5	Whole step
Between notes 5 and 6	Half step
Between notes 6 and 7	Whole step
Between notes 7 and 8	Whole step

The awful truth is that there are three different types of minor scales, but the good news is that you only need to know about one: the scale described by the whole/half step arrangement in the above table. The minor scale in the figure below, and all others that use its sequence of whole and half steps, is called a natural minor scale.

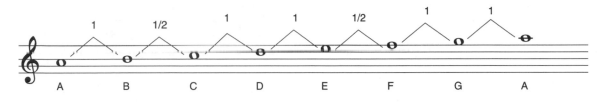

The A-minor scale. Although there are three kinds of minor scales—the natural minor scale one is most important—of which this is an example.

Close Relations

Minor keys (and their scales and key signatures) are closely related to major scales. Remember one crucial fact you know about major keys: that each has a unique key signature. It's true (I'm the honest sort) that no two major keys share a key signature, but every major key does share its key signature with a minor key. Major keys and minor keys that share key signatures are said to be related, so that the minor key with the same key signature as a major key is said to be the relative minor, just as the major key is the relative major of the minor key.

The easiest major and minor keys to remember, when it comes to being related, are C major and its relative minor, A minor. C major and A minor share a key signature of no flats and no sharps. The two keys also provide the key for determining the relative minor of any major key. If you count downward from C to A, you notice that A is three half steps below C. In exactly the same way, any major key's relative minor can be determined by counting down three half steps from the major key's tonic note.

The following illustration shows you key signatures up to five sharps and five flats.

Grace Notes

Okay, time for a juicy snippet of confusion. You now know that modes are extra scales based on ancient musical systems. What you're about to find out is that major and minor are also considered modes. Major mode consists of all major keys and scales, and minor mode contains all minor keys and scales. "Switching mode" generally refers to a change from major key to minor key, or the reverse.

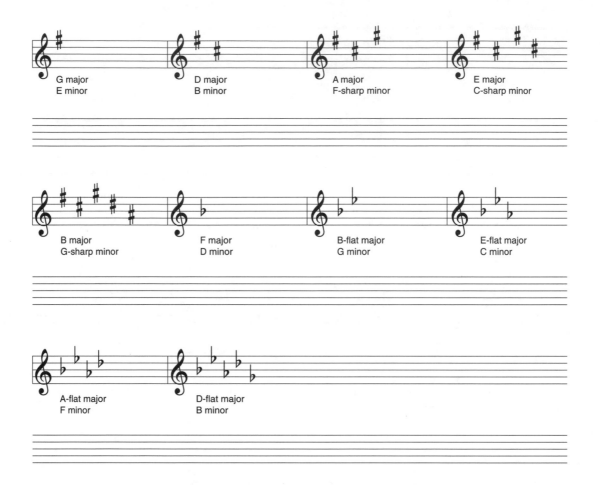

G major
E minor

D major
B minor

A major
F-sharp minor

E major
C-sharp minor

B major
G-sharp minor

F major
D minor

B-flat major
G minor

E-flat major
C minor

A-flat major
F minor

D-flat major
B minor

Scales à la Mode

Some of the smart students sitting in the front row of desks may have heard musicologists refer to modes and wonder how these differ from scales. Well, actually, modes *are* scales, and way back in the medieval era, music was structured around the seven modes rather than the major and minor keys. (You thought learning two scales was hard!) Each mode has a different relation of whole and half steps, determined by the note on which it starts.

Each mode only uses the white keys of the piano. So, the C-major scale, which has no accidentals, is known in Mode-land as the Ionian Mode. Similarly, you can play the other six modes by beginning with each note of the C-major scale, moving up the keyboard using only the white notes. The following table shows you each of the modes with their fancy Greek names.

D	Dorian
E	Phrygian
F	Lydian
G	Mixolydian
A	Aeolian
B	Locrian

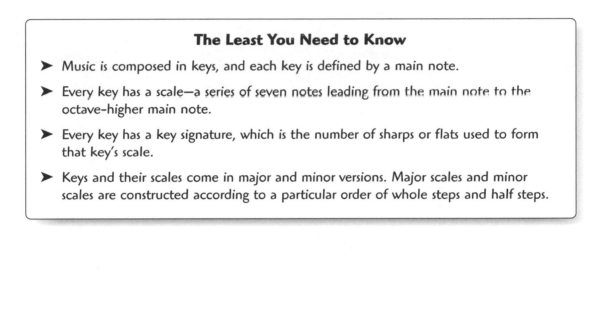

The modes were okay as far as they went, but they weren't too friendly to added harmonies. A piece that was set in the Ionian mode stayed there and didn't stray into the Dorian mode, for example; whereas a piece written in C major can progress into G major or even A minor. By the early seventeenth century, composers were frustrated with modal writing, and longed to freshen their music with harmonies and key changes. The major and minor scales—equivalent to the Ionian and Aeolian modes—won out the battle of bands, and the other modes fell into disuse.

The Least You Need to Know

➤ Music is composed in keys, and each key is defined by a main note.

➤ Every key has a scale—a series of seven notes leading from the main note to the octave-higher main note.

➤ Every key has a key signature, which is the number of sharps or flats used to form that key's scale.

➤ Keys and their scales come in major and minor versions. Major scales and minor scales are constructed according to a particular order of whole steps and half steps.

Give Yourself Another Hand

Part 3 gives the left hand its day in the sun. I'm sure you've noticed that the piano is played with both hands. In fact, that's one of the unique aspects of keyboard instruments—both hands can make notes at the same time. In addition to learning the left-hand notes, the chapters in this part focus on the coordination challenges of playing two-handed music. In addition, I provide a thorough tutorial in chords and other left-hand techniques. Getting familiar with playing and constructing chords makes you a much more capable musician, and enables you to play all kinds of music.

As with Part 2, this part gives you plenty of exercises, framed as Practice Sessions. They are all the more important as you get the two hands working together.

Chapter 10 introduces the notes played by the left hand. Then, in Chapter 11, we put both hands together for the first time! Chapter 12 discusses the joys of accompaniment, and Chapter 13 introduces chord theory, giving you all the chords you need to know.

Learning the Left-Hand Notes

In This Chapter

➤ Finding middle C with the left hand

➤ Learning left-hand notes on the bass clef staff

➤ Exploring time and key signatures in the bass clef

In this chapter, I introduce a whole new dimension to keyboard playing: the left hand. Whether the left-hand notes are useful to you depends on what kind of playing you are interested in. If you have a home keyboard with auto-accompaniment features, you may choose to limit your playing to right-hand notes, supported by the auto-accompaniments afforded by your keyboard. But if you want to explore the full ambidextrous potential of the piano, getting the left hand involved is essential.

Using both hands enables you to play more advanced pieces as well as to accompany yourself. And developing a strong left hand is key to your progress as a pianist.

Middle C for the Left Hand

Chapter 2, "Hammers and Strings," introduced the right-hand notes by starting with middle C as a home base. Conveniently, middle C is an anchor for the left-hand notes, too. Just as the right hand plays middle C with the thumb, so does the left hand. When your left-hand thumb rests on middle C, your other fingers extend downward on the keyboard, ready to play its lower half.

When first finding notes for the left hand, you need to become familiar with saying the alphabet backward. When the right hand plays notes upward from middle C, it's easy enough to recite the alphabet forward as you play successive notes: C, D, E, and so on. With the left hand, the order is backward as your proceed down the keyboard to the left: C, B, A, and so on. The figure below illustrates the keyboard notes extending downward for one octave from middle C.

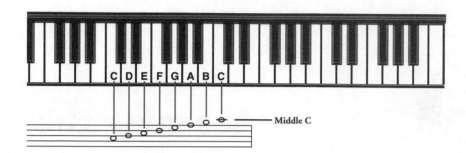

Middle C is both a left-hand and right-hand note. This illustration shows you an octave of notes (without accidentals) from middle C down to the next C.

Practice Session

Time to give your left hand some hands-on experience with the keyboard. Try placing your left thumb on middle C, letting your other fingers rest on the four keys to the left of middle C. No need to actually play any key yet—though if you did, the roof probably won't cave in. Now place your *right* thumb on middle C, without removing your left thumb. That's right—both thumbs are sharing the key, but just resting on it without playing the note.

Your hands are now resting in the classic "ready" position for playing a keyboard, sort of like resting your fingers on a computer keyboard, ready to type. From the middle C position, your hands are best poised to leap into musical action.

Keeping both hands resting in the ready position, thumbs resting on middle C, play the keys downward with your left hand, starting with the thumb and proceeding to the little finger, then reverse direction back up (see the following figure).

Play these left-hand notes with the fingerings indicated. Remember that left-hand fingerings mirror right-hand fingerings—finger number 1 is the thumb.

Now try getting both hands into the act. Start from the bottom—the little finger of your left hand, which should be resting on the F key—and play each note all the way to the little finger of your right hand (resting on G). When you get to middle C, play it twice on the way up—first with your left thumb, then with your right thumb. On the way down you also play it twice, first with the right thumb. Take your time, and don't worry about rhythm or counting. Just play each note clearly, and release each key as you play the next key. The following figure spells out the notation for this exercise.

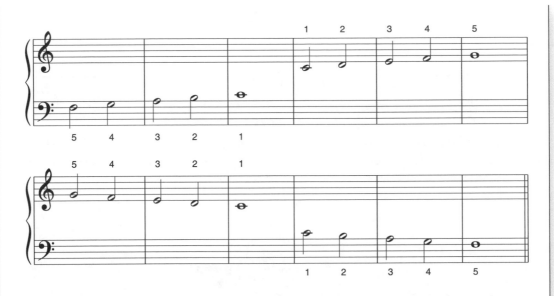

This exercise uses all your fingers. Play the notes slowly up from your left hand little finger to your right-hand little finger, then back down, using the fingerings shown here.

Here's one more thing to try. This exercise is exciting (assuming you're as easily excited as I am) because it starts you playing with both hands at once. Start by playing middle C with *both* thumbs pressing the key down. Using both thumbs on one key may seem like wasted effort, not to mention cramped conditions for your thumbs as they squeeze onto a single key, but it helps your coordination.

Now play both index fingers at the same time—your left index finger should be resting on the B below middle C, and your right index finger should play the D above middle C. Then move on to the middle fingers, then the ring fingers, then the little fingers.

The figure below shows you what this exercise looks like on paper. Don't worry in the slightest about rhythm and counting—just concentrate on playing the notes with both hands simultaneously. Remember to release the keys when you play the next keys. As shown in the illustration, when you get to the little fingers, turn right around and work your way back to the thumbs on middle C.

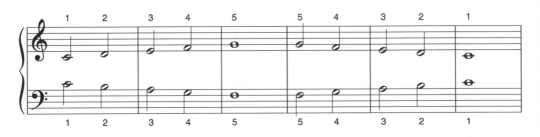

Time to play with both hands at once! Middle C is shared by the thumbs of both hands.

Congratulations: you're now a two-fisted keyboard player!

Grace Notes

While lefties have to make special adjustments to play the guitar, for example, restringing it to suit their left-handed orientation, it makes no difference whether you are right or left handed when it comes to playing the piano. It's a truly ambidextrous instrument!

Key Thought

The thumbs aren't always used to play middle C, but using them now, as you begin to bring the left hand into play (pun fully intended, I'm afraid), helps center your hands on the keyboard. With both hands resting lightly on the keys, each thumb placed on middle C, your hands are in a sort of "home position" from which they can scoot upward or downward as the music demands.

Music Speak

A **clef** is a symbol placed at the beginning of the staff to indicate the position of the notes on it. The most common clefs are the *treble (G clef)* or *bass (F clef)*.

A **double staff** consists of the treble and bass staffs connected together, to indicate two lines that are played simultaneously.

Left-Hand Notes on the Staff

Now that your left hand is finding its way around the keyboard, you need to know how to recognize left-hand notes as they are written in music notation. Learning the left-hand notes introduces the two clefs—treble clef and bass clef—used in keyboard and piano notation. The treble clef is used for right-hand notes, and the bass clef holds the left-hand notes (the following figure illustrates the two clefs).

In real-life playing, you sometimes reach down to the bass clef notes with your right hand, and there's no law saying your left hand can't play treble clef notes. But for most practical purposes, each hand usually stays on its own clef.

The bass clef staff works exactly like the treble clef staff, in that notes are placed on lines and in spaces between the lines. In fact, the staffs are identical (five horizontal lines each), but the clefs make the note placements different. A note placed on the middle line of the treble clef (B) is not the same as a note placed on the middle line of the bass clef (D).

Treble Clef (Right Hand)

Bass Clef (Left Hand)

The treble clef (for right-hand notes) and bass clef (for left-hand notes).

The treble and bass clefs are divided around middle C. You've already learned that middle C on the treble clef is the note hanging beneath the staff on a single leger line. Middle C also exists on the bass clef, and is notated as the note resting *above* the staff on a single leger line (see the following figure). Pretty darn symmetrical, huh? Thank you very much—I wish I could take credit for the notation design, but it was invented several centuries ago when I was only seven years old.

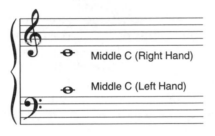

Middle C (Right Hand)

Middle C (Left Hand)

Middle C can be notated on both the treble clef and bass clef.

This is a good time to join the two music staffs into a single, double staff. Huh? Come again? A *single double staff*? That's right: In piano music, the left-hand staff (bass clef) and right-hand staff (treble clef) are joined together with bar lines that extend vertically down through both staffs. To emphasize the bonding of the two staffs, a bracket on the left end of the double-staff joins them together (see the previous figure).

As mentioned above, the two staffs (treble and bass clef) are identical in how they function, but note placements are different. This is undeniably more difficult than if the note placements were the same. If they were the same, you'd only have to learn one staff, then apply that knowledge to both hands. As it is, however, you must learn how to read the staffs independently. This is perhaps the trickiest part of learning to read piano music, but like anything else it just takes some experience and practice.

Key Thought

When you think about it, there can be no other way to notate two-handed playing. Because both hands are often playing at the same time, you must be able to read the notes for both hands at a glance, so one staff must be positioned under the other. It's only natural that the bass clef staff (left hand) be positioned underneath the treble clef staff.

To start, look at the following figure, which spells out all the notes of the bass clef down to the first leger line beneath the staff. You can use this illustration whenever you need a refresher course in reading the bass clef.

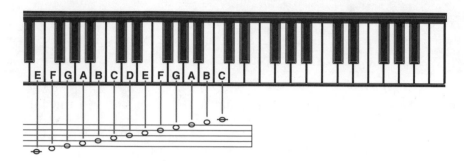

The bass clef notes, and where to find them on the keyboard.

Grace Notes

Just a reminder: The key signature is placed at the beginning of every staff of a piece—that means each clef of a double staff of piano music. The key signature is a constant reminder of which notes are automatically sharped or flatted.

To aid you in learning the bass clef notes, I offer a mnemonic device. This particular mnemonic device is based on the notion that remembering a phrase is easier than remembering a bunch of notes. So, if you take the notes of each of the bass clef lines, bottom to top, they can form an acronym for a memorable phrase. The notes are: G (bottom line), B (next line up), D (middle line), F (below the top line), and A (top line). Here are a few phrases sure to help you remember the order of bass clef lines:

➤ Good Boys Don't Fly Away

➤ Gregarious Babbling Dwarfs Flee Aghast

➤ Gaudy Baubles Demonstrate Futile Agendas

➤ Ghouls Betray Demons, Forestalling Adversity

➤ Gradually But Doggedly, Felicia Advanced

Hope that helps.

Grace Notes

Occasionally, more than two staffs are used to notate piano music. Such an abundant use of staffs is present only when the music is too complex to fit onto the normal two staffs. Orchestral scores connect many staffs, sometimes more than two dozen, to accomodate all the different instrument parts. On the other end of the scale, pop music for piano and keyboards is often notated on a single staff that holds the melody, with chords written above it for the left hand to play.

Practice Session

Now that you know the basics of the bass clef (the bass basics, so to speak), it's a good time to get some hands-on practice (practical practice?) with reading the bass clef and playing its notes on the keyboard. You may remember that I annoyed you with such exercises in Chapter 2, using the treble clef. It might be a good idea to connect the two chapters in your mind, and review the exercises in both chapters now. First, take a look at the following figure:

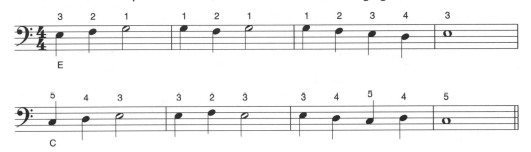

A left-hand playing exercise that may, or may not, move you to tears. Probably not.

If no other piece in this book brings you to cathartic tears, this one will. I'm expecting critics to hail this exercise as a landmark of keyboard composition, worthy of its place in the immortal pantheon; either that, or the critics will ignore it completely. Anyway, get out the tissues and start playing. I've marked fingerings, and the exercise is written in rhythm, so you have a chance to put it all together.

Start by forgetting the rhythm and just figuring out the notes, and playing them with the correct fingers. Once you've got the hang of the notes, start counting and playing in rhythm. As always, go slowly and play evenly. Continue practicing the exercise until you can play it in the correct rhythm and with the correct fingers. It doesn't matter how fast you count and play—slow as molasses is fine. Just for fun (all right, so I'm not exactly a party animal), the following figure gives you another exercise.

This tune may be recognizable as "Here Comes the Bride," which has an alternate title of "Don't Step on the Bridal Train." I've presented the the piece for the left hand with fingerings. It's important to pay attention to the fingerings on this one, because the range covers a full octave—greater than the natural five-key span of your left hand. Again, start by learning the notes and fingerings, then add your counting to play the piece in the correct rhythm. Remember, slow is good. Slow is your friend. Mr. Slow is always there for you.

Time and Key Signatures in the Bass Clef

What's left to round out your understanding of the bass clef, and the left hand's participation on the keyboard? Practice, of course, is what really helps both hands become facile players. When it comes to reading music and recognizing notes placed on both the treble and bass clefs, it's just a matter of getting used to the look of the double staff as two connected single staffs.

You'll be glad to know that key signatures work just the same on the bass clef staff as on the treble clef staff. However, when it comes to the placement of the sharps or flats of a key signature, the symbols must correspond to where the notes lie on the staff. The following figure makes this all clear.

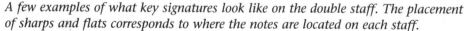

A few examples of what key signatures look like on the double staff. The placement of sharps and flats corresponds to where the notes are located on each staff.

In the first example, the key signature is one sharp (F-sharp), and you can see that sharp indicated on both clefs of the double staff. However, because the F note is located on a different line in each staff, the sharp sign is likewise placed differently. The second example uses a key signature of one flat (B-flat), and here, too, you can see the difference in placement, corresponding to where B is located on both staffs. The other two examples extend this lesson to key signatures with more than one sharp or flat.

Time signatures are very easy: they are simply repeated on each clef of the double staff. The following figure shows what a complete double staff looks like at the beginning of a piece, including the bracket joining the two staffs, the two clefs, the time signature, and the key signature. Remember: The time signature appears only once, at the beginning of the piece, unless the time signature changes during the piece.

The double staff at the beginning of a piece, showing the time signature and key signature.

Making Music

Now that you know the left-hands as written on the bass clef, it's time to get that hand playing some music. In piano music, the left hand plays the melody much less frequently than the right hand does, but with the spotlight on the left hand right now, I've given it a couple of solo melodies to practice.

First is a melody by George Frederick Handel, the German composer who spent most of his career in London during the early eighteenth century. This melody, in it's original form (I've made it a bit easier here) was used by Johannes Brahms, over a century later, in a difficult set of variations for piano.

Next is the American spiritual, "Swing Low, Sweet Chariot," which I think sounds great in the lower range of the left hand, as if sung by a choir of men.

The Least You Need to Know

➤ Middle C is the same for the left hand as for the right hand. When both hands have their thumbs resting on middle C, they are in a basic starting position.

➤ The bass clef has five lines, just like the treble clef, but the lines and spaces of the two staffs don't correlate to the same notes. This chapter reviews the bass clef notes.

➤ Time signatures and key signatures appear on the bass clef just as on the treble clef.

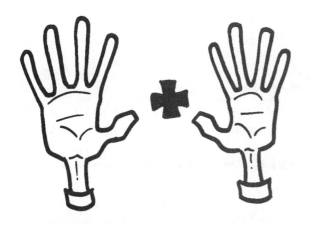

Chapter 11

Putting One and One Together

In This Chapter

➤ Getting acquainted with the grand staff

➤ Understanding how the right-hand and left-hand parts of a piece are notated on the grand staff

➤ Learning how to approach two-handed playing

One of the adventures of playing the piano is that you use both hands to make music. Other instruments are *held* with both hands, or one hand is on the instrument's neck while the other hand strums (guitar) or bows (violin), but keyboards are the instruments for playing two different parts simultaneously.

Pianos (and other keyboards) are the only instruments that let you play a different note with every finger, all at the same time. Such a multinote capacity isn't the easiest thing in the world to master. You can begin slowly when it comes to playing with both hands, and this chapter gets you started.

Starting Simple

The so-called *grand staff*, regal though it sounds, is merely the treble clef staff and the bass clef staff connected in one double staff. You read the grand staff in just the same way as single staffs: from left to right. The left-hand part is on the bottom staff. Bar lines, indicating measures, extend through both staffs, keeping them synchronized according to the rhythm of the piece. The time signature and key signature are the same for both staffs.

Practice Session

Learning to play with two hands involves a couple of distinct challenges. First, there is the sheer physical coordination of using both hands on the keyboard, each playing something different. Then, there is the rhythmic coordination of two musical parts being played at the same time. It's almost enough to drive you to the bongos, but hang in there. These exercises get you started very simply.

The following figure is your first step into the world of two-handed playing. Notice that each hand only plays one note (two Cs an octave apart), and the left-hand part is as simple as it gets. The piece is in 4/4 time, so your counting is to four. Go through the right-hand part a couple of times first. You can also practice the bass clef staff by itself. Then put the two staffs together. Use any fingers to play the notes, and count slowly and evenly.

In this exercise, the right hand does most of the work, and the left hand plays just one note per measure.

The next figure shifts some of the work to the left hand, but doesn't make the two hands do any fancy stuff at the same time. Again, practice each part alone before putting them together, counting all the time. When you put the hands together, keep the counting even, no matter how slow your tempo. I realize these one-note melodies are boring as anything, but if you keep reading you'll get to some more interesting music.

The right and left hands alternate the rhythmic work.

102

The next exercise gives you something to really sink your teeth in. In this heart-rending piece of music, the right hand moves around a little, while the left hand stays anchored on one note. Because the right hand is playing a melody (though not one likely to make Billy Joel put down his pen), it's important to pay attention to the fingering. In fact, two-handed playing requires good fingering more than one-handed playing, because you can't focus all your attention on either hand.

Practice the right hand first, until you can play it easily, almost without thinking about it. Run through the left-hand part once, then put them together.

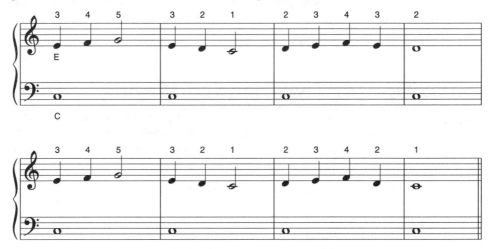

Practice the hands separately first. Count slowly and evenly while playing. Chewing gum at the same time is courting disaster.

You can wrap up this round of exercises with the next figure. This piece is a round, which, if you remember from your sing-along scouting days, is a kind of repetition piece. In this case, the left hand repeats what the right hand plays first. This little study gives you practice playing two melodies simultaneously, but they are composed so that the two hands are not active at the same time. Be sure to try each part several times before trying to put them together, counting evenly all the while.

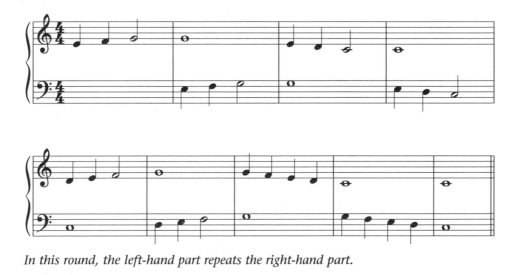

In this round, the left-hand part repeats the right-hand part.

Key Thought

Learning each part separately is good advice from this point on, because the pieces you will be playing will be more and more complicated. Now is a good time to learn the right method of approaching and learning two-handed pieces. And the good habits serve you well later on.

Practice Tips for Two-Handed Playing

The big thing to remember about playing a piece that uses both hands is that you don't have to do it right the first time. In fact, you don't have to play all the notes the first time. The best way to learn a keyboard piece is to take it apart, try the parts separately, practice each hand on its own, then gradually put them together .

Following are the steps you should take when learning any new two-handed piece.

➤ **Note the key signature.** Check out the sharps or flats at the beginning of the staffs. They tell you which notes are automatically sharped or flatted throughout the piece. You need to keep the key signature in mind when you're learning the notes.

➤ **Start with the left hand.** This may be a surprising tip, because the right-hand part is usually the more prominent of the two, containing the melody in most cases. But that's exactly why you want to start with the left hand, which is usually the supportive part. In the end, you may want to concentrate more on the right hand, so you need to know the left-hand part very well.

➤ **Find the notes.** Don't worry about the rhythm right away. Pick out the left-hand notes one by one until you're acquainted with where each note lies on the keyboard.

➤ **Learn the fingerings.** If fingerings are marked in the written music, play the left-hand notes with the correct fingers. There may be no fingerings at all, depending on the helpfulness of whoever prepared the arrangement of the music. In most cases some fingerings exist, giving you the correct finger for certain important notes, and letting you determine the other fingerings based on them.

➤ **Count.** Once you've found the notes and their fingerings, it's time to begin playing the left-hand part with the correct rhythm. Look at the time signature to determine how many beats are in each measure. Use the counting methods of previous chapters, beginning slowly and evenly. A fast tempo isn't important at this stage.

➤ **Look at the right-hand part.** Finally, the right hand! Start by finding the notes, regardless of rhythm. Once you've gotten acquainted with the notes, figure out the best fingering with whatever help the sheet music gives you. Once you can play the notes with the correct fingers, begin counting the correct rhythm.

➤ **Put the hands together.** When you can play each hand independently, begin putting them together. You may want to disregard the rhythm at first, and that's fine. However, continue to use the best fingerings for both hands, no matter how slowly and haltingly you need to play. Gradually even out the rhythm and make it steady with your counting. It's helpful to break up the piece into two- and four-measure chunks, learning each chunk separately, then putting them together into a coherent, whole piece of music.

Making Music

If you've made it this far, this chapter is giving you the first feeling of what it's like to play with two hands. This is what distinguishes the piano (and other keyboards) from most other instruments—using all ten fingers to make notes.

The pieces in this section require more practice than all the previous pieces in the book. About twice as much work, in fact, since two parts must be learned instead of just one. Don't try to play both hands simultaneously at first. Spend some time with the right-hand melody, then try the left-hand part. Go slowly and count carefully with each hand. When you feel comfortable with each part separately, gradually put them together one bar at a time. I have provided suggested fingerings that facilitate some of the harder passages.

You might recognize the first piece, without knowing where it comes from. The melody is a famous theme from the *Symphony from the New World* by the Czech composer Dvorak.

You saw a portion of *Twinkle, Twinkle Little Star* in both Chapters 7 and 8. Here you have the entire melody arranged simply for two hands.

Christmas carols exist in thousands of arrangements, from classical orchestrations to jazzy piano renditions to rock 'n' roll anthems. The following arrangement of *God Rest Ye Merry Gentlemen* uses a fairly simple left-hand part, but one that covers a lot of ground and implies non-traditional harmonies.

The final piece of this chapter is the hardest. Composed to be played in a lively manner, it requires slower practice first, to learn the notes and rests. The second-to-last measure is the hardest, and should be practiced by itself until you can play it up to the speed of the rest of the piece.

The Least You Need to Know

➤ The grand staff is simply a treble clef staff and a bass clef staff joined together. Bar lines connect the two staffs.

➤ Piano pieces are notated on a grand staff, with the left-hand part underneath the right-hand part.

Chapter 12

Basics of Accompaniment

In This Chapter

➤ What is accompaniment?

➤ Understanding basic left-hand playing styles, including walking bass, chords, arpeggios, stride, and broken chords

➤ Beginning to use keyboard auto-accompaniments

Traditionally, the left hand's role in playing keyboards is to provide harmony and rhythm for the right hand, which is usually playing the melody. Sometimes the left hand has a more prominent part in the music, but generally, left-hand parts are supportive of right hand melodies.

In classical piano music of the eighteenth and nineteenth centuries, the melody is usually higher than the accompaniment, and is played with the right hand while the left hand performs various supportive musical phrases. In Baroque music of the sixteenth and seventeenth centuries, composed for organ and harpsichord, the left hand is more independent; the music of the era favored many simultaneous melodies.

This chapter concentrates on some of the standard things the left hand does in various types of music. This is also where you begin learning how to use the one-finger auto-accompaniment feature common to many keyboards. Some of the styles and techniques in this chapter are traditional to classical piano music, but still can be played on electronic instruments.

What Is Accompaniment?

In music, the *accompaniment* is the part (or parts) that plays along with the main musical part. The accompaniment is usually somewhat in the background (lower in volume), so the main part is highlighted. The main part might be performed by a lead singer, an instrumental soloist, or the right hand of a pianist.

Grace Notes

There are a number of spectacular examples of left-hand virtuosity in the musical literature for classical piano. At least one piano concerto (by the French composer Maurice Ravel) and several solo piano pieces owe their existence to the needs of pianists whose right hands had become incapacitated. Is it cheating to play such pieces with two hands? Maybe not, but I wouldn't brag about it.

Music Speak

Accompaniment is the musical part (or parts) that is played underneath, and supports, the main melody. In piano music, the left hand usually plays the accompaniment, though in classical music the accompaniment switches between the two hands.

Grace Notes

In the classic small jazz ensemble, the upright bass provides a harmonic underpinning to the piano part by playing notes that emphasize the piece's harmonies. The bass also helps propel the rhythm by playing a steady, even stream of bass notes on every quarter note.

When Tony Bennett, the jazz singer, gives a concert, he is *accompanied* by a pianist, or perhaps a jazz ensemble with bass and drums. When a violinist plays a concerto, she is accompanied by a symphony orchestra. When a lounge singer performs her solo act, she accompanies herself on the piano. The purpose of an accompaniment is to provide the harmony (chords) and rhythm (beats) of the music, in support of the melody (and, in the case of singers, the words).

Not all accompaniment is always subordinate to the main part. In piano music, the left hand sometimes has the more important and melodic part, while the right hand takes a turn in the background. When a pianist is accompanying an instrumental soloist, say a violinist in a sonata for violin and piano, it is not always the violin in the spotlight. Soloists usually receive star billing in such partnerships, but piano accompaniments are challenging and important in their own right, and often include solo passages of great beauty and difficulty. It's useful to remember that *accompany* means "to go with," not "to hide in the shadow of."

Left-Hand Playing Styles

Over time, many styles of left-hand playing have developed. In classical, jazz, and pop music, the left-hand parts have evolved into certain recognizable patterns. While each piece is different, and many pieces in all genres disregard tradition with unique parts for both hands, accompaniment patterns have developed that can be learned, making it easier to learn new pieces in these genres. In jazz and pop especially, where improvisation is just as important (sometimes more important) as slavishly following the written notes, understanding left-hand accompaniment patterns can really help you play those musical styles.

The following sections describe and illustrate some accompaniment patterns in different musical genres.

The Simplest Accompaniment

Some accompaniment styles provide rich, full harmonies in support of the right-hand melody. In jazz, though, it is stylish to *imply* the harmonies with sparse accompaniments made up of single left-hand notes. The meager accompaniment style is reminiscent of, and probably inspired by, the upright bass—an important instrument in the basic jazz ensemble of piano, bass, and drums. The playing style is called *walking bass*, because of its ambling, continuous style. The following figure illustrates the walking bass style of left-hand accompaniment of a jazz tune.

If you don't care for jazz, take heart. Walking bass isn't just for swing and bossa nova music. Furthermore, it can be simplified, making it easier to play, and single-note bass accompaniment can be applied to just about any popular genre. (However, walking bass is not appropriate for classical music.) The figure below shows how a simple, single-note bass line can be used as an accompaniment for a song.

This simplified arrangement of "The Twelve Days of Christmas" has a simple, one-note-at-a-time left-hand part. Walking bass implies the piece's harmony with just single notes.

Key Thought

Playing with two hands takes a different sort of coordination than playing with just one. The key, as with anything else, is to start simple and practice. The single-finger style of auto-accompaniment featured on many home keyboards lets you create full-blown harmonies to go along with the rhythms that the keyboard is pumping out, just by playing single left-hand notes. That makes coordination relatively easy, but you still must know the basics of harmony and chords. Of course, if you have a piano, digital piano, professional synthesizer, or some other keyboard lacking in auto-accompaniment bells and whistles, you're in for a left-handed learning curve.

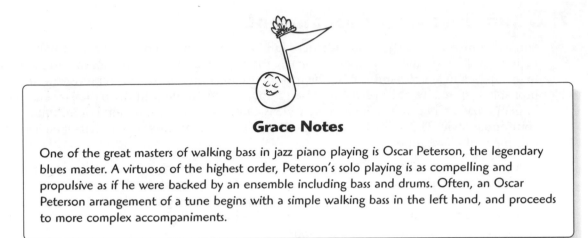

Grace Notes

One of the great masters of walking bass in jazz piano playing is Oscar Peterson, the legendary blues master. A virtuoso of the highest order, Peterson's solo playing is as compelling and propulsive as if he were backed by an ensemble including bass and drums. Often, an Oscar Peterson arrangement of a tune begins with a simple walking bass in the left hand, and proceeds to more complex accompaniments.

Chords

Chords, which are clusters of notes played at the same time, provide the most all-purpose accompaniment. Chords may seem intimidating to play at first, but you get the hang of them with practice.

The following figure shows how chords can be used to accompany part of the melody of "The Twelve Days of Christmas." Try playing the chords if you like, or go to the next chapter for the complete tutorial (the chord curriculum, shall we say). If you do play them, it's easy to notice that they provide a much fuller, richer sound than single notes in the left-hand part. Chords define a full harmony, whereas single notes just imply that harmony.

Another excerpt of "The Twelve Days of Christmas," this time with chords in the left-hand accompaniment.

Music Speak

Chords are clusters of notes played simultaneously. Most chords create a pleasing harmonic effect, but strictly speaking, a chord can be any group of notes, regardless of how awful it sounds.

Chord accompaniments can be altered by playing the notes of chords individually instead of as a simultaneous group. Such an accompaniment is called *broken chords*, and comes in a few varieties. In other words, the notes of the chords may be played in a variety of orders: top to bottom; bottom to top; or all mixed up in any number of ways.

The next example shows a few ways that broken chords derive from regular chords. The beauty of broken chords is that they add a rhythmic element in addition to harmony.

Besides broken chords, another way to play chords is to ripple the notes upward in quick succession, which is called an *arpeggio*. Strictly speaking, arpeggios can ripple either upward or downward, but they usually go from the lowest note to the highest.

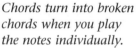

Music Speak

Arpeggios are chords played by rippling the notes quickly from bottom to top.

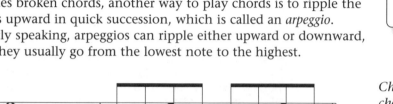

Chords turn into broken chords when you play the notes individually.

The next figure illustrates what an arpeggio looks like in music notation: The wiggly line tells you to play the chord as a very quick, almost simultaneous, succession of notes. There is no hard-and-fast rule about how quickly the arpeggio is played; the speed, force, and character of the arpeggio depends on the mood of the piece.

An arpeggio is a chord played with a rippling effect, indicated with a ripply line before it. The chord is played very quickly from the bottom note to the top.

Repeated chords are the most common style of left-hand accompaniment. The pop music of the fifties featured such chords hammered out through a song, and the music of subsequent decades is only marginally more sophisticated. The typical style for a piano-playing pop star is to pound out chords while singing a song, with very few melodies issuing from the piano.

Chordal accompaniment is a big part of jazz, like pop, but jazz chords are much more sophisticated, usually use more notes, and describe complex, sometimes challenging, harmonies. The master of modern jazz harmony and chord-playing was Bill Evans, a sensitive, introverted, thoughtful musician who helped define what is called the modern jazz harmonic vocabulary. That's a fancy way of saying he invented many of the chords used by jazz pianists for the past forty years. When playing a Bill Evans recording, listen to the quiet chords underneath the right-hand melody.

Music Speak

Broken chords are chords whose notes are played one at a time. A left-hand accompaniment style popular in classical music from the eighteenth and nineteenth centuries, broken chords were used extensively by Mozart and Beethoven.

Striding Along

There's a certain kind of left-hand accompaniment style that is a little difficult to play, but sounds great. The style is called *stride*, and there's nothing like it. Stride playing fits better on a piano than on a small electric keyboard, because the left-hand style requires a large range. The stride style is characterized by the left hand bouncing back and forth between bass notes low on the keyboard and chords at least an octave higher.

The effect of stride is rollicking and jazzy, and is the characteristic left-hand part of ragtime piano pieces. Variations of the simple note-to-chord style of traditional stride involve substituting an octave or a chord for the low note.

Music Speak

Stride is a style of piano playing in which the left hand bounces between bass notes and chords. Stride is used in various types of jazz playing, but was made popular by ragtime.

Ragtime is probably the most popular example of the *stride* style of piano playing. Listen to any recording of Scott Joplin to hear that bouncing left hand—but make sure you get a piano recording, and not one of the many arrangements for orchestra. In a more modern vein, check out the piano stylings of Dave McKenna, a contemporary legend with the best stride left hand in the business.

Using Keyboard Auto-Accompaniments

If you have a home keyboard, as opposed to a digital piano or professional synthesizer, chances are it sports some kind of automated accompaniment with buttons for setting the accompaniment style, tempo, and harmonies.

Basically, auto-accompaniment consists of three aspects:

➤ **Style.** Many keyboards let you choose from many music styles such as swing jazz, various rock beats, waltz, bossa nova, country, and other musical genres. The styles are defined by rhythms, and when you select a style you hear a rhythm section playing the background parts for that genre. Usually, no notes or harmonies are present in the style: You add them yourself.

➤ **Tempo.** The speed at which the style selection plays is sometimes variable. Ideally, you have some kind of slider or dial that lets you speed up or slow down the style as it's playing. Alternatively, and not nearly as flexibly, the styles themselves are defined by speed, such as "slow rock ballad," "medium rock song," and "fast rock."

Grace Notes

Arpeggios were often improvised by keyboard players in the Baroque period of the late seventeenth and early eighteenth centuries. In those days, rippling a written chord up or down was an accepted means of adding flair to a piece's performance, whether or not the composer indicated an arpeggio. Later, composers became more strict in their notations, and arpeggios were written out explicitly in piano scores.

➤ **Harmony.** The chords of the accompaniment are selected with your left hand in one of two ways. The first way is, quite simply, to play the chords. As you play them, a bass sound begins playing in the auto-accompaniment, providing a stylish bass line playing the harmonies you define with your chords. In addition, the harmonies are filled in with other instruments, such as guitar.

Key Thought

DISCLAIMER: Every keyboard brand and model is different, and I can't attempt to describe exactly the features of them all. But, different as the various keyboards are, they have similar characteristics.

The second way is called the *one-finger* or *single-finger* method, and is easier to play but less precise. You just play single notes with your left hand, and the keyboard makes certain assumptions, such as whether the chord you want is a major chord or a minor chord. Every keyboard has its own "intelligence" in the selection of harmonies from the single-finger method, but in most cases major chords are the assumed selection. If you want more sophisticated harmonies, you must switch out of single-finger mode and play actual chords.

Grace Notes

Broken chords have been around, as a piano composer's device, for centuries. Mozart used broken chords constantly in his piano sonatas, as did all his composer buddies. Broken chords became a bit more complex in the early nineteenth century with Beethoven and his frat brothers. Then, later in the century, the so-called *Romantic* composers (Chopin, Brahms, Liszt, Schumann, and other members of the Legendary Composers Lodge) used extravagant broken chords that forced the left hand to sweep up and down the lower half of the piano range. Broken chords are predominantly a feature of classical music, but are sometimes found in arrangements of popular music.

115

Practice Session

If you're working with this book from start to finish—well, first of all, congratulations on your stamina. Second, you should know that Chapter 13 gives you a lot of information about chords that helps you use the auto-accompaniment features of your keyboard. But nothing illustrates like an example, so an example is what you're getting, right here in this chapter. The following figure is one way to play a standard jazz waltz tune using auto-accompaniment. I've written out an arrangement of "My Favorite Things," including left-hand notes for activating the harmonies in the keyboard style. Here's how to go about playing this piece:

Playing the left-hand notes with the "full-fingered" or "chord" setting of your keyboard's auto-accompaniment feature results in correct harmonies for "My Favorite Things."

1. First, select the waltz or jazz waltz style from among your keyboard's auto-accompaniment rhythms.

2. Go through the left-hand part, finding the notes. If the keyboard's rhythm style begins playing when you press a key, it means the auto-play feature is turned on; you might want to turn it off while practicing.

3. Now practice the right-hand part. Become fairly fluent with both hands individually before trying to put them together.

4. Play the piece as written, counting each measure in four. Become confident in playing both hands together before turning on the auto-accompaniment.

5. Now for the payoff. Get that auto-accompaniment going by pressing the start or play button. If your keyboard has an auto-start feature, use that—the auto-accompaniment should begin when you play the first note.

As with other exercises, it's better to play this piece slowly and surely, than quickly and unsteadily. If your auto-accompaniment has a tempo or metronome setting, crank it down until it's playing at a comfortable speed and you can play all the notes without falling behind the tempo. You can gradually increase the speed as you repeat the piece, at least until you get thoroughly sick of it.

Making Music

The pieces in this section are more challenging than anything you encountered earlier in the book. Though I've simplified all of them to some extent, the accompaniment figures used in these examples go some distance toward illustrating fairly advanced piano music from Mozart to ragtime to jazz. The left-hand part is generally more difficult in these pieces than the right hand, so practice it separately for as long as you want. Then, slowly and gradually, put the two hands together.

First, the opening measures of a famous piano sonata by Mozart. The piece gets quite hard very quickly, so I've limited the excerpt to these brief bars. The left-hand part is a thorough styling of the era—the late eighteenth century.

The next piece is an example of stride accompaniment, and you'll probably recognize it as the theme from the movie, "The Sting." In fact, the piece, called *The Entertainer*, was composed by Scott Joplin in the early twentieth century, and I've simplified both the melody and left-hand accompaniment. In the original, the left-hand jumps are larger and the hand must grab more notes at each stop. Much of the right hand is played in octaves, which is an advanced playing technique. But nevermind these changes—the piece survives arrangement exceptionally well, which might be why hundreds of arrangements and transcripts of this ever-popular piece exist.

In the following piece, walking bass is illustrated in a jazz standard. If you feel adventurous, you can try modifying the bass line played by the left hand—this is jazz, after all, not classical.

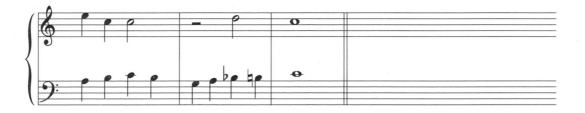

Chordal accompaniment is up next, with a limpidly beautiful piece by the American classical composer Edward MacDowell, called *To a Wild Rose.* In this slightly simplified version, the left hand plays one chord per measure, supporting the right-hand melody. (The next chapter discusses chords in painstaking detail.)

Another, more complex, example of chordal accompaniment is found in a famous Prelude by Chopin. (It's the fourth of fifteen Preludes, if you're counting.) The second half of this piece is dauntingly complex, so I've limited this exerpt to the first half. I've made some slight simplifications to the right hand, but the left-hand part is presented here exactly as composed. It's not that hard to play to any player used to chords, but the slowly shifting harmonies take time to learn. This haunting piece is a perfect example of chords used exclusively to establish the harmony, and even—in this case—the rhythmic pulse.

The Least You Need to Know

➤ Accompaniments are subordinant music parts that provide rhythm and harmony for the melody, vocalist, or solo instrumental part.

➤ Walking bass is a jazz-style accompaniment that mimics an upright bass part.

➤ Chords are the most common type of pianistic, left-hand accompaniment. Chords may be altered into arpeggios, which are rippled chords, and into broken chords, which play the chord's notes individually.

➤ Electronic keyboards have auto-accompaniment features that provide chords and rhythms while you play the melody.

Striking a Familiar Chord

In This Chapter

➤ What are chords?

➤ All about intervals, and why you need to know

➤ Learning what triads are, and how to make them

➤ A review of common chords

I've devoted an entire chapter to chords for two reasons. First, because the International Society of Chord Terrorism told me I had to. Second, and perhaps more important, because chords teach you a lot about harmony and keys.

Chords are the next step beyond scales in musical understanding. Every genre of music uses chords. The most popular contemporary styles—rock, pop, and modern jazz—often notate music using chord marking instead of written-out left-hand parts.

Come to think of it, there are lots of reasons to concentrate on chords and get familiar with how they work. This is one of the most important chapters in the book, and is brought to you by our friends in the ISCT.

A Basic Chord Explanation

A chord is simply a group of notes played together. Following are some basic facts about chords:

➤ The notes could be spread across the whole range of the keyboard, but typically are close enough together to be played with one hand. (Sometimes two-handed chords are called for, in which each hand plays a chord at the same time.)

➤ A chord may have as few as two notes, but three-note and four-note chords are the most common. Two-note chords are called *intervals*.

➤ Any combination of notes may combine into a chord, but the purpose of chords is to create a harmonious blend of notes. Accordingly, like chords strummed on a guitar, keyboard chords come in standard combinations of notes that fulfill specific harmonic functions, and define the piece's harmony.

➤ Chords are often used by the left hand to accompany the right-hand melody.

The next figure illustrates what chords look like when notated.

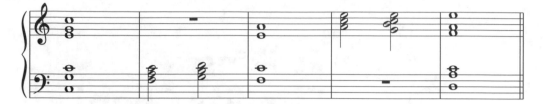

Chords come in all shapes and sizes.

Practice Session

The best way to familiarize yourself with chords is to begin playing them, without regard to their harmonic function. In other words, just get the feeling of chords under your fingers on the keyboard. When you play a chord, it feels almost like grabbing a cluster of notes in your hand. When you get the hang of it, playing chords can feel very satisfying, and sound good, too.

Try playing the two-note chords (intervals) in the figure below. Start by finding each note of the chord independently, then putting them together. Play each interval several times, until you're comfortable with it then move on to the next.

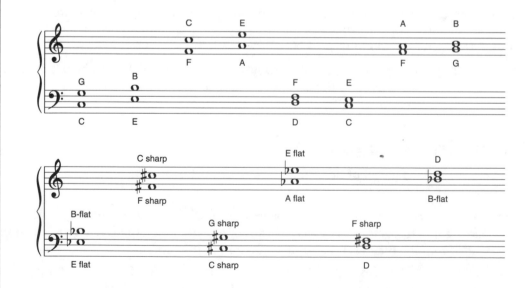

Try playing these two-note chords, also called intervals.

I have deliberately written the above exercise without bar lines, because rhythm is totally unimportant. Don't bother counting—just practice one chord, then proceed to the next. Find fingerings that are comfortable for you, feeling free to experiment with different fingerings on each interval.

The next figure gives you some three-note chords to work with. As with the two-note intervals described above, don't give a thought to rhythm or counting. (There are no bar lines.) Find the individual notes first, then slowly put them together until you're playing all three at once.

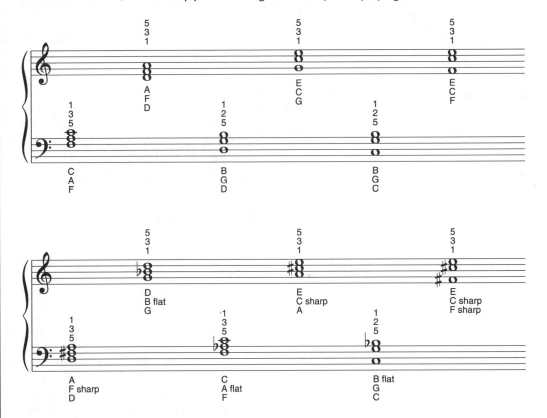

Take your time finding these three-note chords. Keep your arm relaxed from fingers to shoulder, and use the fingerings provided.

The trick to playing chords is to keep your hand and wrist relaxed, but firmly in the position of the chord, so you can lift your hand and drop it down on the chord. It's a lot to ask for, I know! As always, practice is everything. In this exercise I've indicated good fingerings, and using the correct fingers helps keep your hand in a good position for lifting up and dropping down on the chord.

Some of the chords in the exercises included in this Practice Session require you to play black keys for the sharps and flats. When playing a black key and a white key simultaneously, move your whole hand toward the black keys, so that your entire arm moves closer to the base of the keys. Moving your hand like that is especially important when playing a black key with your thumb, the shortest finger. If you don't move your hand forward, you must twist your wrist to reach the black key with the thumb, and that twisting is not only bad form, but stressful to the tendons in your arm. When you shift your whole hand forward, your fingers can play the black keys at the ends of the keys, and your fingers are reaching the white keys in the middle of the key length.

Key Thought

Why, you ask, do you really need to know how chords are constructed? Because some pop and jazz sheet music doesn't use full music notation, but indicates the left-hand part through chord symbols. When you see such a chord symbol, it's up to you to play the chord, even though the notes aren't spelled out for you. For example, you might see "CM" (a C-major chord) or "Dm" (D-minor chord), and you need to know which notes make up that chord.

Music Speak

A **triad** consists of the first, third, and fifth notes of the scale played simultaneously.

Triads and Intervals

It's all well and good to play chords from an exercise illustration, but it's more important to understand how chords are created in the first place.

Learning about chords has two stages. First I'll show you the fundamentals of how chords are created in any key, based on any scale. Understanding the fundamentals gives you the tools to construct a chord in any situation, even if it takes a bit of time to work out the notes.

The second stage involves memory, as you become familiar with the basic chords used in most popular music, and no longer have to refer to scales or the chord-construction techniques you've learned. Knowing the chords automatically is the goal, of course, because when you're playing a piece there's no time to stop and figure out the chords—ideally, you know them so well that playing them is almost second nature.

Learning the Basic Triad

By far, the most common type of chord is the three-note chord, called a *triad*. Now, before you start thinking this is going to be too easy, let me notify you that not all three-note chords are called triads—just those whose notes are stacked up in a certain formation. Simply put, this is the formation of a triad: first note of a scale on the bottom, third note in the middle, and fifth note on top of the chord (see the next figure).

Triads are formed by taking notes from a scale and playing them together. The spaces between the notes are called *intervals*. I've mentioned intervals in earlier parts of the book, but this is where you learn how they work, what the specific intervals are, how to find them on the keyboard, and how they fit into chords. (Whew! All that in one chapter? Yes, thanks to the miracle of modern technology. Or modern book publishing. Modern authorship? Oh, the heck with it—just keep reading.) Intervals and chords are closely related, and it's impossible to learn about one without covering the other.

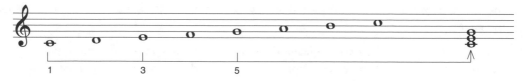

The C-major triad is formed by taking the first, third, and fifth notes of the C-major scale, and playing them together.

Intervals of the C-Major Scale

An interval is really two notes, or, more precisely, the distance between two notes. By "distance" I don't mean physical distance on the keyboard, but pitch distance. Pitch distance is measured by the number of half steps between any two notes. You got acquainted with this concept in Chapter 9, "Unlocking Keys and Scales," and practiced constructing scales by counting half steps and whole steps on the keyboard. Finding intervals is pretty much the same. As with scales, it's best to start in the simplest way possible, which is to restrict yourself to the white keys of the keyboard.

The next figure reminds you of what a notated C-major scale looks like, with each note assigned a number in ascending order.

Armed with this illustration, you can easily form and name intervals by using the bottom C as your bottom note. From C to D (the second note), for example, forms the interval of a *second*. (Intervals are named after ordinal numbers: *second*, *third*, *fourth*, and so on.)

From C to the third note, E, is a third. C to F is a fourth. You get the picture—just go from the bottom C to any step of the scale, and the interval is defined by the number of the top step. What about C to the upper C? That's one interval you learned about as early as Chapter 3, called "The Keyboard in Black and White": the octave. The octave is the only interval not named after an ordinal number. It's called an octave instead of an eighth.

Music Speak

An **interval** is the distance between two notes. For example, the distance between C and G is a fifth (G is the fifth note of the C scale).

The C-major scale, with each of the ascending steps numbered.

Now look at the figure below, to see the intervals of the C-major scale written in music notation.

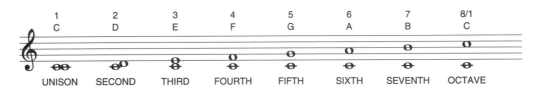

The intervals of the C-major scale.

Intervals in Other Keys

Admittedly, finding intervals within the C-major scale, when the bottom note is C, is the easiest interval exercise in the world (maybe in the whole galaxy). Your mission is not completed until you can find intervals from *any* note on the keyboard. There are two ways to find an interval from any note:

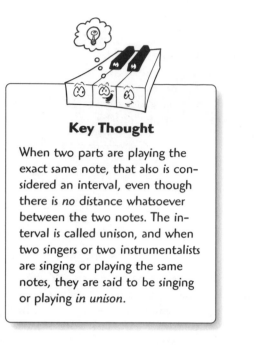

Key Thought

When two parts are playing the exact same note, that also is considered an interval, even though there *is* no distance whatsoever between the two notes. The interval is called unison, and when two singers or two instrumentalists are singing or playing the same notes, they are said to be singing or playing *in unison*.

➤ Construct a major scale from that note, as described in Chapter 9, then number its steps and find the intervals just as with the C-major scale. The process is exactly the same with all major scales, the only difference being that you end up using some black keys, because C major is the only major scale played on white keys only.

The next figure shows the major scale, and its intervals, for D major. Note that D major has a key signature of two sharps (F-sharp and C-sharp), so those two notes are used in the intervals as well as the scale.

➤ Count half steps. Counting half steps is how you find intervals without regard to keys, scales, and key signatures. Intervals are independent beings, and though they relate to keys and scales, they exist separately. It's important to be able to find them separately, and the only way to do that is by counting half steps between the two notes of the interval. Keep reading to see how it's done.

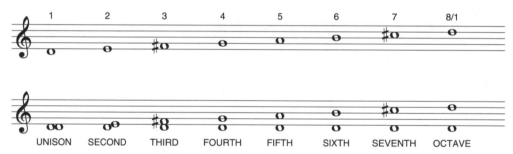

The scale and intervals of D major, which uses two sharps.

Grace Notes

The Society for the Prevention of Interval Discrimination (SPID) has asked me to inform you that *perfect* intervals are really no better than major or minor intervals. The term *perfect* is just that—a musical term with no implication of superiority.

Different Types of Intervals

Counting half steps to find intervals reveals a very interesting fact: Intervals come in different types, just like scales and keys have major and minor modes. There are three main types of intervals:

➤ Major intervals

➤ Minor intervals

➤ Perfect intervals

I should mention that there are two other types of intervals, called *augmented* and *diminished* intervals, but they are part of advanced music theory, and you won't deal with them in this book. You must know about major and minor intervals because they are identified by differing numbers of half steps. I'll get to the half steps very shortly, but for now, please absorb these important facts about major and minor intervals:

➤ Major intervals are one half-step larger (more space between the two notes) than minor intervals. Naturally, minor intervals are one half-step smaller than major intervals.

➤ You can turn a major interval into a minor interval by *subtracting* one half step from between the two notes. (Either raise the bottom note or lower the top note.) Conversely, you can turn a minor interval into a major interval by *adding* a half step between the two notes. (Either lower the bottom note or raise the top note.)

The next figure is an illustration of how major and minor intervals are related, and can be turned into each other. The process only works with intervals that can be major or minor intervals: seconds, thirds, sixths, and sevenths.

Music Speak

Only seconds, thirds, sixths, and sevenths can be major or minor intervals. Unisons, fourths, fifths, and octaves are called **perfect intervals** because they cannot be major or minor.

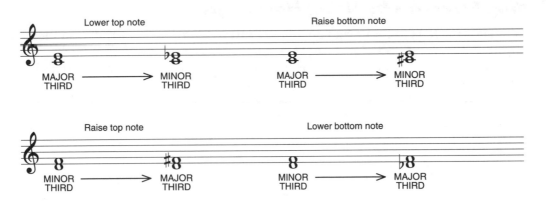

Major intervals turn into minor intervals by subtracting a half step between the notes, which can be done by lowering the top note or raising the bottom note. Minor intervals turn into major intervals in just the opposite way, but adding a half step between the two notes.

Other intervals (unisons, fourths, fifths, and octaves) are the so-called perfect intervals, and cannot be made major or minor. Take a look at the next illustration.

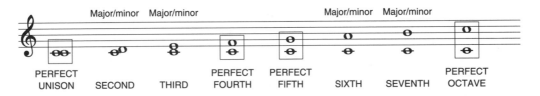

The perfect intervals—unisons, fourths, fifths, and octaves—can never be major or minor intervals.

129

Key Thought

Counting half steps to identify intervals may seem laborious, but after doing it for a while the ol' memory kicks in and you begin to recognize intervals (in their major and minor versions) just by seeing them in music notation or in their position on the keyboard. But for now, counting half steps is the best way to get started.

Finding Intervals by Using Half Steps

Even knowing how to turn major and minor intervals into each other, the question remains how to find a major third, for example, or a minor sixth, starting from any note. To do that, you need to count half steps. The next table shows the number of half steps between every major and minor intervals in any octave.

	Major	Minor	Perfect
Unison	—	—	0
Second	2	1	—
Third	4	3	—
Fourth	—	—	5
Fifth	—	—	7
Sixth	9	8	—
Seventh	11	10	—
Octave	—	—	12

Count up (or down) from any note by a specified number of half steps to find these intervals. Don't count the original note.

Practice Session

The next figure spells out the process of counting half steps to find intervals. Use the illustration to find the interval in each example. Start by finding the bottom note (generously spelled out for you by you-know-who), then count up the half step on the keyboard as indicated. When you find the interval, play both notes simultaneously.

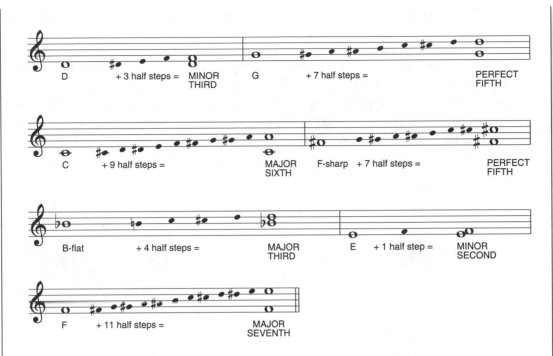

Major, minor, and perfect intervals can be determined by counting half steps.

Now it's time to put you to work. In the next example, I've given you the bottom or top note of each interval, and it's up to you to find the other note. Make sure you do this exercise in front of your keyboard, and count the half steps with your finger on the keys. The direction you should count is indicated by the arrows, but for added fun, count in both directions from each note.

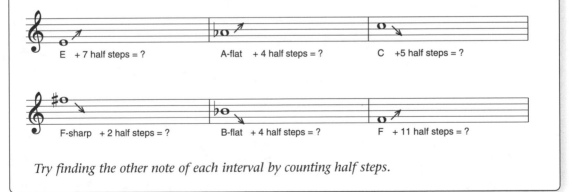

Try finding the other note of each interval by counting half steps.

Major and Minor Triads

You've learned that major triads are created with the first, third, and fifth notes of any major scale. But when push comes to shove, it's actually a little cumbersome to figure out an entire scale just to find a triad.

Here's an easier way. Triads, being three-note chords, consist of two intervals, one on top of the other. Here's how major and minor triads are constructed through intervals:

➤ **Major triads.** The bottom interval is a major third, and the top interval is a minor third. That formula gets you a major triad every time, regardless of what note you start with on the bottom. Just count up four half steps from the bottom note (major third), then count three half steps from the new note (minor third), and you have the three notes of a major triad.

➤ **Minor triads.** Making a minor triad is just as easy as a major triad, but the intervals are reversed. Minor triads have a minor third on the bottom, and a major third on top. Pick a note, and count up three half steps to find the triad's middle note, then count four half steps from the middle note to get the top note.

The following figure shows what happens when you create both a major triad and a minor triad using middle C as the bottom note. You can turn a C-major triad into a C-minor triad by simply lowering the middle note. Conversely, it's no problem to alchemize the C-minor triad into a C-major triad by—you guessed it, Merlin—raising the middle note. Best of all, you can accomplish the major/minor transformation with any triad, just by altering the middle note.

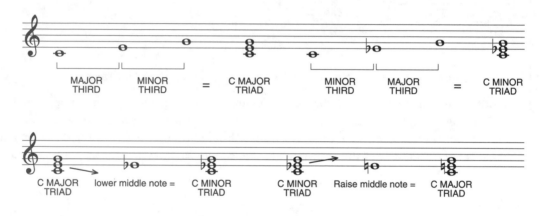

Creating major and minor triads.

Practice Session

Time to practice those major/minor chord shifts that make life so fulfilling! The next illustration presents a few examples of triads, with instructions to change each major to minor, and each minor to major.

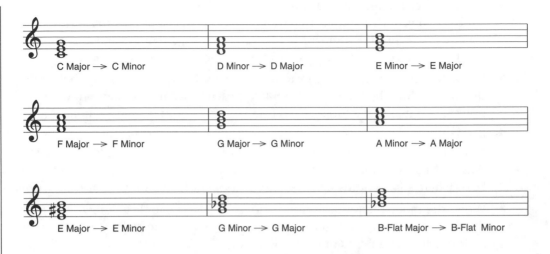

Alternate between major and minor triads by altering the middle note.

All you need to do is alter the middle note of each triad. Raise the middle to change minor to major, and lower the middle note to change major to minor. Play the triads on the keyboard, both before and after the change, using the fingerings I've written above each triad.

The Common Chords

Most of this chapter has been devoted to the *theory* of chords: how to construct them, and understanding the intervals that make up chords. All of that music theory stuff is valuable, but this section cuts to the chase by giving you the most common chords used in everyday sheet music. These are the chords you need to get your fingers on quickly when reading a pop music sheet. The chords you should practice are notated in the next illustration, one of the most important illustrations for learning chords.

When studying the common chords, please keep these points in mind:

➤ Each sequence of chords is in a different key, with a different key signature. The chords of each example are the most common chords in that key. However, this is not to say that you don't see many other chords in pieces written in that particular key. These examples are not meant to be comprehensive—rather, they are a sort of first-aid kit to chords in the most common keys.

➤ I've included examples for several keys, but not all the keys. Most pop music is written in a few basic keys, but if you browse through sheet music you're bound to find many a song with a different key signature than you see in the illustration.

➤ The chord examples presented here only use three-note chords, but it's easy to notice that some of them look different from the triads shown earlier in this chapter. That's because it's sometimes easier to play chords when the notes are re-arranged—for example, taking the bottom note and raising it an octave, putting it on the top of the chord. Such rearrange-ments of the order in which chord notes are stacked are called *inversions*.

Music Speak

Inversions are different varieties of the same chord, with the notes stacked in different orders.

133

➤ The chord examples are meant to be played! Don't just look at those chords: Get your hands involved. I've written the examples for the left hand, as that is the hand that usually plays chord accompaniments. Take your time figuring out the notes, and take this tip: Observe how the notes move from one chord to the next.

➤ In the first example, moving from the first chord to the second, the bottom note stays the same, while the middle and top notes each move up. Noticing how the individual notes move makes it a lot easier to find the next chord on the keyboard.

➤ Remember to look at the key signatures! The examples are written just as they would be in sheet music (except there are no bar lines), without reminders of the sharps and flats written as accidentals. The exception to the no-accidental policy is in the minor keys, where some chords must be altered in order to sound harmonically correct.

➤ When the mode (major or minor) is not indicated, major is assumed. (Major is usually the default mode in sheet music.) Minor chords are indicated with a lower-case "m" after the chord name, as in *Em* for E-minor.

Key Thought

The inversions that I've presented here are not the only way to play the inverted chords; in fact, throughout the figure you can find the same chords inverted different ways. You can rearrange the notes any way you please. Whole books have been written about how to construct chord inversions that sound great and are easy to play, but I'm determined that this book should weigh less than fifty pounds. I've given you good inversions for these examples, but feel free to experiment with how the notes are stacked.

Common chords used in different keys.

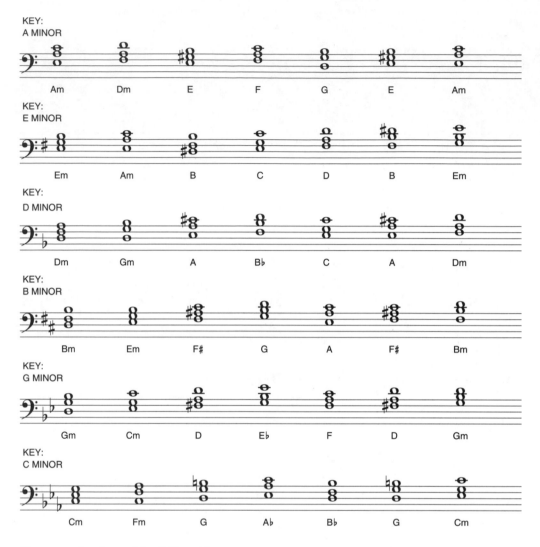

Common chords used in different keys.

The Least You Need to Know

➤ Chords are groups of notes played simultaneously.

➤ Intervals are the distances (number of half steps) between pairs of notes. There are major and minor intervals, as well as *perfect* intervals.

➤ Triads are made by stacking one interval on top of another. Major triads have a minor third on top of a major third. Minor triads have a major third on top of a minor third.

Part 4

Master Class

Playing the piano is such a large topic, I could write a book about it. Oh, wait–this is a book. Well, thank goodness there's room for the chapters in this part, which take you beyond the elementary basics into some of the fun, and slightly more advanced, techniques and knowledge of music and keyboards. In Chapter 14, you'll learn about the details of music notations–the marks, squiggles, and strange abbreviations found on almost all sheet music. Chapter 15 gives you a complete tutorial in using the pedals, including the all-important sustain pedal, which requires a certain technique to use well. (Yes, I provide Practice Sessions for the pedals.)

In Chapter 16, I divulge secrets of playing tunes from "fake book," and improvising left-hand arrangements of songs. When you get in a highbrow mood, check out Chapter 17 for descriptions of different types of classical music and some pieces to play. You may not realize it yet, but practicing is almost as much of an art as performing, and Chapter 18 discusses several ways to maximize your practice sessions. Chapter 19 is stuffed with technical tips that help you gain keyboard facility. And, when you feel like you're at the end of your rope, you can find some great motivational tips and techniques in Chapter 20.

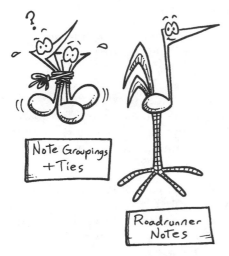

Note Groupings
+Ties

Roadrunner
Notes

Chapter 14

Details of Music Notation

In This Chapter

➤ Introducing sixteenth notes

➤ Tying notes together

➤ Tricky triplets

➤ Getting the hang of repeat signs

➤ Crescendos, decrescendos, and other expression markings

➤ A basic glossary of Italian words found in classical sheet music

Earlier parts of this book deliver the goods about basic music notation. Notes, the staff, rests—they're all covered earlier (in a prose style brilliant enough to awaken slumbering Nobel jurors.) But in fact there is quite a bit more to music notation than the fundamentals—details that may seem inconsequential when you're learning about them, but which are commonplace on the printed music page. Knowing about them really helps turn the circles, lines, and spaces into music.

This chapter gives you all the information you need to understand fairly advanced music notation, as used in classical piano music, jazz, and non-EZ arrangements of popular songs.

Note Groupings and Ties

In Part 2, I introduced note values from very long (whole notes, equal to four beats) to the relatively quick (eighth notes, equal to a half beat). I also described the principle of dotting notes to add half their value. Presumably you've become fairly familiar with all those types of notes, but if you need a refresher course, please review Chapter 7, "Whole Notes and Their Offspring," before diving into this section. Here, I introduce note values less than an eighth note; notes that are tied together; and groupings of notes such as triplets.

Key Thought

If you're feeling lost, review Chapter 7, to refresh your memory of how note values are determined.

Music Speak

Sixteenth notes have half the time value of eighth-notes, or a quarter of a beat. They are indicated by a stem with two flags on the end.

Roadrunner Notes

The speed with which a sequence of notes plays is determined by two things: the tempo of the piece, and the value of the notes. Notes with small values, like eighth notes and quarter notes, move along at a speedier clip than notes with large values, like half notes and whole notes. However, everything gets played more slowly in a rock ballad, for example, than in a fast, foot-stomping ragtime number. The quarter notes of a slow piece may end up being played more slowly than the half notes of a fast piece, even though quarter notes have half the value of half notes.

As the heading of this section implies, I'm about to introduce note values that get played very quickly, but only when the tempo allows it. We're going deep into fractions now, dividing eighth notes (worth a half beat each) into pieces.

The following figure shows just how fine we're getting with note values, starting from a single whole note, worth four beats, to a type of note you haven't seen yet: the sixteenth note. Sixteenth notes, being worth half the time rhythmic value of eighth notes, are counted with one quarter beat each.

Sixteenth notes, like eighth notes, may appear two ways on the music staff. When separated from surrounding notes, they appear with a stem that has a flag on the end—except that sixteenth notes have two flags. When several eighth or sixteenth notes are connected, they appear with horizontal bars linking their stems—and in that case, sixteenth notes have a double horizontal bar.

1 per 4/4 measure		Whole note = 4 beats
2 per 4/4 measure		Half note = 2 beats
4 per 4/4 measure		Quarter note = 1 beat
8 per 4/4 measure		Eighth note = 1/2 beat
16 per 4/4 measure		Sixteenth note: 1/4 beat

The basic note values, from whole notes through sixteenth notes.

Now that you know whole notes, half notes, quarter notes, eighth notes, and sixteenth notes, the question naturally arises how far you can go cutting note values in half and arriving at a new type of note. The answer, in theory, is that there's no limit. I have seen 256th-notes on classical sheet music for the piano. Practically speaking, though, sixteenth notes represent the limit in normal music notation. You may occasionally see thirty-second notes, which have three flags when separated and a triple horizontal bar when connected. Thirty-second notes appear primarily in classical piano music, which seems to delight in confounding the natural limits of human tolerance for tiny notes. In most keyboard arrangments of popular music, jazz, and classical, sixteenth notes represent the small end of note values.

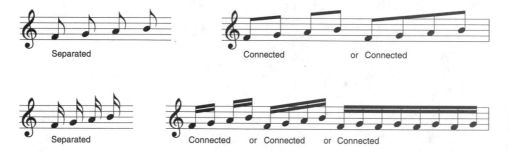

Eighth notes and sixteenth notes may appear two different ways on the music staff.

Practice Session

Understanding how ties work in theory is fine, but you need to practice them so you don't get thrown off when you see a tied note on sheet music. Actually, that's just my excuse—my real purpose is to torment you with further exercises. But these practice pieces are useful, I promise.

The following example is another piece destined for induction in the Boring Music Hall of Shame. I want to start you off with an exercise that doesn't complicate matters by making you search for notes. The point here is to count accurately, and play the tied notes correctly.

The following exercise is for separate hands; the time signature is an easy 4/4; and the key signature is an equally easy no sharps or flats. Remember to count in groups of four beats, and to start slowly and evenly. After playing the right-hand piece several times, try the left-hand piece. The two pieces are not meant to be played together.

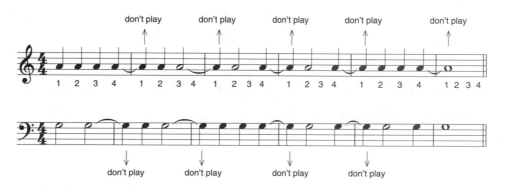

Play the right hand and left hand separately, as they are two exercises. Count slowly and evenly.

The next exercise raises the stakes by putting both hands in action at once. Start by learning the right hand, then get familiar with the left-hand part. When you can play each hand comfortably and without faltering, try putting them together slowly. Evenness is more important than speed. If this piece moves you to sentimental tears, you obviously don't listen to enough music.

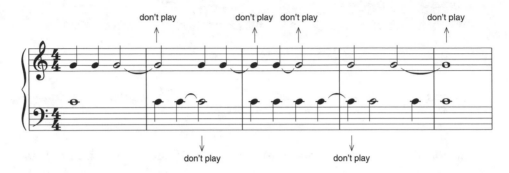

Try each hand separately first, then put them together.

The next one is actually a pretty piece of music, but I can't take credit for it unless I was Frédéric Chopin in a previous life. The exercise is an adaptation of a piano piece by Chopin, and gives you a good workout in tying right-hand notes. I've kept the left-hand part simple to let you focus on the job at hand, which is counting the right hand correctly. Practice the right hand first, and repeat it several times, counting carefully, until you're comfortable with it. Work out the two hands together, first without counting, then in the correct rhythm.

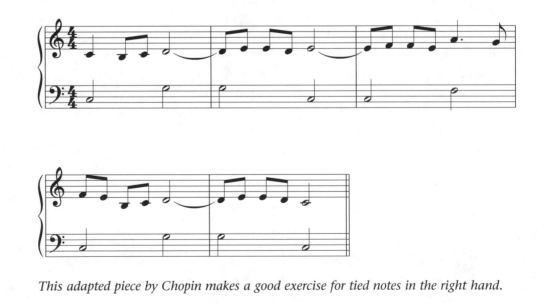

This adapted piece by Chopin makes a good exercise for tied notes in the right hand.

Tying Notes Together

The rules of written music sometimes get in their own way. For example, when a piece is in 4/4 time, every measure must contain exactly four beats, filled with either notes or rests. But what if a note, played on the fourth beat of the measure, lasts for more than one beat? In that case, the note doesn't end when the measure does, so how does it appear on the staff?

To solve that dilemma, as well as other fascinating challenges in music notation, a feature called a *tie* comes to the rescue. The tie is a graceful mark drawn between two notes whose values are added together. The tie may be drawn across a bar line, or reside within the measure. The effect is that when you see two notes tied together, you play only the first note, but hold it for the rhythmic value of both notes. Here are a few examples of ties.

Here are a few things to remember about tied notes:

➤ Ties are mostly used across bar lines to extend the duration of the last note of a measure into the next measure.

➤ Ties are also used within a single measure to add the note values of notes that couldn't be written as a single note.

➤ In some cases, ties are used when not absolutely necessary, as in tying together two quarter notes instead of writing a half note. Ties are used this way to make the piece's notation easier to read for one reason or another. Sometimes tying two notes makes it clearer how the note is held against whatever is happening in the other hand.

Music Speak

Tied notes are connected by a curved line, indicating that the time value of the two notes is added together. You only play the first note, but hold it for the duration of both notes.

Grace Notes

There is no limit to how many notes can be tied. In all cases, no matter how many notes are tied, only the first note actually gets played, but it is held for the duration of all the tied notes.

Ties add together the note values of two (or more) notes. You play only the first note, but hold it for the duration of both (or all) tied notes.

Music Speak

A **triplet** is a group of three notes grouped into a certain rhythm. Quarter-note triplets are played in the time value of a single half note, and eighth-note triplets are played in the same number of beats as a quarter note.

Triplets

I'm not talking about babies here, although if you have the squirming variety, congratulations. The *triplets* I'm referring to are clusters of notes grouped in threes, that create a peculiar rhythm. Triplets are usually formed from quarter notes or eighth notes, but are sometimes sixteenth notes, and in theory can be *any* type of note. A triplet is market on sheet music in a pretty obvious way; with a numeral 3 above or underneath the cluster of three notes. Here are some examples.

Triplets are groups of three notes, marked with a numeral 3. A triplet's note value is equal to two of the three notes.

The rhythmic value of triplets.

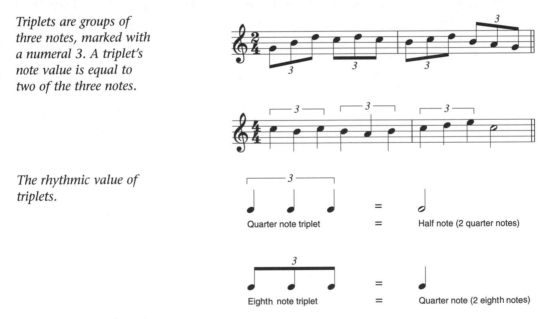

What makes triplets special, and tricky, is their note value. One triplet is equal to two of the three notes in the triplet. Therefore, an eighth-note triplet is equal to two eighth notes, or one beat. (A single eighth note is worth a half beat.) A quarter-note triplet is equal to two quarter notes, or two beats. (A single quarter note is worth one beat.) The illustration above clarifies the rhythmic value of triplets.

Practice Session

The only way to learn triplets is to play them. The first figure below is a very basic exercise, but helpful if you really learn it well. I've provided the counting points in the illustration, to help you count through the triplets. The two parts of the exercise show you the rhythmic difference between quarter-note triplets and eighth-note triplets. (The eighth-note triplets are twice as fast, so you can fit twice as many into a measure.)

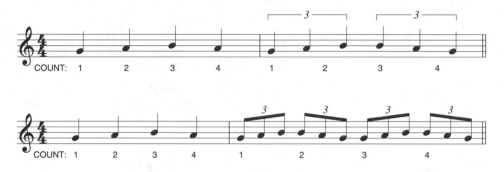

A simple exercise for playing quarter-note and eighth-note triplets.

Ready for another exercise? The next figure mixes quarter-note and eighth-note triplets for a truly frustrating—I mean, a highly educational—experience. Play slowly, because the eighth-note triplets go by pretty quickly if your tempo is too fast. Count a *slow* four before you start, then proceed with the piece. I've indicated the timing of the counts to help you cope with the triplets.

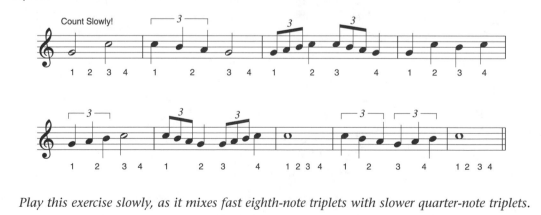

Play this exercise slowly, as it mixes fast eighth-note triplets with slower quarter-note triplets.

Play It Again

Imagine if you were composing a piece of music—a popular song, for example (at least you hope it will be popular). As with most pop songs, repetition is crucial to the catchiness of your masterpiece. Verses and choruses both must repeat several times to drive home the sublime musical meaning.

But how tedious it is to notate the same portions of the song over and over again! Fortunately, composers through the ages have been there before you, and a solution is in place. Music notation has something called a *repeat sign* that indicates when a portion of a piece should be repeated. Here's what a repeat sign looks like.

The special bar line at the end of the staff, with the odd dots on each staff, is a repeat sign. When you reach a repeat sign, return to the beginning of the piece and play it again.

Repeat signs work very simply. When you run into one as you're playing a piece, bounce right back to the beginning and start again. That is, unless you've passed a *reversed* repeat sign on your way through the piece. The following piece shows what a reversed repeat sign looks like. It indicates the place at which you start over when you reach the normal repeat sign. In other words, the portion of the piece between the two repeat signs—first the reversed sign, then the normal repeat sign—is the portion of the piece that gets repeated.

Do you notice something else about the following piece? Around the repeat sign, the measures are delineated and marked 1 and 2. Those numbers stand for *first ending* and *second ending*, and indicate which measure is played when you repeat the portion. Here's how the musical example of the following piece works:

1. Play the first ending when you first play through to the repeat sign.

2. Go back to the reverse repeat sign and replay the four-bar portion of the piece.

3. This time, as you approach the repeat sign, you skip the first ending entirely (don't play that measure) and play the second ending instead.

Repeat signs and multiple endings are very common in popular sheet music. In fact, I hesitate to break the news, but I must: there are even third endings. Many pop songs have verses or choruses that repeat three times, so it makes sense that the music notation would indicate that repetition somehow. The following example illustrates how third endings work. In most cases, you play the same measure for the first and second ending, then you play the third ending on your last time through the repeated portion.

Music Speak

Repeat signs bracket portions of a piece that should be repeated. Repeat signs make music notation more compact, especially in pop music, since the repeated portion doesn't have to be written out a second or third time.

In this example, you would replay the portion between the repeat signs, playing the measure marked 1 the first time through, and replacing it with the measure marked 2 the second time through.

First, second, and third endings.

Grace Notes

Repeat signs save time and paper by telling you what parts of a piece to play over again. The re-iterated portions can be as short as a single measure (though that is very rare) or as long as the entire piece, which is likewise rare in popular music. Repeating an entire piece is not too un-common in classical music, though, demonstrating without question that the great masters of the past were just lazy bums.

Expression Markings

Music is subtle; notation is cut-and-dried. Music is flexible; notation is rigid. Music is horizontal; notation is vertical. Expression marks help bring the life of music into the dry notes and bars of music notation. Expression marks indicate when to get louder and softer; when to play faster or slower; when to pause; when to play smoothly or sharply; and, in the case of classical sheet music, when to dig out an Italian dictionary to see what the heck those strange words mean.

Key Thought

How many times do you repeat a portion when you see a repeat sign? Instrumental composi-tions—pieces without words—assume a single repetition only. However, there is no such limita-tion on the number of repeats in pop songs. There is an informal and somewhat obvious method for determining how many repeats are called for—just keep your eye on the words, and repeat whenever there is another verse to be sung.

Dynamic Markings

In music, *dynamics* refers to volume—in other words, how loudly or softly to play. The dynamic range of a piece is indicated in the sheet music by abbreviations of Italian words, even in modern popular music. (Some arrangements of pop music forego the traditional Italian for plain English.) The following table illustrates the dynamic indicators used in music notation, the full Italian words they stand for, and what they mean.

Dynamic Markings in Music Notation

What You See	What It Stands for	What It Means
pp	*pianissimo*	Very soft
p	*piano*	Soft
mp	*mezzo piano*	Medium soft
mf	*mezzo forte*	Medium loud
f	*forte*	Loud
ff	*fortissimo*	Very loud

These dynamic markings are used to generally indicate the volume of a section of a piece. When it comes to dynamic fluctuations within sections, from one measure to the next, other indications come into play. Called *crescendos* (get louder) and *decrescendos* (get softer), these two important expression markings are illustrated in the following figure, using their abbreviated forms.

In addition to *cresc* and *decresc*, the same indications can be given with symbols. You usually see the symbols when the composer (or arranger) wants to indicate a precisely timed crescendo or decrescendo, since the symbols can be stretched as long, or compressed as short, as needed. The spelled-out abbreviations, on the other hand, are more general indications that the piece should get louder or softer, without telling you exactly when the dynamic destination is reached.

Music Speak

The **crescendo** sign indicates that you should play gradually louder; the **decrescendo** sign indicates to gradually play softer.

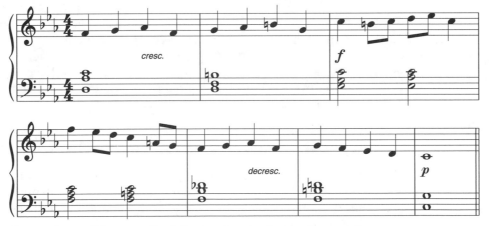

Crescendos and decrescendos tell you when to play louder or softer.

Crescendos and decrescendos may be indicated by symbols that define how gradually you should increase or decrease your playing volume.

Pass the Dictionary

At the beginning of most pieces is some indication of the tempo and spirit with which the piece should be played. In classical music, traditional Italian expressions are used, whereas in twentieth-century pop music and jazz English expressions are used. You don't need any help from me interpreting an English expression like "Slowly" or "With bounce." But the Italian words used in the classics need some translating. Here are many of the most common tempo markings and what they mean.

Italian Tempo Markings in Classical Piano Music

What You See	What It Means
Lento	Very slowly
Andante	Moderately slowly
Allegro	Happily
Allegretto	Lightly; not as fast as *Allegro*
Presto	Quickly
Vivace	Very quickly
Dolce	Sweetly
… ma non troppo	… but not too (slowly, quickly, or whatever)

As you can see, Italian tempo markings indicate attitude as well as sheer speed or slowness. In classical music, interpretation of the written music is important, and conveying the spirit of the music is more important than adhering slavishly to a certain tempo indication.

Some composers (and many editors of classical music collections) enhance the Italian tempo markings with specific metronome settings to indicate exactly how fast the piece should be played. When you see such an indication at the start of a piano piece, if you have a metronome you may set it at the required point and even practice the piece with the metronome on to keep the tempo.

Music Speak

Metronomes are mechanical devices that audibly tick the beats of a piece, and can be set for a certain number of beats per minute.

Miscellaneous Expression Markings

Music notation is filled with expression markings that attempt to bring life to the notes. In addition to dynamic markings and tempo indications, symbols above, below, and around the notes indicate subtleties in the performance of the piece.

Slurs (But Not Insults)

Probably the most common expression marking in music notation, the *slur* is a sweeping, graceful indicator that helps you phrase the notes of a piece musically and smoothly. (Slurs are also called *phrase marks*.) Whether you're looking at classical or popular sheet music, if the playing level is at least intermediate, slurs are all over the page.

Slurs indicate unbroken musical phrases. By "unbroken," I mean that the notes within a slur should be played very smoothly, with each note lasting exactly until the next note is played. You shouldn't let little spaces of silence intrude between the notes within a slur.

Here's what slurs look like. Phrase marks can apply to both left-hand and right-hand parts, but usually appear over single-note lines, as opposed to chords.

When interpreting these phrase marks, imagine that you're a singer (unless you really are a singer, in which case no imagination is necessary). Singers need to take a breath every so often during a song, and the notes that are sung before taking a breath are all part of the same musical phrase. Keyboard music can be thought of in the same way, as a series of phrases.

Music Speak

Phrase marks, or **slurs**, indicate when groups of notes should be played without any breaks between the notes. The effect of a slurred phrase is smooth and seamless.

Play the notes within the slurs in a smooth, unbroken manner.

Slurs, or phrase marks, indicate where the unbroken phrases are. As you play melody parts shown with slurs, imagine singing them (or actually sing along while you play), and don't take a breath (or break the phrasing of your playing) until the end of a phrase mark.

Legato and Staccato

Another word for playing smoothly is *legato*. Yes, another Italian word. Playing phrase marks well is called *playing legato*. In fact, the word itself is used sometimes in classical sheet music to indicate a generally smooth approach to a piece or a passage within the piece. There may also be phrase marks in a legato piece (or passage), even though the overriding instruction is to play smoothly.

The opposite of legato is *staccato*, and there's an indication for that, too. Staccato notes are shown with little dots underneath or above

Music Speak

Legato means smooth playing, without undue breaks between notes.

Staccato means sharp, detached playing, with breaks between the notes.

them. When you see those dots, make an effort to play the opposite of an unbroken, smooth, legato style. Play each note shortly, letting your finger bounce off the key as soon as you play it.

Staccato notes are indicated by dots above or below the note, and are played detachedly, each note separated from the notes around it.

Making Music

The five pieces in this section present classical melodies you've probably heard (plus one you may not be familiar with), and illustrate the notation elements described in this chapter. It's easy to notice that these pieces are a little more complex. And difficult to play. than earlier pieces in the book. Remember to start slowly, one hand at a time. The recognizable melodies are all in the right-hand parts. Add the left hand gradually, or jus stick to the right had for now.

The first example, a short keyboard Air by Henry Purcell, shows show repeat signs were often used in the Baroque era to divide a piece in half, requiring the player to repeat each half. I've added slurs and dynamic markings to suggest how the piece can be shaped and phrased, but never forget the slurs are subjective, usually added by editors, not composers.

Beethoven's *Fur Elise,* composed for a child and a perennial favorite among students and teachers is a longer piece than I have room to show here, but requires no simplification. The excerpt below is almost exactly as Ludwig penned it, and I've added some expression marks to guide your interpretation. One beauty of this piece is that the two hands almost never play at the same time, making it easier to learn than many others requiring two-hand coordination. The tempo marking, "Moderato", means (unsurprisingly) "Moderately." The piece shouldn't drag, and neither should it move too quickly—keep an even-paced flow.

Triplets abound in *Jesu, Joy of Man's Desiring* by Bach. This piece wasn't originally composed for piano solo (in fact, Bach didn't write anything explicitly for the piano), but many keyboard arrangements exist. This excerpt gives you enough triplets to get you dreaming about them, and gives you plenty of practice counting them. Triplets don't have to be played fast, so you needn't rush. Note that I've supplied a suggested fingering for every note of the right hand. The right-hand part covers such a big range that many crossovers facilitate playing it smoothly. The fingerings may seem odd at firs, but once you get comfortable with them they will help you manage the melody's intricacies—and give you practice with standard scale fingerings to boot.

The following melody of Russian composer Borodin is one of my favorites, and has become a Christmas instrumental (no words) classic. Whether in orchestral or keyboard arrangements, it is often played in a sharp manner, using staccato notes mixed with legato phrases. I've indicated one way of playing that way, with the first two notes of each melodic phrase (every four measures) marked for staccato playing.

Key Thought

I can't beat around the bush about one crucial fact: counting triplets is difficult. It's something you have to get a *feel* for. Triplets are played perfectly evenly through the whole triplet. The result is a syncopated rhythm that seems to go against the rhythm of the piece, and yet fits into it. Triplets are definitely cool-sounding, but it takes practice to play them effectively.

Finally, why not play a symphony on the piano? (Admittedly, only a tiny excerpt in a sim-plified version.) Symphonic transcriptions are a long-standing tradition in piano music. In this case I've taken the first statement of the thunderously famous theme from Beethoven's *Fifth Symphony* and arranged it for moderately easy playing. Notice all the octaves—if play-ing octaves is troublesome, reduce them to single notes in either hand, or both the tied B-flat in the left hand illustrates that more than two notes can be tied together; in fact, there is no limit to the number of notes that can be tied into a single, long sustained tone.

The Least You Need to Know

➤ Sixteenth notes are worth one quarter beat, and get played twice as rapidly as eighth notes in the same piece.

➤ When two or more notes are tied together, even across a bar line, only the first note is played. But it is held for the counting value of all the tied notes combined.

➤ Triplets are groups of three notes indicated by the numeral 3. A quarter note triplet has a time value of two beats, and an eighth note triplet has a time value of one beat.

➤ Repeat signs tell you which portions of a piece to repeat, without writing that portion a second time.

➤ Crescendos tell you to gradually play more loudly, and decrescendos indicate gradually softer playing.

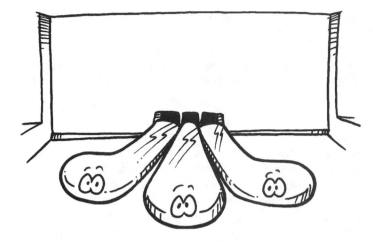

Chapter 15

Pedals: Where's the Clutch?

In This Chapter

➤ Understanding the three pedals of a piano

➤ Plugging in and using the sustain pedal of an electronic keyboard

➤ Practicing with the sustain pedal

➤ How pedal markings are notated in sheet music

You play the piano with your hands, right? Well, that's only partly true. Sure, you make the notes play with your fingers, but a big part of any pianist's sound comes from the feet. Working the pedals is an important part of playing the piano, and even most home keyboards include one of the piano's three pedals.

Keyboard pedals came into being at around the time the piano was invented. Before the piano, early keyboards like the harpsichord (I'm talking about centuries ago) didn't have pedals—they were hands-only instruments.

The piano changed everything. The earliest pianos, though not as powerful-sounding as modern pianos, nevertheless had a much more sustaining sound than harpsichords or clavichords. Pedals were added to the piano to take advantage of its sustaining power.

Pianos have three pedals, which I briefly describe in Chapter 2, "Hammers and Strings." Most electronic keyboards only have one pedal, which works like the right hand piano pedal, and is the most important pedal. (Digital pianos often have two pedals, and occasionally three.) This chapter is devoted mostly to learning how to use that most important pedal, which is called the *sustain pedal*.

Plugging in the Pedal

Pianos are big, totally integrated mechanisms with the pedals built right into the machine, as it were. Actually, the piano's pedal mechanism *can* be disassembled and removed, but when you buy a piano it comes to your home either with the pedals attached or with a helpful technician who'll put the darn things on for you. It's not an operation to be attempted by someone without experience in piano maintenance.

Key Thought

Some keyboard models call the jack something else, like *sustain pedal* or *avocado*, though the latter is rare.

Digital pianos sometimes create more of a headache than their acoustic counterparts. The pedal mechanisms of digital pianos usually come packaged separately, and the appearance of a solicitous technician is entirely dependent on the generosity of the store from which you bought the instrument—and, in most cases, extremely unlikely. If you are stuck with putting together your new digital piano's pedal assembly on your own, I wish you good luck, the grace of the electronic instrument god, and long-suffering patience. The only thing that may prevent you from throwing your new digital piano out the window in frustration is that it's too heavy.

Home keyboard owners have it easy. Their instruments may not sound as much like a real piano as a digital piano does, but at least attaching the pedal is a breeze. The first thing you must do is find it. The pedals of small keyboards are themselves rather on the small side, so you might have to rummage through the box for a while. The pedal has a longish cord attached to it, with a plug at the end. The pedal itself is usually a small, black device with a rubber bottom that's placed on the floor under the keyboard. Home keyboard pedals are not attached to the main instrument with a wood or plastic construction—it's just a dangling cord connecting the pedal to the keyboard.

Once you find the keyboard pedal, simply place it on the floor where your right foot naturally falls when you sit at the keyboard. The part of the pedal that depresses should face your seat. Then plug the cord into the back of the keyboard, into the jack marked *pedal*.

Some keyboard pedals suffer from their small size and light weight, skittering easily across the floor as they are used, requiring facility with a modern keyboard skill of retrieving the pedal with your feet while you play. With practice, you can get so orthopedically dextrous that nobody will notice you swiftly pulling the pedal back in its place as you play your tunes. I have found a couple of tricks useful:

➤ Wrap the pedal chord around something so that there is very little slack. In other words, keep the pedal on a short leash. If the keyboard is resting on a table, use one of the table legs; if the keyboard is on a keyboard stand, use whatever part of the stand is handy to wrap the cord.

➤ Place something heavy on the floor behind the pedal, as a roadblock. If you've placed the keyboard against a wall, that's ideal. If the keyboard is against open space, you must decide whether you want a possibly unsightly pedal-stop cluttering up your floor.

Trying Out the Pedal

The sustain pedal has a unique function: It holds your notes for you. You still must do most of the work playing, of course, but the sustain pedal makes it much easier than it would be otherwise. When you depress the sustain pedal, any notes you subsequently play, plus any notes you're holding down when you depress the pedal, continue sounding even if you lift your hands off the keyboard.

It's pretty convenient when you think about it, as it lets you sound as if you had more than ten fingers, or more than two hands. You can play a massive chord low on the keyboard, then move both hands to the upper range to play there, and the low chord is sustained as your hands take their new playing position.

The best way to get acquainted with the pedal is to simply try it randomly. I'll get to specific pedaling technique a bit later in this chapter. For now, just experiment. Sit comfortably at the piano; if you're using an electronic keyboard, the pedal should be under your right foot when your leg is bent at about a ninety-degree angle.

Play a note, and while still holding down the key, depress the pedal (that's the right-most pedal on the piano). Release the key, and thrill to the sustained sound of the note being held by the pedal. (It's all right if you're not exactly thrilled.) Play other notes with the pedal still down, lift your hands, then release the notes by lifing your foot from the pedal.

When working the pedal, it's important keep your right heel on the floor. Press the pedal by pushing down on it with the ball of your foot, and release it by pivoting up from your heel. It should take only a slight motion to press and release the pedal, though some piano pedals require more effort.

Practice sustaining random notes on the keyboard, concentrating on minimizing your foot motions when controlling the pedal. Efficiency is key, because you don't want to expend a lot of body movement on the pedal. There's no need to lift your foot *off* the pedal.

Piano players have an easier time of it when getting the feel of the pedal, because piano pedals offer more resistance and spring than keyboard pedals. Furthermore, piano pedals are higher off the floor, making it less tempting to lift the foot way off the pedal.

Pedal Technique

The purpose of the sustain pedal is to connect notes together for a smoother-sounding playing style. The purpose is not, as you may suspect from your first experiments, to create a cacophony of endlessly sustaining notes clashing with each other. Using the pedal effectively takes some practice, and practice is the goal of this section.

There are no universal, hard-and-fast rules about when to use the sustain pedal and when to lay off. To a large extent, using the pedal is a personal decision that has a big effect on your playing style. Sparse use of the pedal contributes to a dry, clear style, while a heavy foot creates more liquid-sounding music. Using the sustain pedal too much causes a muddy blur of notes, while using it too little results in musical discontinuity and ungraceful phrases. These

Key Thought

It's possible to use the sustain pedal too much, the result being a muddy-sounding mess of notes blending into each other. The important thing to remember is to lift the pedal from time to time, clearing away the notes it was holding. How often should you lift the sustain pedal, and when should you press it down in the first place? The next section, Pedal Technique, gives you some rules and exercises.

Key Thought

You may, in time, develop a preference for a pedal position that stretches your leg out, but the easiest way to start is with the ninety-degree angle. Piano players and most digital piano players don't have a choice, because the pedal mechanisms are in a fixed position.

Key Thought

Piano pedals may seem *too* far off the floor, especially if you have small feet or if the piano lives on rollers that lift the whole instrument up. If the pedal forces your right foot into an uncomfortable position, simply place a book or some other object (pets are not recommended) under your heel.

pages show you a basic pedal technique that will stand you in good stead; from there you must use your own ears and musical taste.

Suggested pedaling is sometimes marked in piano notation, using two symbols you should be aware of. The first symbol is simply an abbreviation of pedal: *Ped.* It means: push the sustain pedal down! The second symbol is the pedal-off asterisk, which indicates releasing the sustain pedal. Both symbols are illustrated in the following figure.

The pedal-on and pedal-off notation symbols usually appear beneath the double staff, underneath the left-hand part, and more often in piano music than keyboard arrangements.

More often that not, pedal notations in sheet music used the *Ped* symbol and not the asterick. When this is the case, the *Ped* notation refers to a quick up/down movement of the pedal. That quick flip of the pedal releases previously held notes and begins holding new notes. Experienced pianists flip the sustain pedal very often during the course of a piece, and all those "pedal off" asterick would clutter the pages. Keep in mind, also, that pedal markings are editorial additions to sheet music, and almost never added by the composer. Take them as suggestions and develop your own pedaling style.

PEDAL DOWN PEDAL UP

Pedal markings give suggestions of when to use the sustain pedal.

Pedal notations are fine, and helpful in giving a basic indication of when to pedal. In all cases, though, you must use your own taste in deciding when to sustain notes with your foot. In this section I want to introduce you to a basic pedaling technique that is useful on any type of keyboard or piano. There is one fundamental, most important trick to good pedaling:

➤ The crucial technique of good pedaling is holding the pedal down, sustaining a note, until just *after* you have played the note on which you're releasing the pedal.

In many cases you are holding the pedal through the playing of several notes, not just one. The point is to release the pedal a split second after playing a note.

Here are two alternating notes, too far away from each other on the keyboard to be played smoothly without using the pedal.

Grace Notes

Pedal notations sometimes consist of only the *Ped.* abbreviation, without any pedal-off asterisks. The missing asterisk doesn't mean that you should never lift the pedal up, however. It just means that you should *change the pedal*—an expression meaning lift the pedal quickly and depress it again—every time a *Ped.* notation occurs. Occasionally, the asterisk is used alone, without the *Ped.* abbreviation.

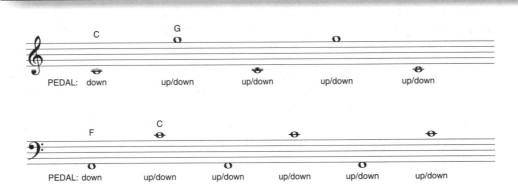

Play this pedaling exercise with just one hand. Then try it with the other hand.

Try the first part of the above example with the right hand. It doesn't matter which fingers you use—you can even use a single finger for both notes. Don't worry about counting, either, as this is strictly a pedaling exercise. The lower note is middle C, and the upper note is the second G above middle C. Play the first note and immediately depress the pedal. Lift your hand from the keyboard and play the upper note. The moment you play the G, lift the pedal and depress it again in a quick up/down motion. Lift your hand and go back down to middle C, once again using the quick up/down of the pedal the moment you play the note.

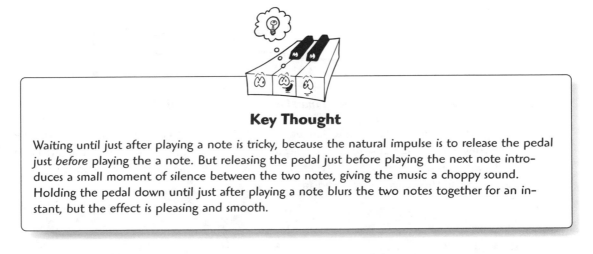

Key Thought

Waiting until just after playing a note is tricky, because the natural impulse is to release the pedal just *before* playing the a note. But releasing the pedal just before playing the next note introduces a small moment of silence between the two notes, giving the music a choppy sound. Holding the pedal down until just after playing a note blurs the two notes together for an instant, but the effect is pleasing and smooth.

Continue in this fashion several times until you're comfortable using the pedal this way. Whenever you're ready, proceed to the second part of the exercise, which is for the left hand. Use the pedal in exactly the same way. The upper note in the left-hand exercise is middle C, and the lower note is the second F below middle C.

Practice Session

Time to exercise your new pedaling skill in a musical manner. The first illustration in this Practice Session is a little piece for the right hand that will in all likelihood resonate throughout musical history in its poignant beauty. Either that, or it is totally insignificant. Whichever is the case, your destiny is to learn it with the pedal markings I've provided.

I have used the *Ped.* abbreviation to indicate the quick up/down pedal motion I describe in this chapter. Because your foot is probaly not depressing the pedal before the first note, that particular marking obviously means just *down*. (The truth is, when playing the piano, I often depress the sustain pedal before playing a single note, in which case the first marking would be an up/down.) Likewise, the last pedal indication can mean just *up*.

The pedal marking of this right-hand exercise indicates a quick up/down pedaling motion.

When you get thoroughly sick of the above exercise—I mean, when you've mastered its subtle intricacies—move onto the next one.

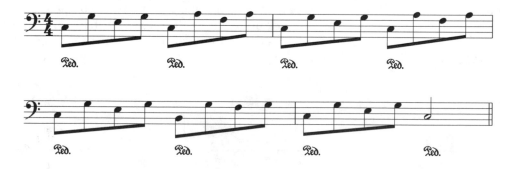

This left-hand part, and its pedal markings, are typical of classical music pieces.

This exercise is also for pedaling technique, but should be played by the left hand. As with the previous exercise, the pedal markings indicate the quick up/down of the pedal. The left-hand part written in the above figure is typical of accompaniment parts written by Mozart and Beethoven in their easy-to-intermediate piano sonatas.

The final exercise of this Practice Session puts both hands together in the famous opening passage of a Mozart sonata for piano. (I've adapted it slightly to make the notes simpler to learn, because you have your hands full—or your feet full—getting the pedaling correct.)

A simplified excerpt of a Mozart sonata. Practice the pedalings while playing the left hand alone, then add the right-hand part.

Approach this exercise gradually and in parts. Try the right hand first, alone and without the pedals, just figuring out the notes. I've given you right-hand fingerings. Then move to the left-hand part, working out the notes without the pedal. The next step is to play the left hand alone *with* the pedal. Because the left hand has more notes, use it to learn the pedaling part. Finally, add the right-hand melody. Go as slowly as you want, building up speed ever so gradually as you repeat the exercise. (Don't speed up while you're playing the piece.)

Using the sustain pedal on a piano has an added acoustic effect besides sustaining any notes you play. The pedal mechanism lifts the entire damping mechanism off the strings, which normally stops the strings of unplayed notes from vibrating when you play. All the strings of the piano are free to vibrate when you depress the sustain pedal, and many of them do, ever so slightly, when you play even a single note with the pedal down. The vibration of unstruck strings is called *sympathetic vibration*, and it adds a subtle but unmistakable richness and sonority to the instrument's sound.

You can test this yourself by playing a single note with the pedal up, then playing it again with the pedal down. Alternate a few times to hear the difference.

Keyboards, on the other hand, don't have strings, and the pedal effect is much simpler. The sustain pedal on electric keyboards and digital pianos simply sustains notes that are played, without enhancing the sonic effect of the instrument as a whole. This phenomenon is one reason digital pianos cannot sound precisely like the real thing.

Using the Piano's Other Pedals

Most of this chapter discusses the sustain pedal, because that's the one pedal of the piano used by electronic keyboards. Cleary, it's the most important pedal, used by keyboard players in all styles and genres. But this section focuses on the two other pedals that lie underneath pianos.

The left-hand pedal is called the *soft pedal*, and does just what the name implies it should do: It makes the piano softer. Of course, you can make the piano softer with your hands by simply playing the keys less forcefully, but the pedal makes the piano sound like you've just thrown a blanket around the whole instrument. The tone changes, and the notes become less sharp, and slightly muffled.

The degree of difference made by the soft pedal varies from one piano to another. With some instruments it's hardly noticeable, while in others the soft pedal makes a startling difference in tone and volume.

The middle pedal on grand pianos and some uprights is called the *sostenuto pedal*, and is similar to the sustain pedal, but with a crucial difference. The sostenuto pedal sustains notes, but *only* those notes whose keys are depressed when you push down the pedal. As those notes are continuing to sound, you can play the piano without other notes "sticking," and even use the sustain pedal normally. This feature lets you play a two-handed chord in one part of the piano range, then play other music above or below it while the chord sustains, without muddying the air with a discord of notes clashing against each other.

The sostenuto pedal is not used very much, and some pianos don't have one. Smaller uprights with three pedals have a middle "practice" pedal that inserts a strip of felt between the hammers and the strings, muffling the sound of the piano drastically. It's great for apartment dwellers or anyone who's self-conscious about practicing loudly enough to be heard.

Grace Notes

Most classical performers use the soft pedal very sparingly, if at all, because the change in tone is undesirable in most pieces. One musical genre in which the soft pedal attains importance is New Age piano music, in which "soft pedal artistry" places an emphasis on producing tonal shadings with the soft pedal down.

Music Speak

In classical piano music, very occasionally, you see a notation marking indicating use of the soft pedal. That marking is the phrase *una corda* (Italian for "one string") written into the music. By and large, though, players use the soft pedal whenever they desire the softest touch possible in a delicate musical passage.

Making Music

As a rule of thumb, the sustain pedal is used more when playing music composed in later centuries that when playing Bach, Haydn, and Mozart. The statement is a gross generalization, but there is no question that Chopin, Schumann, Liszt, and other composers of the Romantic era wrote music that requires a liquid, pedal-intensive playing style, far more than the relatively dry and pristine music of the Classic era in the eighteenth century. And Impressionistic music—the watery, highly textural compositions of early twentieth century French composer—requires an even heavier foot on the sustain pedal.

The following piece is by Impressionism's most famous proponent, Claude Debussy. Most of Debussy's music is extremely complex and difficult; beginning pianist are lucky to have this gorgeous and relatively easy piece. Notice how the left-hand part reaches up into the treble clef—the notes aren't difficult to play, but it might take some time to figure them out. (Remember that all Bs are flatted.) I've added suggested pedal timings, corresponding to every right-hand note. These suggestions shouldn't be etched in stone; use the pedal more sparinngly if the notes seem to be blurring into each other too much. (If you play on different pianos, you may notice that you must adjust your pedaling to the instrument's individual sonorities.)

Play *Reverie* as slowly as you like; it's not meant to move too quickly.

The Least You Need to Know

➤ Every piano has a sustain pedal (the right-hand pedal) and a soft pedal (on the left). In addition, some pianos have a middle sostenuto pedal. The sustain pedal is the most important, and it makes notes continue to sound after you've released the keys. The soft pedal makes the piano a bit softer and changes its tone. The sostenuto pedal sustains an initial note or group of notes, but then lets you play subsequent notes normally.

➤ Most electronic keyboards come with a sustain pedal, which must be plugged into the back of the keyboard.

➤ Pedal markings in sheet music are indicated with the abbreviation *Ped.*, and sometimes, with an asterisk.

Faking It

In This Chapter

➤ All about charts and lead sheets

➤ Tips for "faking" an arrangement of a pop or jazz song

This may come as a surprise, but "faking it" is an honored tradition among piano and keyboard players. However, lest anybody get the wrong impression, I should point out that faking it in music refers to a specific skill when playing jazz and pop music. Laziness in general is not universally respected among musicians!

Jazz and pop music have very different requirements and traditions than classical music. Whereas when playing a classical piece every note is important as written, jazz and pop songs consist of a melody, words (if the tune is a song and not an instrumental piece), and chords. How the chords are played, and the arrangement of the whole song, can be left to the discretion of the player. Improvising an arrangement of a jazz or pop tune is sometimes called *faking it*, and the books that help you do so are called *fake books*.

This chapter concentrates on the specific skills needed to play music out of a fake book. These specialized books of tunes, when approached with a bit of knowledge and an open mind, let you expand your playing range to a large number of songs instantly. Knowing how to fake it makes anyone a much more competent keyboard player.

How Music Charts Work

The word *chart* sounds so unartistic, like a blueprint. In fact, charts (also called *lead sheets*) are very much like blueprints, showing the schematic structure of a song. A song's chart consists of the melody, notated on a single treble cleff staff, plus chord symbols either above or below the melody. (Words are sometimes present if the tune isn't an instrumental.) Some charts work equally well for guitarists and keyboardists, by placing guitar chord symbols next to the keyboard chord symbols. Keyboardists call the chart's chord symbols the *changes*, as in "What are the changes for this tune?" The following figure shows a chart for "Greensleeves," using piano chord symbols only.

A chart for "Greensleeves," showing piano chords above the melody. This tune is simple, but some song charts have much more frequent chord changes.

Music Speak

Fake books are volumes of sheet music for songs. Each song in a fake book consists of the melody, written in music notation, and chord symbols above the notes. Taking cues from the chord symbols, the player must improvise (fake) an arrangement for the song.

Music **charts**, also called **lead sheets**, notate the melody of a song, with chord symbols above the notes to indicate the accompaniment harmonies for the left hand. Charts (lead sheets) are compiled in fake books.

In playing a music chart, use your right hand to play the melody, and your left hand for the chords. If playing the chords is too much to cope with at first, just play single bass notes underneath the chord symbols. Sticking with our "Greensleeves" example, the next example shows the easiest possible way to fake the tune from the chart, playing one bass note for each chord symbol.

The next step is to play full chords underneath the chord symbols, as shown in the following example.

The next step in creating an interesting arrangement from a fake book is to fill in the left-hand part with some embellishments—extra notes or chords—to give the piece interest and rhythmic movement. The first three examples showed the simplest ways of playing a chart, by changing the left-hand part only when a chord symbol appears above the melody. Skilled keyboard fakers keep the left hand playing almost all the time, as if they were reading a complicated arrangement from the sheet music. Playing with complexity isn't required or even preferable in many cases, but in examples such as the "Greensleeves" chart I'm using in this chapter, which has two-measure gaps between most chord changes, there's plenty of room for the left hand to fill in.

The final version—still "Greensleeves"—shows what you can do by playing broken chords instead of solid chords.

Here is one way to play the "Greensleeves" chart shown on the previous page. This is the simplest possible arrangement, using single left-hand notes instead of chords.

Music Speak

When in doubt, simplify. Remember, you're faking it! Perfection is not a requirement. If you can't come up with a good chord, just hit the bass note, or even leave the left hand out entirely for a couple of beats until you can catch up with the melody. Using fake books should be fun: Don't spoil the experience by stressing out.

Fakery Tips to Remember

Here are a few things to remember about playing charts and lead sheets from fake books:

➤ The chords indicated in a chart are just suggestions. True, they are often the best possible suggestions, and represent the chords originally intended by the song's composer. But that doesn't stop musicians from changing them (using what are called *alternate chords*) and inserting additional chords into the chart spontaneously. It takes a good knowledge of chords and some musical experience to substitute or insert chords, but you know the old-world proverb: "The only way to get experience is to go for it, big-time, with utter disregard for consequences." (Those old world folks really have a way with words.)

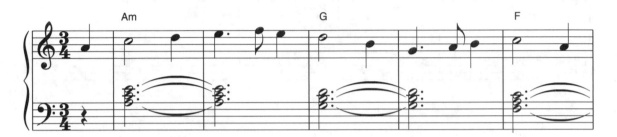

Using chords in "Greensleeves."

➤ You can assume that any chord symbol refers to a major chord if not indicated otherwise. Minor chords are indicated with a lower-case "m" next to the chord symbol.

➤ The right-hand part of a chart is open to some leeway as well as the left hand. Charts and lead sheets are meant to give you the bare bones of a song, not tie you to a literal interpretation of the notation. The important thing about playing a chart is to make the song recognizable, and many keyboard players throw in a lot of improvisation in *both* hands along the way.

Using broken chords can spice up a faked arrangement.

Making Music

Holiday music illustrates a couple of enhanced music charts. I say "enhanced," because I've supplied chord notation in addition to chord symbols. Don't get too used to such kind treatment—fake books give only the symbols. These chords give you a few ideas of how to translate the symbols, but feel free to deviate from them and make up your own arrangements.

The traditional Christmas carol *We Three Kings* is a favorite of jazz players because of its flexibility. The tune can be interpreted slowly and hauntingly, or fast and jazzy. In the following arrangement, I've used many open-fifth intervals to imply chords, giving the song an antique sound characteristic of ancient music from the Renaissance period. Note also, toward the end, the sort series of single notes in walking-bass style. This sort of shifting from style to style is perfectly typical when faking a tune. Do what works; do what occurs to you at the moment.

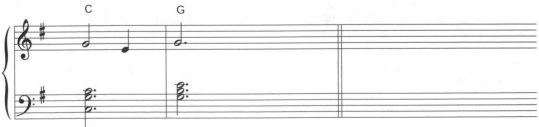

After you've entertained friends for Christmas, they'll come running back for New Year's. the traditional ringing –in song *Auld Lang Syne* lends itself to fake-book arrangement. Once again (in the holiday spirit), I've provided notated chords in addition to symbols.

The Least You Need to Know

➤ A music chart, or lead sheet, consists of a melody written on a single staff, above which are chord symbols indicating what harmonies should be played with the left hand. If the song has words, they are printed beneath the staff.

➤ Chord symbols on a chart are just suggestions, and you can experiment with using other chords, or playing single bass notes.

➤ When playing a chart for the first time, keep it simple until you get familiar with the song.

Chapter 17

The Rigors and Joys of the Classics

In This Chapter

➤ Discussing the difficulties and rewards of learning classical piano music

➤ Surveying the easy and intermediate classical repertoire

Everybody wants to play the classics—that's what makes them *the* classics! But, seriously, all keyboard players should be exposed to the very best music ever written for the instrument; and you can't deny that Bach, Beethoven, Mozart, Chopin, and the boys were no slouches when it came to composing keyboard music.

How Classical Music Works

Let's review a few common (mis)perceptions about classical music.

➤ Classical music is high-brow

➤ Classical music is difficult

➤ Playing classical music requires extensive training

While it's true that advanced classical music can be very difficult, and some people do indulge in extensive training to master the genre, there is such a thing as relatively easy classical music for the keyboard, and anyone who can read music can play it.

As to the high-brow nature of the classics, it's worth remembering that some of the music we call classical was the popular music of its day.

Adhering to the Letter and Spirit

One reason classical music has a rigorous reputation is its literalness. In other words, classical music is composed, and must be played, down to the individual note and expression marking. The explicitness of classical music is opposed to the informality of popular composition, which consists of just a melody, words, and chords; the exact arrangement of notes is made up by the publisher and/or the player. When you learn a classical piece, every note must be in its place, whereas there can be quite a bit of fudging and simplifying when you play a pop song, and quite a bit of improvisation when you play a jazz tune.

Grace Notes

In modern times there is a clear division between classical and popular music, never mind genre schisms like jazz, R&B, hip-hop, rock, new age, and many others. Before the twentieth century, classical music appealed to the aristocracy that had the leisure and money to enjoy it, but the great composers also wrote music for the masses. Bach produced church music every Sunday; Mozart composed operas for the popular theater; Beethoven churned out piano sonatas to be played in private homes.

Why would anyone want to play classical music if there were no room for the player's musical personality? The answer is that nobody would. The fact is, there *is* room for personality when playing classical music. Personal playing style, when applied to a classical piece, is called *interpretation*.

The interpretation of a piece usually affects the following aspects:

Music Speak

The **interpretation** of a classical piece of music is defined as the individual player's approach to its tempo, dynamics, and articulation/phrasing.

➤ **Tempo.** The exact speed at which a classical piece moves is usually left up to the player. Sometimes you see pieces whose tempos are explicitly defined by metronome settings at the beginning, but even those pieces are subject to some variation. In most cases the tempos of classical piano pieces are indicated by vague descriptors such as Allegro (happily) or Lento (slowly). While it wouldn't be appropriate for a Lento piece—to be played fast, the indicators are general enough to allow considerable leeway.

➤ **Dynamics.** Even more than with tempo markings, the dynamics of a piece—how loud or soft it should be played at any given point—can be taken as suggestions rather than rules. If you question whether a composer's indications should be disregarded or changed, consider that many dynamic markings you see in classical sheet music—such as crescendos and decrescendos—were placed there by the publisher or editor of the music, not the composer.

All kinds of dynamic indicators infest the notation of most classical music, and if you listen to recordings while following along with the music, you can see that much of is completely ignored volume (loudness and softness) is one of the main ways of expressing mood in music, which is the most personal aspect of a performance.

➤ **Articulation and phrasing.** Articulation is the degree to which notes are disconnected from each other, and phrasing refers to the way in which notes are connected. Articulation and phrasing are related concepts, and difficult to learn except through experience.

Grace Notes

One of Bach's most famous collections, the *Clavier-Büchlein für Anna Magdalena Bach*, was a collection of student-level pieces for his second wife to practice her keyboard technique.

If you have any recordings of Bach piano music, played by different performers, listen to them with an ear to how the notes are articulated and phrased. Some performers play the lines of notes with the utmost smoothness, seamlessly and without any breaks between the notes. Other players, seeking to distinguish the notes from each other, use a more detached touch that separates the notes from each other. What did Bach want? It's hard to say, since he just wrote down the notes, often without any phrase markings, and since he was composing for the harpsichord which has a more detached sound than the piano. In all cases, classical music is *old* music played on modern instruments, and it is up to the player to make it sound good with whatever techniques and styles are available.

Even the Masters Wrote Easy Music

The question of difficulty in classical music deserves further discussion. While it's true that the reputation for difficulty is largely due to its rigorous notation, I can't deny that a lot of piano/keyboard classics are treacherously hard to play. Some pieces were composed for piano virtuosos, and in the nineteenth century the great piano composers *were* the performing virtuosos of the day, and they naturally wrote music with which to show off their glorious keyboard technique.

Believe it or not, the great classical composers actually wrote some easy music. In some cases they composed for students, in other cases they met publishing requests. As someone who has dabbled in composition myself, I can testify that there is a pure satisfaction in composing simple music for its own sake, as well. Whatever the many reasons, there is a wealth of classical music that doesn't crunch the player's knuckles. Once you've become very familiar with the basics of reading music and two-handed playing, you can graduate yourself to the classics with some easy pieces.

Begin With the Baroque

Piano music begins with the *Baroque* era, a European artistic period that lasted from roughly 1600 to 1750. Baroque architecture is highly ornate, and was often expressed in elaborately chiselled cathedrals. Classical music of the period was likewise complex and ornamental, and the predominant keyboard of the period was the harpsichord (see Chapter 2). Why then do I call it the beginning of piano music? Because modern performances of Baroque keyboard music are usually on the piano, not the harpsichord.

Baroque music is not very emotional, though it can be stirring. The Baroque style did not feature lovely melodies set against a chordal accompaniment, like a piece by Chopin, a jazz ballad, or a George Winston piano song. Baroque composers fitted melodies against each other ingeniously, forging music of great precision that has a mathematical quality. *Contrapuntal* music, or music written in opposing parts, is the highlight of Baroque compositional style. It is almost abstract in its devotion to a labyrinth of musical rules.

Grace Notes

If you were to buy several recordings of a famous classical piece, such as a Beethoven sonata or a Chopin étude, you'd find that in each case the tempo indicator is obeyed with a variety of personal styles that represent slightly different specific tempos.

Grace Notes

Playing classical music, with its combination of rigorous notation and personal interpretation, offers a challenge to find a balance between mechanical playing and artistry. You may think that musical artistry is beyond you, but anyone who learns a single piece of classical music has the right to interpret it, and in so doing bring a personal artistry to the fore, even if only for personal pleasure.

Music Speak

The **Baroque** period of music ran through the seventeenth and early eighteenth centuries, and featured complex, ornate music. Typically, composers fashioned multiple melodies to play at the same time, fitting them together with mathematical accuracy in pleasing harmonies. Bach is the most famous Baroque composer.

Baroque music sometimes sounds dry, like an exercise. Indeed, contrapuntal music really is an exercise in composition. However, the great Baroque composers transcended the technical aspects of their art, and delivered immortal music. (Sounds corny, but it's true.)

Johann Sebastian Bach lived at the end of the Baroque period, and composed contrapuntally even as his younger contemporaries were moving into new, more hip styles of music. Near the end of his life Bach was considered something of an old fogey, and his music was quickly forgotten when he died—only to be revived in the nineteenth century. Bach's profession was writing church music, which he cranked out in weekly batches. Lucky for pianists, Bach wrote quite a bit of keyboard music for young students, some of whom were his own kids.

To explore Bach's music, look for any compilation of pieces for beginning or intermediate players. There are many *preludes* and other pieces that require good counting, but are not fast or complicated. The following piece is a simple Minuet for keyboard (originally composed for harpsichord), which I've presented without any abridgment or editing. Note the dual repeat signs that divide the piece into two sections—the whole thing is played in AABB form.

Bach's best-known collection of keyboard pieces is The Well-Tempered Clavier, a title that needs some explanation. Well-tempered refers to the system of music we are familiar with today, including keys, scales, half steps, whole steps, and the modern method of tuning a keyboard. Music wasn't always composed according to the current system, and Bach celebrated the liberation all composers felt from more primitive systems of music theory by writing a prelude and fugue for every single key, both major and minor. (That's twenty-four keys.) Then he did it again—Book 2 of The Well-Tempered Clavier. (*Clavier* is a generic name for a keyboard instrument.)

The following musical examples present the entire first prelude of The Well-Tempered Clavier, preceded by two alternative notations of the first two measures. I've written out these optional notations because the original sheet music looks more complex and intimidating than it really is. (Thanks a bunch, Johann.) The notes are rather easy to play, and many beginning piano students latch onto this lovely and instructive piece. Go straight to the original notation if you like, then back up and see how it works with the alternative excerpts if you run into trouble.

Music Speak

Contrapuntal music features separate melodies that sound good when played against each other. (Contra means against.) One of the most mathematical styles of music composition, it has many rules that the composer must follow. (Otherwise the contrapuntal police get you.) Bach was a master of counterpoint music.

Bach is the best-known Baroque composer, but Handel and Scarlatti also wrote lots of beginning and intermediate keyboard music.

Classic Classics

Classical music refers to the entire tradition of the strictly composed, refined music practiced by trained musicians for several centuries. Within that long tradition have transpired several phases, or styles of music, as this chapter surveys. The Classical period is one such phase, and it shouldn't be confused with classical music generally. The Classical period extended from the mid-eighteenth century to the mid-nineteenth century (more or less) in Europe.

The styles of Classic composers different from their Baroque predecessors very distinctly. The contrapuntal style of pitting melodies against each other faded out of chic, and a new rigorous tradition took its place. Composers from this period were more concerned with structure than anything else, and stuck fast to their definitions of pieces like *symphonies, sonatas,* and *concertos.* Within the pieces, the compositional style was elegant but less intellectual than the Baroque composers had been. There was more emphasis on single melodies supported by accompaniments.

So what effect does music from the Classic period have on modern ears? Some piano music from that era sounds excessively polite, but the best has a marvelous innocence and purity. Later in the period, the music is earthy, strong, bold, serious, and strict. It is not a musical period known for its overt emotionalism, but it provides many memorable melodies.

After the movie *Amadeus,* most people became familiar, to some extent, with the life of Wolfgang Amadeus Mozart, perhaps the most precocious music prodigy to ever live. Mozart represented the near-beginning of the Classic period. Considering Wolfgang died in his thirties, his prodigious output is all the more amazing. The piano sonatas are among the most lucid and limpid piano music ever written. If you need some sonic simplicity in your day, go for the effortless innocence of an album of Mozart sonatas.

The next piece is a simplified arrangement of a famous melody in one of Mozart's piano sonatas—the so-called Turkish March. Although I have not placed staccato marks throughout the left-hand part, most pianists play the left hand in a markedly detached fashion. The melody is unusually exotic for Mozart, who was not generally known for composing melodies inspired by the musical traditions of other countries.

Music Speak

Symphonies are pieces composed for an orchestra, usually in three movements, like a piano sonata. **Concertos** are similar to symphonies, but composed with a solo instrument accompanied by the orchestra. The piano part of a piano concerto, for example, is usually virtuosic, with the intent of showing off the pianist's skills.

Music Speak

A **sonata** is a piano piece written in three connected parts. Each part is called a *movement.* The movements may sound like entirely separate pieces, and in a sense they are. Ideally, the entire sonata hangs together as a satisfying musical experience. Handel, Haydn, Mozart, and Beethoven wrote famous sonatas.

Here are some other great Classic composers you should be aware of:

➤ **Haydn.** Haydn was an early master of the Classic period, whose music contains lingering traces of the Baroque period. Haydn's piano sonatas are much shorter than Mozart's, and less developed. They are somewhat more ornate, and don't have the translucent Mozart genius.

➤ **Beethoven.** Most people have heard of Ludwig, and know the poignant story of his deafness, which occurred during his adulthood and didn't stop him from composing. Beethoven was a gruff composer who brought a kind of peasant earthiness to refined classical forms. If you really want a challenge, make it a project to listen to all thirty-two of his piano sonatas. (I know I'm recommending a lot of sonatas in this section. What can I say—it was a ragingly popular musical form back then.) The early sonatas sound like a coarse version of Mozart. The middle sonatas include the famous Moonlight Sonata and Appassionata—both deservedly enduring in their beauty and power. The late sonatas are phenomenally challenging pieces, both to play and listen to. Beethoven composed his music a bit later in the eighteenth century than Mozart, and while the two composers sound similar, Beethoven had more fire and brimstone compared to Mozart's limpid innocence.

➤ **Schubert.** Franz Schubert was one of the most spectacular melodic composers of all time—a hall of famer in the tune-humming department. He wrote many songs for classical singers accompanied by piano, and also—guess what?—piano sonatas.

Grace Notes

Consider that much of Bach's so-called piano music was composed for the harpsichord, which has a completely different dynamic range, and is played with a different technique, than a modern piano. Yet today the piano is, more often than not, the instrument of choice for playing Bach's harpsichord music.

Grace Notes

It has been said of Mozart's music that it should be played either in childhood or old age, because only innocence or long experience can bring out the purity of the music. But don't let that stop you from playing Mozart if your age falls somewhere between nine and ninety. The music is refreshing and disarmingly simple.

Virtuosity Emerges

The title of this section may be misleading. Keyboard virtuosity was certainly celebrated in the Classic and Baroque eras. But it's hard for us to relate to ancient virtuosity, performed as it was on ancient instruments that were very different from our modern pianos. The music itself was influenced by the instruments. The string-busting virtuosity that we think of today emerged in the nineteenth century during a period called the Romantic era of classical music.

Why Romantic? Melody was king during this period—tear-jerking, swoon-worthy melodies dripping with moonlight that leave listeners weak in the knees and gasping for more. It was during the Romantic period that the melody-and-accompaniment style of composing reached a height of sophistication and beauty.

Romantic piano music was composed for instruments very close in range, sonority, responsiveness, and power to modern pianos, and composers went to town. In fact, the great composers of the nineteenth century were also the most dashing pianists, unlike the twentieth century, during which composition has spun off into a separate and somewhat reclusive art.

Frederick Chopin was perhaps the most famous and beloved Romantic composer, and he enjoys a special regard among pianists and piano lovers because he composed almost exclusively for the instrument. Chopin was himself a great pianist of his day, and he adored the instrument. He is the piano's great champion of the nineteenth century, even of all time.

Chopin wrote no symphonies, no operas, and even his two piano concertos have boring and perfunctory orchestral parts. Where to start with the piano music? Chopin invented forms like *mazurkas,* nocturnes (he actually popularized this previously invented form), polonaises, and ballades. His two sets of piano études (technical studies whose gorgeous musicality transcends their studiousness) are astonishing. If you're new to Chopin, your best bet is one of the many compilation albums featuring a mix of several works.

In the next musical sample, I've simplified a portion of Chopin's famous Raindrop Prelude and transposed it down one half-step from its difficult original key. As originally composed, the piece is too much of a handful for beginning players. In this version, you can enjoy the ravishing melody.

In addition to Chopin, the following major Romantic composers wrote great listening music, most of which resides in the advanced piano repertoire:

➤ **Liszt.** A contemporary of Chopin, Franz Liszt was considered the greatest virtuoso of his day, and in retrospect was one of the hottest piano stars of all time. He practically caused riots when he performed in concert. His compositions are less profound than Chopin's but you might want to pick up a compilation CD just to enjoy unbridled, unapologetic, virtuosic flash.

➤ **Brahms.** A very refined woman with impeccable taste once said to me she didn't like Brahms because he had no sense of humor. Reflecting on that critique, I realized it's true—Johannes Brahms has no playfulness in his compositions. By all accounts not a playful man in person, he nonetheless wrote soulful, inspired music for orchestra, combinations of instruments, and piano. The best way to get a handle on Brahms's piano persona is to buy an album that contains many of his short pieces for solo piano. His moods range from quietly introspective to tumultuous and assertive.

➤ **Rachmaninoff.** Sergei Rachmaninoff was born late in the Romantic period, and composed well into the twentieth century, by which time he was rather a throwback to a previous era. A Russian composer, Rachmaninoff recently gained popular allure when his Piano Concerto #3 was featured in the movie *Shine*, then featured again in David Helfgott's chart-busting recording. That particular concerto has been my favorite since I was a young teenager, so I recommend it. Rachmaninoff is perhaps best known for his concertos, but he also composed many shorter solo piano pieces such as preludes and études. They are crushingly difficult to play, and it's fun to listen to master pianists dispatch them as if they were easy.

➤ **Scriabin.** Another Russian, and, like Rachmaninoff, born late to the Romantic era. Scriabin's early piano music sounds like a Russian Chopin, but it didn't take him long to develop a highly individual and almost modern style. His later pieces veer almost into atonality—a style of composing that can sound as if the notes were picked at random. Scriabin pushed the envelope, but he wasn't a capricious or trivial composer. His piano music is deeply sensual and evocative. Try an album of études, preludes, or miscellaneous short piano pieces.

Grace Notes

Chopin was impressed with, and influenced by, folk music from the villages of Poland, and those simple tunes inspired some of his melodies. Chopin composed a series of *Mazurkas* for piano—the mazurka is a type of folk dance. Some of the slower mazurkas are fairly easy to play without any simplification. Chopin's waltzes are good for intermediate-advanced players, as are the nocturnes. Pretty much everything else is hard.

The Impressionists

Music and art follow each other throughout the ages. Just as French turn-of-the-century painting took on a *impressionistic* flavor, with fuzzy washes of color and indistinct images, so did classical music have its own impressionistic period championed by Maurice Ravel, Claude Debussy, and many other French composers. Impressionistic music features flowing, watery music with harmonies that sound more modern than in the Romantic pieces of the mid-nineteenth century.

As you can gather from the name, impressionistic art and music was created to convey an impression—not necessarily a concrete impression, and certainly not one based on realism. Paintings from the period are fuzzy and imbued with a wash of colors. Music from those days shares the same sensibility, as harmonies were stretched in new directions and the rhythmic pulse of previous generations became vague. Impressionistic music doesn't generally have a strong beat. Instead, it is a watery-sounding melange of shifting sonorities and evocative harmonies. Some of the pieces from this

Grace Notes

Some of Ravel's and Debussy's music is available in simplified versions. One piece you might want to search out is Ravel's *Pavane pour une infante défunte* (Dance for a Dead Princess), which, despite the morbid title, is one of the loveliest piano pieces ever.

period attempted to convey, musically, underwater scenes or landscapes. Harmonic rules that had been in place for hundreds of years were thrown out the window, and smashed on the Parisian streets below.

For the listener, impressionistic piano music is extremely moody. It bears a certain resemblance to new age music, but with far greater complexity and sophistication. Impressionistic melodies don't stick in your head, and the pieces definitely don't make you tap your foot. Rather, music from that period sends you on mental journeys filled with lovely and fantastic imagery.

Ravel and Debussy are the two most famous Impressionists. Claude Debussy was influenced by many musical traditions, including jazz. His piano music sounds much simpler than it actually is—his pieces are densely filled with notes, but must be made to sound transparent. Maurice Ravel was an Impressionist with a stronger sense of melody than some others, and as such is a good introduction to the period. His piano music is fastidiously crafted and especially lovely.

The following piece is a simplified excerpt of what is, to many listeners, Ravel's most lovely piano piece, the *Pavane pour une Infante Defunte* (Pavane for a Dead Princess). A pavane is an ancient, slow dance. Don't be put off by the morbid title. This famous melody has been adapted to popular songs and movie themes.

Two other Impressionist composers who wrote somewhat easier music:

➤ **Erik Satie**. You may be familiar with Satie's work, or one of his works, without being aware of the composer's name. Satie wrote the so-called *Gymnopédies* that has been used over and over in all kinds of recordings, including rock songs. It is bittersweet, poignant, and—most important—fairly simple to play. It is one of several easy but hauntingly beautiful pieces Satie wrote for the piano. Take note that his work has a broad range that often can't be fit into the five-octave range of home keyboards.

➤ **Charles Gounod**. Gounod lived and composed a bit earlier than the pillars of French impressionism, but his music is still atmospheric without being overly complex. Some of Gounod's pieces are downright simple, and are found in collections of easy French piano music.

➤ **Gabriel Fauré**. Perhaps best known for his evocative *Requiem* for orchestra and chorus, Fauré lightened the mood in some of his piano pieces. Though not as simplistic as Gounod or Satie, Fauré's piano music is manageable for intermediate players.

Music Speak

Ragtime was one of the first forms of jazz piano, developed early in the century in southern urban centers like New Orleans. Featuring a *stride* left hand, bouncing back and forth between bass notes and mid-range chords, set against jaunty melodies in the right hand, ragtime is joyful and playful music.

Jazz–America's Music

Twentieth-century piano music in America has been dominated by a single, diverse, sprawling art form: jazz. Jazz is America's home-grown music genre, born from a confluence of Afro-American spirituals and urban street music early in the century.

Ragtime was the first organized expression of early jazz piano that you can listen to today. The happy, rhythmically syncopated type of music enjoyed a renewal of popularity after the movie *The Sting* was released, featuring ragtime prominently in the soundtrack. Since then, Scott Joplin has been firmly installed on the musical map of the twentieth century.

You can find albums with collected ragtime pieces, called *rags*, by Joplin and others. Scott Joplin was a genius of melody and mood, but any ragtime composer you come across will give you some joyful listening. Ragtime has bittersweet moments, but overall is some of the most purely happy music you can find.

The Least You Need to Know

➤ Classical music is more literal than popular music or jazz, and that's one reason it seems intimidating: You can't fudge it.

➤ Some of the greatest classical composers wrote easy music that beginning pianists can enjoy, including Bach, Mozart, Beethoven, Chopin, and some of the French impressionists.

➤ Classical piano music is sometimes available in simplified arrangements that let you play immortal music without studying for years.

Power Practicing

Playing the piano is an art. Successful art depends on practice. In a sense, art *is* practice. We hear of great performers "practicing their art." I propose in this chapter that practice is an art of its own. I have practiced piano for almost my entire life, and I've learned that ten minutes spent practicing *well* is worth more than an hour of practicing badly. This chapter explores habits of good practicing.

Repetition is the most common form of practice. If you want to do something well, after all, it makes sense to do it over and over again, until the performance is almost automatic. But there is a difference between rote repetition and constructive repetition, and that is the difference this chapter is all about. All practice involves repetition, but the value of your practice depends on what other techniques are layered onto the sheer repetition of musical passages. Read on to learn some fresh practicing techniques.

The Goal of Practicing

What is the purpose of practicing, anyway? Throughout this book I present exercises that are primarily geared to learning the basic elements of playing and notation. The exercises are not entire pieces in most cases, and they are not oriented toward eventual performance.

Now, I don't mean to imply that public performance should be anybody's goal, necessarily. But even if you're playing for personal satisfaction alone, and you'd rather hang upside down from a tree than let anybody hear you perform, being able to play music with some expertise is a great feeling. So, whatever your musical goals, using practice techniques geared toward performance excellence enhances your personal musical art.

Practicing, and practicing efficiently, has several goals:

➤ **Smoothness.** Music needs to proceed unhaltingly to be effective. Pauses in the musical flow are distracting and disconcerting. It's natural, when learning a piece, to stumble over notes and stop to get your bearings. One point of practicing is to smooth out those rough spots until you can play the piece through entirely without pausing.

Smoothness also refers to the continuity and musicality of individual phrases within the piece. Using good fingering helps you play musically and unbrokenly, and practicing involves finding and learning the best fingerings for the piece.

Key Thought

You shouldn't play a rollicking ragtime piece such as "The Maple Leaf Rag" at the same tempo that you'd play a slow torch song like "As Time Goes By," or the whole musical point of the rag is lost.

Musical Mouthful

"To stop the flow of music would be like the stopping of time itself, incredible and inconceivable."
—Aaron Copland

➤ **Playing the right tempo.** Throughout this book, in the exercises, I emphasize that playing fast is your least important consideration. Evenness and steadiness are more important than speed when practicing the exercises. That rule of thumb is generally true with more musically meaningful pieces as well, but tempo is more important with real pieces than exercises.

A piece's effect is conveyed partly by its tempo, and one of your practicing goals is to get the piece "up to speed." Speed isn't much of a concern with rock ballads, slow jazz tunes, or classical piano pieces with the Largo or Lento tempo marking. But faster pieces need to steam along at a good clip, or they just don't sound right.

➤ **Clarity.** It's tempting to fudge your way through a piece, or a part of a piece, that you haven't learned perfectly. Hey, it's not a problem—music is fun, and perfection isn't necessarily the goal. Nevertheless, playing every note of a piece clearly is an ideal, and one of the goals of practicing. Clarity is hardest when a piece throws a lot of fast notes at you, like some classical pieces do when you have to zoom up and down the keyboard with speedy scales or arpeggios. In addition to a glut of notes, using the sustain pedal too much can cause lack of musical clarity. Whatever the cause of muddiness, good practicing technique can help bring distinctness and clarity to your playing.

➤ **Expressiveness.** Music is emotional. At some point in your practicing, it becomes time to move beyond the rote learning of notes, to conveying the emotional point of the piece. All kinds of music have sentiment as the core value. Good practicing takes into consideration the emotion of the notes you've worked so hard to learn.

Knowing How Much to Practice

Adults take piano lessons for different reasons. Some with to recapture a piece of their childhood; others start from scratch with what they hope will be a fulfilling hobby. Some are determined to become accomplished players; others are in it for the the fun and relaxation of making music. How you practice should be determined by your goals. Nevertheless, a few rules of thumb apply to everyone.

Contrary to what might seem like common sense, practicing every day in not necessary. Daily practice doesn't hurt; don't get me wrong. But one substantial practice session every few days (or even once a week) moves you further along than a short daily session, especially if the short session is distracted. Naturally, frequent serious practice makes the most progress, but you shouldn't feel that your skills will erode if you don't get to the piano every day.

Setting musical goals is more important (for Adults) than sticking to a certain time schedule. In other words, forcing yourself to sit at the piano for 60 minutes when you're not in the mood is less valuable than getting a handle on that troublesome single measure that makes you stumble every time, when you're in the mood to break it down and work it out.

Speaking broadly, practicing two or three hours per week will keep most adults progressing toward better technique and more advanced pieces, how those hours are spaced throughout the week isn't so important, as long as you find time for one or two well-rounded sessions with plenty of repetition. More advanced students need more time to continue progression, and intermediate players work up to about an hour of practice each day.

Take Apart the Parts

When learning to play a new piece, there often seems to be too much happening at once. Both hands being asked to play different parts, there's a key signature to remember, plus you must count the rhythm. The best way to cope with a piece's complexites, and begin to master each element of the performance, is to disassemble the piece.

There are two ways to take a piece apart:

➤ Separate the two hands. Expert players can sometimes play a new piece at sight, both hands going at once. But most mortals need to examine each hand separately at some point during the practice process.

➤ Isolate the piece's different portions. Usually, keyboard pieces have easy sections and hard sections. Whether you're working with a jazz chart, the lead sheet of a pop standard, or a classical piano piece, some portion of the music is likely to give you more problems than other portions. Isolating the hard parts and treating them like self-contained exercises is the best way to master them. Many of the tips in this chapter give you ideas for practicing portions of a piece.

Imagine walking down the hall of a music conservatory, a college-level school for aspiring musicians. Practice rooms—small, badly soundproofed rooms with a piano in each room—line both sides of the hall. The sonic atmosphere is a cacophony of conflicting musical passages. As you walk down the hall, the music pouring into your ears shifts, rises, and falls as the nearest rooms become more audible than the others, then fade away as you walk along. If you were to concentrate on each room in turn, there is little doubt what you'd hear. In

Key Thought

Just as you want to practice the more difficult hand first, so you want to find, isolate, and attack the most difficult part of a piece first. Don't make the mistake of putting off working on a hard passage precisely because it *is* hard! Use the advice in this chapter to make hard passages easier, then enjoy how relatively easy the rest of the piece seems.

Grace Notes

I remember attending a classical piano class led by the Jorge Bolet, the famous, and quite astounding, piano virtuoso. He constantly exhorted the students who played for the class to slow down their playing of fast pieces. He finally confided, "I'm the slowest player in the world. It only seems like I play fast because I play so evenly." Of course, in the case of Jorge Bolet and others of his skill level, they play both evenly *and* lightning-fast. But the point is that by practicing slowly and evenly, you can both increase your speed and your polish. Keyboard virtuosity is a matter of control, not just raw velocity.

every room, would-be musicians practicing isolated passages of pieces over and over, often one hand at at time. In other words, combining the techniques of separating the hands and isolating the piece's portions is a common and effective way to practice.

Here is a rule to remember when practicing hands separately:

➤ Practice the more difficult hand first.

There are a few reasons for this rule. First of all, the most difficult part requires more time to learn, so it makes sense to start with it. Second, if you can learn the difficult hand well enough to play it semiautomatically, it makes it easy to add the other hand. Thirdly, the facility with which you can play the difficult part determines how fast and smoothly you eventually play the whole portion.

When it comes to maintaining the tempo of a piece all the way through, you can only go as fast as you can play the most difficult portion of the piece. By isolating the hardest passage, and practicing the hard hand separately, you zero in on the most crucial part of the whole piece: the part that sets the pace.

Slow, Slower, Slowest

A primary rule of practicing is: Slow it down. Hard pieces (or parts of pieces) become easier when played slowly, of course, but that's not the real reason for developing a habit of practicing slowly. There are two important reasons for habitually practicing at a slow tempo:

➤ The first reason is evenness. Fast passages with a lot of notes definitely need to be slowed down for practicing. The emphasis, as I've repeated often through this book, should be on playing evenly, not quickly. When practicing, play only as fast as you can stay faithful to the rhythm. Playing with rock-solid evenness—no pauses, slowdowns, or speeding up during the passage you're practicing—is great training for eventually playing the part full speed.

➤ The second reason for practicing slowly involves the natural intelligence of your fingers. Yep, you heard me—your fingers have their own smarts. I doubt if your fingers can balance the checkbook without a little help from your mind, but they have a sort of independent memory for motion. Just as your hands seem to tie shoelaces without much thought, using a kind of learned autopilot facility, so it is on the keyboard.

Your fingers can learn music and play it back semiautomatically. Practicing slowly etches music into your finger-memory. Ironically, practicing slowly teaches your fingers more quickly than practicing fast.

When I was a teenager, my piano teacher told me the story of how he prepared a difficult piece by Chopin for a performance. He learned the piece fastidiously, working on it with very slow tempos, concentrating on clarity and even-ness. The astounding part of the story is that his discipline was so great that he didn't play the piece at full speed *even once* before the day of the performance, and the concert went without a hitch. Whether this account was an exaggeration meant to impress me is irrele-vant. It *did* impress me with the importance and power of practicing slowly, whether the story is literally true or not.

A great tool for slow practice is the *metronome*. Metronomes make a deeply annoying clicking sound, certain to drive you and anyone in earshot to rash acts of violence. The clicking torture is worth it, however, because you can set the metronome to a fast or slow rate of clicking, in very small increments.

Metronomes are practice tools for developing evenness. It's like having a conductor standing next to you, or a teacher rapping on your keyboard with a pencil. The worst thing you can do when practicing slowly is to speed up when the going gets easy, and slow down during tough passages. The relentless, machine-ticking of the metronome helps keep you at one steady speed.

There are two kinds of ticking metronome: electronic and mechani-cal. The mechanical metronomes use a pendulum device that swings back and forth, creating the ticks. A weight attached to the pendulum stalk regulates the tempo. Electronic metronomes plug in and work their magic with a dial to adjust the tempo. The elec-tronic type is more reliable, ticks more evenly, and is usually more expensive. Digital quartz metronomes are now available, some with built in electronic tuners.

One type of metronome to avoid is the kind that blinks a light at you. The blinking light is fine if the device also ticks, but don't get a metronome that has only the light, as the visual indicator isn't enough to really help when practicing. You've got to hear the tick, or it doesn't do the trick. (I made up that rhyme. Just now. All by myself.)

Making Things Harder

When you're wrestling with a hard keyboard piece, or a hard pas-sage within a piece, what's the thing to do? Why, make it harder, of course. That may seem like advice from a masochist, but it's actu-ally good practice technique, and one used in other disciplines.

Prizefighters, for example, train extensively in ways that don't re-late exactly to what they do in the ring: by running, lifting weights, and dieting, in addition to hitting punching bags and sparring with suicidal ring partners. In other words, boxers do *more* than they are required to in the ring, over-training for each fight. In music, eating raw eggs and jumping rope for an hour doesn't help much with those tricky left-hand passages. In music, the same principle can be applied, and is sometimes called *overpracticing*.

Overpracticing takes whatever is most difficult in a piece, or a portion of a piece, and makes it more difficult. By magnifying

Key Thought

Start with the metronome set very slowly, and play the entire passage you're working on at that speed. Then gradually edge the ticking speed higher, playing the entire passage at each new tempo. In this fashion you are soon playing the piece (or por-tion of the piece) at a perform-ance speed, having polished your evenness in the process.

Grace Notes

Anyone who has ever played with a metronome has had the strange sensation that it's the metronome that's slowing down (rather than the obvious fact that they're speeding up)! It's kind of like the notion that the sun revolves around the earth; your perspective as a player can fool you! Metronomes, however, are machines—they don't speed up or slow down, so if you're falling off the steady "click," you must be at fault!

Key Thought

This technique is especially effective with passages for either hand that involve lots of quickly played consecutive notes. After spending some time overpracticing with high fingers, you should find that the passage zips along pretty well when played normally. Reminder: always play evenly!

Grace Notes

The piano teacher I studied with as a teenager believed in making things harder to an unearthly degree. He was always giving me tips for making hard passages harder. Before important concerts, he really poured on the torture, making me practice my performance pieces under very strange conditions indeed, just to make life difficult and strengthen my concentration. I practiced with a bright light shining in my eyes. I placed a record player next to the piano and played my classical pieces with rock 'n' roll blaring in my ear. I played my concert pieces standing up. I practiced while wearing gloves. By the time I was through, sitting in front of a large audience and playing the pieces normally seemed like the easiest thing in the world.

whatever you find hard, and practicing it that way, you begin to make the original music seem easier to play. And it's more than just appearances: the original music *is* easier to play after practicing it in some more difficult form.

Here are some ways to make difficult types of playing even harder for practice purposes.

➤ One basic method of overpracticing that works in almost all keyboard situations is to exaggerate the movements of your fingers. Consider this technique to be a kind of aerobic exercise for your hands.

Normally it doesn't take much finger movement to push down a key, especially the light plastic keys of an electronic keyboard. When practicing a difficult passage, though, play slowly and lift each finger as high as possible before dropping it down on the note. Gradually, through repetition, increase your speed, but continue lifting your fingers as if they were stepping over high hurdles. It is your *priority* to lift your fingers high, so don't go faster than you can while exercising your fingers this way.

➤ Here's one: jump higher and leap farther. This overpracticing technique is for when you have a difficult leap to execute on the keyboard. A leap is a quick jump from one part of the keyboard's range to a higher or lower part with the same hand. Landing accurately on the correct notes at the end of the leap can be tricky. The solution? Add an octave to the leap. Add two octaves. Make it brutally hard.

Go very slowly when you start this particular form of overpracticing. Be very deliberate as you make the leap and land on your destination note(s). Gradually add some speed to the maneuver, until you're playing it almost at full speed. Use the same fingerings as in the original leap. Finally, when you return to the correct leap as written in the piece, it seems much less treacherous.

➤ Too many notes? Play twice as many. When you have a fast passage of notes, usually in the right hand, with some zig-zagging configurations that make learning and playing the passage difficult, slow down and practice doubling up the notes. That's right—play each written note twice. If that doesn't seem frustrating enough, play each note three times. (Use the same finger for each repetition.)

This particular brand of sadistic overpracticing helps ingrain the position of the notes in your mind and finger-memory, plus it forces you to slow down.

No Strain, Big Gain

One of the most difficult parts of playing the piano is staying relaxed while learning a new physical skill. Your wrists, arms, and shoulders should be at ease while playing. Like anything else that's difficult, it takes practice. It may seem strange, but relaxation is a keyboard skill that can be practiced just like any of the musical challenges discussed in this chapter.

Here are two ways to encourage relaxation in your hands and arms:

➤ One of the bottlenecks of tension for many keyboard players is the wrist. Ideally, your wrist should be in a state of near-liquid relaxation, enabling you to raise your hand from the keyboard without lifting your forearm. One good exercise for encouraging such relaxation is to, indeed, lift your hand from the keyboard without using your forearm.

Just rest your hand on the keys—don't worry about hitting any particular notes or chords. Now, lift your hand by pivoting upward from the wrist, and drop it down on the keys. After several repetitions, try the same thing with the other hand. This exercise can be extended by dropping your hand down on predetermined notes or groups of notes. The next figure shows what notes to aim for with the right hand, then the left hand. (You can try both hands together, too.)

This one simple exercise can be repeated often—even every day if you like. Gradually, you should notice that your wrist is naturally more relaxed when you play.

➤ The second exercise is really is just a common sense relaxer. Every once in a while, remember to check whether you are in a relaxed state from your shoulders down through your fingers. Adjust your posture by sitting directly in front of the keyboard, both feet on the floor, and your back straight. Are your shoulders hunched? Unhunch them. Are you carrying tension anywhere in your upper body? Do a physical inventory, and deliberately relax any tense spots. Shake your forearms out as if you were doing the French "ooh-la-la" gesture quite vigorously with both hands. In every way you can think of, reestablish your relaxed demeanor before beginning to play again.

> **Key Thought**
>
> Increase leaps only in increments of an octave. You must be aiming for the same note(s), just an octave or two farther away.

> **Musical Mouthful**
>
> "You cannot imagine how it spoils you to have been a child prodigy."
> —Franz Lizst

> **Key Thought**
>
> Overpracticing leaps in this way is especially useful in ragtime pieces which traditionally have a left-hand part that bounces between a low bass note and a higher chord. Practice by lowering the bass note an octave, or raising the chord an octave, or both. Leave the right hand out of it while practicing.

The following figure is an exercise in overpracticing a left-hand part.

ORIGINAL VERSION:

OVERPRACTICE VERSION:

Play with left hand only

Overpracticing leaps requires increasing the size of the leap by an octave (or two). Remember: leave your right hand out of it. Play the overpractice version with just the left hand.

ORIGINAL VERSION:

OVERPRACTICE VERSION:

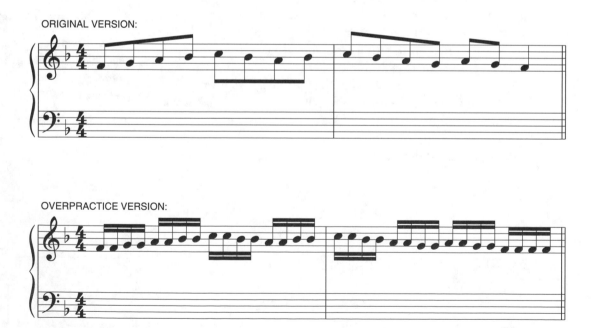

Overpracticing by doubling notes.

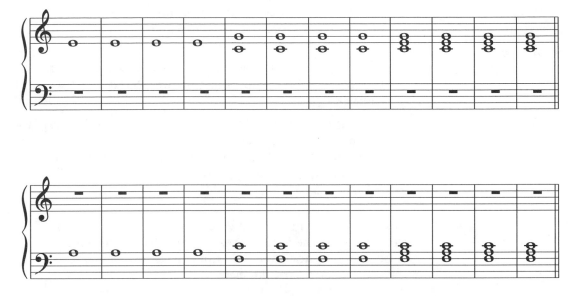

Play these notes and chords by dropping your hand down on the keyboard from the wrist, keeping your arm, wrist, and hand as relaxed as possible.

Facing the Music

Most of the practice techniques in this chapter focus on physical concerns like overcoming difficulties in a piece or relaxing your arms for better overall playing habits. Lest we forget the emotional side of music, this last section offers a practice technique designed to improve the expressiveness of your playing. It's a simple exercise, but in a way the most grueling, because it's the most revealing.

Here's the exercise in a nutshell: Record yourself playing. You can record yourself with a portable cassette recorder, or, if you're learning on a keyboard with a built-in *sequencer*, use that. Sound quality isn't the point here, so it really doesn't matter what method you use, as long as you can hear the result and learn from it.

Recording yourself play is difficult for every pianist and keyboardist, regardless of your experience or playing level. Hearing your own playing is hard because it rarely sounds like what you expect. Oddly, our ears deceive us while we're actually playing, leading us to believe we sound like what's in our head, rather than what's truly coming out of the instrument. Because we all have an ideal sound in our head, the truth is likely to hurt a bit. But for exactly that reason, recording is a great tool for improvement.

The time to record is when you've learned a piece well. There is no point in adding insult to injury by recording a half-learned piece, so you can witness objectively how much work you still have to do! Wait until you can play the piece smoothly, all the way through.

Remember, the point of recording is to improve your *expressiveness* in playing, so it should be done when you've gained some mastery over your material. As you listen to your playing, make notes (mentally or on paper) of what you want to change. Here are some considerations you may notice:

Key Thought

When aiming for particular notes during the hand-drop, the wrist tends to tighten up, so concentrate on keeping it as loose as possible, even as you form your hand into the position necessary to play the correct notes.

Musical Mouthful

"I am astounded ... at the wonderful power you have developed, and terrified at the thought that so much hideous and bad music may be put on record forever."
—Arthur Sullivan, on seeing a demonstration of Edison's phonograph

➤ Is your playing uneven where you thought it was even? You need to overpractice that passage with the "high fingers" technique described above.

➤ Does the piece sound tentative, as if you lacked confidence in your playing? Make sure your arms are relaxed, and try counting while you play.

➤ Would you characterize the playing as stiff or mechanical? You may be placing too much emphasis on counting, and not playing freely enough. Relax your internal metronome (and turn off the real metronome if you have one) and play the piece with a more relaxed attitude.

Of course, you may notice that your playing is far better than you expected! Whatever the result, it's exciting to record yourself and hear your own playing. You should do this exercise occasionally, as a final check when you've learned a piece.

Grace Notes

Everyone has had the experience of hearing their voice on a tape recording and saying, "That can't possibly be me!" The same is true with your playing—what you hear when you're playing may not be the same as what you hear, objectively, when you listen to a tape of your playing!

The Least You Need to Know

➤ The goals of practicing are smooth and even playing, playing at the correct speed, playing clearly, and playing expressively.

➤ The first rule of practicing is to work on a piece in sections, hands separately. Always attack the hardest part first.

➤ It's not necessary to be the fastest player in the world, and playing with great evenness simulates speed.

➤ Find ways to make hard passages even harder. Then when you play them normally, they don't seem so hard.

➤ Check often to see if your hands, wrists, arms, and shoulders are as relaxed as they could be. Take a moment to reduce any tension in your upper body.

➤ Try recording your own playing to evaluate whether the piece really sounds like you think it does.

Chapter 19

Technical Tips

In This Chapter

➤ Keeping your hands and arms relaxed

➤ Tips for playing octaves

➤ Attaining speed and power on the keyboard

➤ All thumbs

➤ Playing repeated notes, chords, trills, glissandos, and arpeggios

➤ Sight-reading and memorizing

This chapter is devoted to tips and advice to make you a stronger player in all kinds of ways, from using your thumbs effectively (you might have noticed that they are rather on the stubby side) to injecting more speed and power into your playing. You might not find gold in every section in this chapter, but I hope that everybody finds something helpful here.

Getting Relaxed

Your assignment: coordinate two hands, ten fingers, and both your feet while taming an instrument that weighs at least twice as much as you do—and relax while you're doing it! Playing the piano isn't easy, and tension is the player's biggest downfall. (Besides having a piano dropped on your foot, which would ruin anyone's day.) A pianist's entire body is subject to tension, but tightness especially gathers in the shoulders, arms, and wrists. Wrist tension alone can inhibit you from gaining a greater command of keyboard technique.

The greatest tool you can use to unlock constriction is simple awareness. The surprising truth is that the most tense players are often unaware that they are, in fact, constricted.

When practicing, develop a habit of checking your tension level—a tension reality check. Lift your hands from the keyboard and shake them out by the wrist. Take a few deep breaths and relax your shoulders and arms; ease of movement is organic, and must involve the whole body.

The wrists are gathering points for playing tension. The strain of positioning the hand to avoid playing wrong notes consolidates tension in the wrist. Try this exercise to release tension and build more relaxed playing habits. Pick a note, interval, or chord on the keyboard—one that's easy to play. Use just one hand. Play the note, interval, or chord repeatedly, using only your wrist motion. Keep your forearm still, and pivot your hand up and down by the wrist. Let your fingers *fall* onto the keyboard—don't push the hand down with your muscles. Hitting the right notes doesn't matter at first, just stay relaxed. Gradually concentrate on getting the chord right without letting tension creep into your wrist.

Key Thought

As much as possible, try to play the keyboard using the weight of your arms, not by strength of muscle. This partly mental, partly physical skill helps you stay relaxed.

Key Thought

Getting the piano to sing under your fingers in your own style is a matter of keyboard "touch." Remember that weight is more important than muscle, and approach the keyboard peacefully. Follow-through is an important part of keyboard touch, just as following through is important to a tennis stroke. Even though the follow-through happens after the sound has been initiated, it helps affect the sound.

Mastering Octaves

Playing octaves (the keyboard distance between a note and the next-higher or next-lower identical note) is an important part of most types of piano music. The octave is a unique keyboard interval. Because it is two versions of the same note, the octave is, of all the intervals, uniquely resolute and unambiguous. Octaves are put in the right hand to hammer out a melody strongly, and the left hand uses octaves to deepen and anchor a strong bass line.

If your hands are small, and spanning an octave is difficult, it's best not to strain to reach it. In many cases you can substitute single notes for octaves in pop, jazz, and ragtime. Changing the notation of classical music is forbidden in professional circles, but perfectly fine for amateurs playing at home.

For those who want to improve the facility and accuracy of their octave playing, the trick is to develop a firmness in your hand while keeping your wrist relaxed. Play any octave, and keep your hand on the keyboard, the two keys depressed. Concentrate on maintaining a locked distance between your thumb and fifth finger, as if you were holding a pencil between them. At the same time, relax your wrist and arm. Move your wrist up and down to encourage fluid movement, while keeping your fingers on the depressed keys. Now lift up your hand by the wrist, keeping your fingers separated by the distance of the octave, and move one note up on the keyboard—play the next octave and hold it a while. Continue in this fashion up the keyboard, encouraging firmness in your fingers and relaxation in your wrist.

Octaves are often consecutive, and sometimes played rather rapidly. In those cases, it's important to develop a technique for accomplishing rapid-fire octave playing. The trick is to keep your fingers firmly shaped to play the interval while your wrist is relaxed so it bounces up and down quickly and without strain. Make sure your forearm and upper arm are loose, too. Another hint lies in proper fingering. It is natural to use the fifth finger to play the top note of right-hand octaves (bottom note in the left hand). But when the octave falls on black keys, it's helpful to use the fourth finger—if your hand is big enough to stretch the octave with the thumb and ring finger. Doing so avoids the need to move your whole arm forward to reach the recessed black keys. Using the fourth finger leads to faster and smoother octave playing.

Speed and Power

What's the first thing that comes to mind when you think of a piano virtuoso? Probably sheer speed—the ability to play blindingly fast. But the truth is that speed, while important sometimes, is largely a matter of perception. And nothing contributes to the perception of speed like evenness. When you have a fast passage to play, an even performance—with each note precisely spaced from each other note—sounds faster than an uneven performance at a quicker tempo.

When practicing for speed, concentrate on mastery of evenness. You can do this by starting slowly, and gradually building up to faster tempos. While practicing, concentrate on absolute, even mechanical, timing precision. Your performance shouldn't sound robotic, but your practicing should. Don't indulge yourself by practicing full-speed too often. (It's irresistible sometimes.) The more time you spend mastering playing fast passages evenly, the more they will sound like lightning when you bring the piece up to tempo.

After speed, piano virtuosity is expressed through power—the ability to make the piano roar. Actually, playing power isn't an absolute characteristic. That is to say, power is relative. It is really dynamic range that creates the impression of power, and the pianists who can play most mightily are also the ones who can play the most delicately and softly. Great pianists never bang; rather, they control our expectations by managing the piano's extraordinary range of volume.

Nevertheless, you can increase your power (and dynamic range) by

Key Thought

Are scales necessary? They are the bane of every piano student. The thought of practicing scales makes piano lessons seem dull. The sad truth is that scales—or some form of similar exercise—are important in developing finger agility and independence. One of the most useful things about practicing scales is that they familiarize you with crossing the thumb underneath other fingers during sequences of notes.

Grace Notes

One old style of piano teaching (perhaps still used by some teachers) places a penny on the back of the student's hand. Ideally, you should be able to play a scale, up and down, without letting the penny slip off. That's how stable and level your wrist position should be.

learning one basic fact of power playing: It's weight, not muscle. Do not slam your hands on the keyboard to play loudly. Instead, lean into it, and imagine your power proceeding from your torso, along your shoulders, and down your arms. Your whole body is involved when playing with strength.

Key Thought

The thumb is the runt of fingers, and because of its shortness cannot play black keys easily. When determining your fingerings, try to avoid that situation. However, sometimes its unavoidable, especially when playing chords. In those instances, when the thumb must reach for a black key, move your whole arm forward so your knuckles approach the back of the keyboard. Avoid twisting your wrist when getting your thumb on the black key.

Repeating Notes and Chords

Playing a single note repeatedly on the keyboard isn't hard if the notes don't repeat too quickly. But if the tempo is fast, repeated notes do present a problem—it's hard to move the wrist up and down quickly, which you must do to play repeated notes with one finger. You can get around this challenge by using different finger for the repeated notes. A famous piece called "Bear Dance" by Bela Bartok, the Hungarian composer, has a left-hand part that consists almost entirely of sequences of *staccato* repeated notes. It is simply impossible to play that left-hand part without rotating the fingers you use. A 4-3-2-1 fingering is best when faced with a long string of repeated notes, and you can cycle through that sequence repeatedly (4-3-2-1-4-3-2-1-4-3-2-1). The pinky is almost never used in quick repeated notes.

Music Speak

Staccato is a musical notation for playing very short notes. Effective staccato playing requires a supple wrist. Don't try to lift your whole forearm quickly from the keyboard—a few repeats in that style shows you how exhausting it is. Instead, use your wrist as the pivot point, darting your hand down to the key and letting it bounce back up from the wrist. Try that with both hands, with individual notes, two-note intervals, and three-note chords. Keeping your wrist relaxed is more important than hitting notes accurately (for now). Try playing a scale in this staccato fashion. To keep your forearm still, you can even try holding it with your free hand.

Repeated chords are another challenge. Have you ever listened to the piano parts of old rock 'n' roll from the 1950s and early 1960s? Piano players in those days often used a rapid chord-playing technique that demanded a certain skill. In some classical music (including a famous Beethoven Sonata), a similar "running chord" figure is sometimes found. To play a repeated chord rapidly, try to develop the same firm-hand, loose-wrist style that comes in handy when playing octaves. It's important to keep the fingers firmly in position around the chord's notes, while using the wrist as a flexible lever that moves the hand quickly up and down. Don't raise your fingers off the keys unnecessarily high. Start slow, and gradually build up speed—but don't let your wrist or arm grow stiff. If you feel tension stop, shake your arm out, and start again slowly.

Out of Thin Air

Until the twentieth century when the practice faded, improvising was considered an essential keyboard art. Bach improvised gloriously on church organs. Mozart improvised famously on the harpsichord. Beethoven's piano improvisations were thunderous and ingenious. In the modern world, making up music from thin air is a skill that resides mostly in the jazz realm.

Improvising on the piano can be fun, yet intimidating. Even if you're alone, there is a self-consciousness about playing spontaneously, without any music or goal. It helps to adopt a childlike attitude of discovery about the instrument and music itself. Imagine you're a child, running your hands over the keyboard for the first time. Don't take the experience for granted—there's something wondrous about pressing a key and hearing sound come out! Try to forget whatever you've learned about notes, intervals, scales, chords, and all the rest. Approach the piano with utter naiveté. Remember that when improvising, there are no mistakes. There's no such thing as a wrong note or shaky tempo. Explore different ranges. Cluster notes together outrageously. Play in a free-form manner or establish a simple beat. Be happy with repeating a single note for a while—get your ears inside the sound. The key to improvisation is freedom, for both you and the music.

If you've tried improvising freely on the piano, and enjoy it, there may come a time when you have an urge to organize your keyboard meanderings. This doesn't necessarily mean composing pieces or writing down the music. But you may want to tighten the perimeter of your improvising—it's amazing how clear boundaries can create freedom.

One good technique is to establish a simple repeated part in your left hand, and improvise over it with the right hand. It's important to keep the left hand ultra-easy so as not to distract your imagination from improvising. Even a single note, played in a simple counting rhythm, gives your right hand a structure to play upon. Or, you can try an unchanging chord in the left hand, or a two-note interval. Keep it easy enough to play automatically. You might want to spend some time just playing the left hand until you're solidly on auto-pilot. When you add the right hand, keep that simple, too, at least at first.

Another way of anchoring your improvisation is to use a metronome as a rhythmic anchor. The left hand can function as a rhythmic anchor, but it takes more effort to keep up the beat yourself.

Grace Notes

Improvisation is such a lost classical art that it's difficult to conceive of the expertise once expressed by master musicians. Improvisation was extremely stylish—even required—among musicians in the Baroque era of the early eighteenth century. It was nothing for Bach to sit down at the harpsichord or organ and extemporize a five-part fugue—one of the most complex and mathematical forms of music ever invented.

The beauty of using a metronome is that it stays effortlessly unvarying, and leaves you both your hands to play on the keyboard. The downside is that annoying ticking, but think of it as an exotic percussion instrument. (If you can do that, you have the perfect imagination for improvising!)

Sight-Reading Tips

Sight-reading is the ability to play a piece of music from sheet music, without practice. It's not easy! Typically, sight-reading and memorization (which I cover in the next section) are complementary skills, and many people who can accomplish one easily have trouble with the other.

It may seem obvious, but when sight-reading you should keep your eyes on the music as much as possible, without glancing down at the keyboard. Most players look at the keyboard with quick glances when playing from music. Keeping your eyes glued to the music is a skill similar to touch-typing, and it takes practice. The value in this skill is emphasized when sight-reading because you aren't familiar with the piece, and you don't have any spare moments to look away from the sheet then find your place again. Furthermore, forcing yourself to play without glancing down trains you to navigate the keyboard intuitively, not by sight.

All piano music (except for ultra-modern avant-garde pieces) is written in a certain key, defined by the key signature. The first thing to do when presented with a piece to play at sight is look at the key signature (the flats or sharps placed at the beginning of each staff) and identify the key. Once you get the key in your mind, lock the sharps or flats into your mind before you start playing. Understanding what key you're in makes the reading go smoother. You might even play a scale or two in the key before starting, or a few chords, to get your hands positioned in that key.

Key Thought

The most important requirement of sight-reading, especially if anyone is listening or trying to sing along, is to keep the tempo going at all costs. Never mind if your drop notes or make mistakes—the beat is the important thing. The temptation is to slow down to get the notes right, but that doesn't teach you to become a better sight-reader. Forcing yourself to keep going at the tempo trains you to make good compromises, choosing what to leave out and what to include. It also encourages you to keep your eyes up on the sheet music, because there's simply no time to look down!

Perhaps the most important sight-reading skill involves recognizing note relationships. There are two ways to read and recognize a note on the printed page. One is to identify the actual note (C, B-flat, F-sharp, or whatever) and play it. The other is to see each note as related to the previous note. In other words, the B-flat or F-sharp may be right next to the A or E that preceded it. Why is this relationship important? Because with practice, you can train your hands to play correct notes without necessarily identifying the notes. It's a quicker process to see notes in relationship to each other than to identify each note individually. This technique isn't used all the time, even by the most expert sight-readers. Fluent sight-reading combines note identification with note relationships.

Try relating notes to each other by sight-reading just one hand of a piece. Don't look down at the keyboard, and don't attempt to name each note in your head as you play. Instead, your mental chatter should be along these lines: "This note is two steps above the one I just played, this one is one step up, now three steps down, now one step down ..." With practice, you may find your sight-reading becoming more instinctive.

Grace Notes

Sight-reading is an essential skill when playing for sing-alongs. Whether you're reading full piano scores or song charts, you need to keep the music going, at tempo, for the enjoyment of the group singing. Accordingly, you may think that the melody is the most important pretty part. Surprisingly, it is often the case that the left-hand part is more important than the right-hand melody, especially when the singers know the melody well. The left hand sets the beat and establishes the harmony, both of which the singers need to stay on track. If you need to drop out one hand for a few measures, make it the right hand and keep pumping out that left-hand accompaniment.

Committing It to Memory

Classical music is traditionally performed without sheet music. Memorizing a piece can cause anxiety, and playing in public (even just for a friend) without relying on the sheets can be traumatic. Following are some tips to help the process and ease your mind.

Clearly, weaning yourself from sheet music is a key to memorization. In a process just the opposite of the sight-reading exercise of keeping your eyes glued to the music, you must now begin forcing your gaze downward to the keyboard. When learning a piece from sheet music, a certain addiction can develop to the music, making it oddly difficult to break your eyes away. Your ability to play may seem tied to having the music in front of you, but chances are you have already memorized portions of the piece without knowing it. Try lowering your gaze until a memory lapse forces you to stop playing, then refresh your memory of what comes next and continue with your eyes on the keys. Gradually, phrase by phrase, develop your confidence in playing the piece without referring to the music.

Memory is not just mental. It may sound odd, but a pianist's hands have their own memory by which they can play a piece that has been repeatedly practiced. If you struggle to play a piece from memory, you may be trying too hard to think your way through it. It's a tricky hint, but try to shut your mind off and let your fingers take over. Try this: Close your eyes. This unusual tip might help set your muscle memory in motion, though you'll probably smack a few wrong notes with this particular technique. In the long run, memorization is both mental and physical. Ideally, a performance doesn't require a lot of thought or conscious recollection. Develop your trust in the muscle memory you have established by practicing.

Just as developing muscle memory is important, so is cultivating the purely mental aspect of memorization. For a real challenge, try playing the piece entirely in your head, visualizing the keyboard and your hands moving over it—and the feeling of the keys under your fingers. You can attempt this cerebral exercise anywhere—no need to sit at the piano. Close your eyes and visualize playing the keyboard, from the piece's beginning to the end. It's best to try this in a quiet room. Be as detailed as your power of visualization will allow, and try to "see" every note played with both hands. If you can approximate the playing experience in your mind, actually playing the piece will be a breeze.

If memorizing a piece is really important, there are ways you can strengthen your memory by testing it. The best and most difficult memory test involves starting a piece somewhere in the middle. All players have a tendency to memorize pieces whole, and have trouble when the memory flow is interrupted—so interrupt it deliberately. Pick natural break points first, such as the end of a repeated section or the beginning of a key change. Then, as an advanced test, try starting the piece up in the middle of a phrase—it's not easy! You might also want to try playing the final eight measures from memory (refer to the sheet music to count the measures, but don't look at the music while playing). Then take it back sixteen measures, and so on backwards through the piece.

Ornaments and Flourishes

Trills, glissandos (sometimes called glissandi), and arpeggios are ornamental playing techniques favored by composers throughout the history of music notation, since the seventeenth century.

Trills

A *trill* is the quick alternation of two notes—so quick that the two almost blend into a single note. Sometimes trills (especially in Baroque music) are measured, as if the alternating notes were written out in time. They rarely are written out in that fashion, and most trills are executed at a speed determined by the player.

Effective trill technique takes practice. Like anything else, slow practice is helpful. Most people prefer to trill with the second and third fingers (index and middle fingers) when the piece's fingering allows. But other players get better results using the thumb and another finger, and getting the wrist more involved in the trilling action. You can practice trills even when they don't occur in the pieces you're learning. Just pick any two consecutive white keys, two consecutive black keys, or a white key and the next black key on either side. Don't cheat by using two hands! Trill slowly at first, and build up speed.

Glissandos

Glissandos (or, to be linguistically correct, glissandi) are sweeps up or down the keyboard, usually on the white keys only. These flourishes are not usually notated note-for-note on sheet music, but indicated by a range—top and bottom note—and the word Glissando or the abbreviation "Gliss." If you've ever seen rock keyboardists accomplish their glissandos with their palms and the fleshy part of their fingertips, you might be tempted to try the same stunt on a piano. You'd regret it! Pianos have much stiffer actions than electronic keyboards, and that maneuver is likely to give you bruised or cut fingers.

Most piano glissandos are played with the fingernail. Going upward with the right hand, turn your hand over and use the nail of your third finger to sweep upward a short portion of the white keys. (Don't play black-key glissandos. The black keys are raised too high from the keyboard and are spaced too far apart from each other to be "gliss'd" without risking damage to your fingers.) Going down, try the thumbnail of your right hand, then the middle fingernail of your left hand. Don't do too many at first—it takes gradual practice to build up the toughness of the cuticle under your nail and, even more important, to learn to avoid the cuticle.

Arpeggios

Arpeggios are "broken" chords, rippled upward (or sometimes downward) from the bottom note to the top. (See Chapter 12, "Basics of Accompaniment," for an illustration of arpeggio notation.) This figuration is used deliberately by composers who want to create a harp-like effect, as in the famous Étude by Chopin, Opus 25, Number 1. It's useful to have good arpeggio skills if your hands are on the small side. It is traditional to quickly "roll" chords that can't be spanned by the hand, thereby getting in all the notes almost simultaneously. Arpeggios sometimes involve both hands, sometimes just one. Either way, you want to develop a facility for breaking chords in this fashion. Practice with any chord—first, with chords you can easily span with your hand. The notes you use don't matter (except perhaps to anyone listening while you practice). Then increase the size of the chord, until it's slightly wider than you can reach with your hand. Arpeggiate it slowly at first, then increase the speed until the notes are almost simultaneous.

> **Music Speak**
>
> **Trills** are quick alternations between two notes, played so fast that the notes sound like a blur. "Glissandos" also sound like a blur, but involve many notes as the player runs a finger up or down a portion of the keyboard. **Glissandos** usually occur on white keys only. **Arpeggios** are rippled chords, played quickly from bottom not to top, or top to bottom.

> ### The Least You Need to Know
>
> ➤ Becoming aware of your tension level helps keep your arms and wrists relaxed while playing.
>
> ➤ Keep your hand position firm when playing octaves and use the fourth finger (of either hand) when playing black-key octaves.
>
> ➤ Fast playing is really even playing. Concentrate on control more than blind speed.
>
> ➤ Use your wrist as a pivot when playing repeated chords. Rotate fingers when playing a string of repeated single notes.
>
> ➤ Force your eyes up when sight-reading; force them down when memorizing.

Next Steps

In This Chapter

➤ A few ways to take a break from practicing

➤ How to find a piano teacher

➤ Questions to ask before taking the first lesson

➤ Learning about MIDI and digital keyboards

➤ A quick survey of jazz and classical pianists

This book is, by necessity, just a first step toward playing the piano. If you've explored a number of chapters, you've probably learned how to read music and play simple (and a few not-so-simple) pieces. This chapter points toward the future, and toward a few nontechnical aspects of having keyboards in your life. This chapter is where I discuss tips for staying motivated, finding a teacher, experimenting with digital keyboards, and listening to piano music.

Keeping It Interesting

There's no denying it—practicing can wear a little thin over the long haul. Much as you may love the piano, and be excited about playing, there are two facts that rub against each other:

➤ Developing skill on the piano requires regular practice.

➤ Regular practice sometimes gets boring.

What can you do? Well, here are some suggestions:

➤ **Take a break.** Okay, this is a no-brainer, I admit it. When you're sick of practicing, stop practicing. What you may not know—and this is going to sound loony—is that you can actually get better by not practicing. Paradoxical as such a statement seems, there is truth to it. Take five, or quit for the day, or rest your fingers for a week, or even lay off for a month from time to time.

➤ **Try different kinds of music.** If you're getting bored with practicing classical pieces, get a collection of pop tunes—maybe music from your teen years—and try something completely different. By the same token, if you feel saturated from playing too much popular music, have a crack at some classical stuff, which requires a completely different kind of concentration and skill. (See Chapter 20, "Next Steps," for specific suggestions.)

➤ **Stop playing and listen.** Adopting the piano into your life is a two-way street. There's playing, and there's listening. Both thrive on attention and dedication. When you get bored with practicing, you tend to lose appreciation for the piano generally. Listening to favorite piano music—or exploring new recordings—is an ideal way to renew your appreciation. And when it's possible, there is absolutely nothing better than going to a piano concert for getting inspired again.

➤ **Switch instruments.** Switching from keyboard to trombone is good. (Just kidding.) The point I'm making is that if the piano has you under its thumb, and if you have the means, try getting a home keyboard to play around with. The various buttons and electronic features of home keyboards are a lot of fun to experiment with. In the process, you would certainly gain a fresh appreciation for the wonderful aspects of the piano you might have been taking for granted.

➤ **Find a music partner.** The best solution of all to tired practicing is to find a music partner to share this venture with. The person needn't be another keyboard player—in fact, another pianist or keyboardist would limit the possibilities for collaboration. If you know someone who sings, or plays another instrument like flute or violin, you can make music together. Playing with another person, relying on each other to keep the musical flow going, choosing and exploring new music together—these are fulfilling activities that keep the routine from ever going stale.

Key Thought

When you work repeatedly on something with your conscious mind, you can hit roadblocks and never seem to get past a certain point. If you put the project away for a time, it's as if the unconscious mind continues working on it. When you return to your practice, the playing is sometimes mysteriously easier. I have experienced this phenomenon so many times that I now rely on it.

Never forget that you're in this for fun. You're not a kid anymore, and nobody is making you practice. So do whatever you need to keep music fresh and hassle-free.

Finding a Teacher

Hard though it may be to fathom (especially for me), this book may not provide enough instruction for a lifetime of learning. Even if you continue getting value from these chapters for the next, say, seventy-five years, you may want to have a live teacher to stay motivated. Furthermore, it's good to ask questions of someone who can actually answer. (You can try asking questions of this book, but I can't guarantee a response.)

The question is, how do you find a teacher? Here are a few ways to locate one:

➤ Call up a local school and say you want a piano teacher, and you want one now! Well, no need to be obstreperous. Just politely ask if any music teachers on the school faculty give private piano lessons. If there is a music school nearby, all the better.

➤ Check the classifieds of your local paper.

➤ Look on bulletin boards around town—many local teachers use that free means of advertising.

➤ If all else fails, try the Yellow Pages.

For a beginner, there is almost no such thing as a bad teacher, as long as you both speak the same language and the person doesn't have any pathologies you find disagreeable. (Chewing on the curtains during the lesson, for example, would be disturbing.) Nonetheless, you should ask a few questions over the phone before committing to the first lesson:

➤ **How long are the lessons?** Some teachers offer two lengths: thirty and sixty minutes. Others play around with weird times like forty-five or fifty minutes. Some teachers show more flexibility than others. Beginning students do best with half-hour lessons—longer isn't necessary. Don't let a teacher force you into an hour if you don't feel you're ready for such intense lessons.

➤ **Who does the driving?** Most teachers work out of a studio, either in their home or a separate location. If driving isn't a problem for you, going to a studio is preferable all the way around: the teacher probably has a good piano, lots of sheet music, and you don't have to make sure the house is clean every week. (That would be a big consideration for me.) However, if your schedule or transportation resources make it inconvenient to travel to a lesson, find a local teacher who makes house calls. Many piano teachers still do this, though you might have to pay a bit more for the lesson.

➤ **What kind of music?** Needless to say, the teacher should teach the sort of music you wish to play. Now, if you're a beginner, and simply want help learning your way around the keyboard, then just about any teacher can help you. But even at the beginning a good teacher can focus on tips and tricks that apply to the type of music you eventually want to play. So make sure, at the beginning, that you and your teacher are on the same page.

➤ **How many students, and what ages?** Ask the prospective teacher point-blank how many private students he or she currently is teaching. Make sure they're talking about *private*, one-on-one students, not classroom students. Chances are that a bustling practice indicates a good teacher.

Musical Mouthful

"I will gladly give lessons as a favor, particularly where I see that my student has talent, inclination, and anxiety to learn."
—Wolfgang Amadeus Mozart (1778)

Key Thought

Once you've made an appointment for a lesson, don't think that you're committed to this teacher for life. Take a first lesson, and see how the two of you get along. The lessons should be fun, as well as informative. Above all, if you feel self-conscious or uncomfortable learning and playing with this person, find someone else. You should feel completely comfortable and trusting during your lessons.

Once you've found a teacher, remember that you and he (or she) are not married. If the lessons aren't working for you, no matter what the reason, bring them to a gentle close and find somebody else.

MIDI and Home Music Studios

Digital music equipment, as part of the computer revolution, brings an astonishing degree of musical power and capability right into the home. For some people it's nothing more than a fun hobby; for others, such equipment brings out musical ability that was hidden for years; and for some people, advanced keyboards and related equipment actually opens up new career doors. This chapter has modest ambitions—it gives you a rundown on what is available, what it does, and why people are buying it.

Any discussion of keyboards and home studios must start with the strange musical term, *MIDI*. MIDI (pronounced MIH-dee) is an acronym for Musical Instrument Digital Interface, but don't worry—that's as technical as I'm going to get in this chapter. Actually, you may be somewhat familiar with MIDI, if you've looked at the back of your keyboard or in the owner's manual. The back panel of almost every home keyboard has jacks labeled MIDI, though you may have to squint hard to read the label. If the MIDI jacks are there, the owner's manual certainly talks about how to use them.

Music Speak

MIDI is an acronym for Musical Instrument Digital Interface—a fancy way of saying that MIDI connects keyboards to other keyboards, and keyboards to computers. There are other types of devices using MIDI as well, including drum machines, tone modules, and sequencers.

Basically, MIDI lets you hook musical devices to each other for various purposes that I describe in this chapter. The only things you need, in order to use MIDI, are a MIDI cable and a second MIDI device. (Your keyboard is a MIDI device if it has MIDI jacks on the back panel. Keep reading to discover other types of MIDI devices.) There's no limit on the degree to which you can expand a MIDI setup, except perhaps budgetary and space limits.

But what *is* a MIDI setup? In the most general terms, a MIDI setup is two or more connected MIDI devices. The two devices could be two keyboards, a keyboard and a computer, a keyboard and a recording device, a keyboard and a drum machine, or any number of other possibilities.

There are two basic reasons for having a MIDI studio:

Grace Notes

Many television shows use scores completely created in MIDI studios. The well-known score of *Seinfeld*, combining musical themes with pops and bursts of sound, is one current example.

➤ **Enjoying lots of different sounds.** If you own a home keyboard or digital piano, you can make it sound like a number of different instruments just by pressing buttons. This is definitely fun, and prompts the more-is-better syndrome to kick in. If one keyboard with a hundred instrument sounds is good, wouldn't the addition of a second keyboard, with one hundred fresh sounds be better? This reasoning is especially compelling if you grow tired of your keyboard's sounds.

Furthermore, some keyboards specialize in one type of sound, much as digital pianos have excellent acoustic piano sounds, but sometimes fall short when it comes to emulating other instruments. If you have been playing a digital piano for a while, you may begin to crave the tones of a digital synthesizer; if you've been learning on a home keyboard with a cheesy piano sound, you may begin eyeing digital pianos.

➤ **Recording original compositions.** Recording is the second big reason for accumulating space-eating, budget-consuming MIDI gear. For many people, recording is the name of the game with MIDI, thanks to devices that keep track of every keystroke you play, then let you correct mistakes and alter your own performance in many ways. MIDI recorders (which I describe in more detail later in this chapter), have the added enticing benefit of letting you record in simultaneous tracks, just like a professional sound studio. With all the sounds at your disposal thanks to your keyboard(s), and with the multitrack capability of MIDI recorders, home MIDI studios amount to virtual orchestras. And having a virtual orchestra in your home, let me tell you, is a blast. MIDI recording is very appealing to composers, both amateur and professional.

MIDI is so much fun, many pianists have small hobby studios in their homes for musical recreation apart from the challenging work of serious piano practice.

Grace Notes

MIDI is a digital language—basically a specialized kind of computer language. As such, the stuff transmitted through MIDI cables and MIDI jacks is called *MIDI data* or *MIDI information*.

The Many Types of MIDI Keyboards

I want to make clear right from the beginning that MIDI is not some exotic feature that you must search for when shopping for keyboards. There is almost no such thing as a modern keyboard made today that doesn't have MIDI jacks built in. The presence of MIDI jacks is all you need to see to determine that a keyboard is a MIDI keyboard. Only the very least expensive, ill-equipped home keyboards lack MIDI jacks. Other home keyboards, sporting the crucial MIDI jacks, may differ widely in the features they offer, but they all share one essential ability: They can send and receive MIDI information.

Here are the basic types of MIDI keyboards.

➤ **Home keyboards.** These small keyboards are cheap, light, and easier to operate than pro keyboards. Home keyboards always have built-in speakers; in fact, that's the distinguishing feature that *makes* them home keyboards. Many of them contain built-in auto-accompaniment features that can sound quite good or quite cheesy. These small instruments represent a good introduction to digital music-making, as they bring an effective range of features without forcing you to pay for perks you might never use.

➤ **Professional synthesizers.** A synthesizer is a kind of keyboard that can create (synthesize) its own sounds. Synthesizers come with a selection of built-in sounds (often called *factory sounds* or *presets*), just as home keyboards do, but you are not limited to the presets. Synthesizers let you create new sounds, or modify the factory sounds, or even buy new banks of instrument sounds from the manufacturer or a third-party company. The result of this flexibility is that synthesizers have a virtually unlimited sound palette if you go to the trouble and/or expense of using its capabilities.

Grace Notes

It's easy to confuse samplers with MIDI recorders, but they are not the same. Samplers digitally record real sounds like a flute or a drum. MIDI recorders record keystrokes played on MIDI keyboards. MIDI recorders do not record real sounds at all. I describe MIDI recorders in more detail a bit farther ahead in this chapter.

➤ **Samplers.** Samplers are unique. The one thing samplers do that no other MIDI instrument does is record sounds. (Recording with a sampler is called *sampling.*) With a sampler, you can record your dog barking, then play the bark on the keyboard. You can record the wind, and play the *whoosh.* Such sampling escapades may not be the most musical use to which technology can be put, but are fun nonetheless. In professional studios, samplers are used to record real instrument notes, which then are played on the keyboard. Talk about an unlimited sound palette! With sampling, the entire real world of sound is at your disposal. All you need is a microphone, which plugs directly in to the sampler, and you're in the sampling business for fun and profit. (Well, probably not for profit.) Samplers tend to be more expensive than synthesizers, thanks to their specialized circuitry, plus the built-in hard drives and floppy drives needed to store samples.

Key Thought

When it comes to synthesizers, there is some blurring of the line between home keyboards and professional models. For the sake of clarification I am grouping all synthesizers (which are sometimes called *synths,* by the way) as professional keyboards, because the ability to create new sounds is usually a matter of professional interest. However, the truth is that making a new sound is fun no matter what your level of experience, and some inexpensive home keyboards let you "tweak" the factory sounds to some extent. Professional synths give you helpful features like memory slots for storing new sound creations, and even computer-style disk drives for longer-term storage.

MIDI Recorders

Earlier in this chapter I have made reference to MIDI recorders. I didn't want to muddy the waters before, but I'll tell you now: MIDI recorders are called *sequencers.* Sequencers get such a nerdy name because they perform the geeky task of recording *sequences* of keystrokes. If you hook up a sequencer to a MIDI keyboard, then play something on the keyboard with the sequencer in Record mode, the sequencer keeps track of every key you play, when you play it, and how hard you play it. After you've finished the recording, you can play back the sequence, hearing your performance reproduced exactly, and even make corrections to the notes.

There are three basic types of sequencers:

➤ **Sequencers built into keyboards.** Some home keyboards have simple sequencers, and professional keyboard workstations have fancier, more advanced sequencers.

➤ **Stand-alone sequencers.** These devices are box-like MIDI components, sometimes called hardware *sequencers,* that sit next to your keyboard, or even on top of it (but not covering the keys), and plug into the keyboard's MIDI jacks. They are usually more powerful than sequencers built into home keyboards, but not as powerful as software sequencers described in the next paragraph.

➤ **Software sequencers.** Software sequencers are computer programs that run on personal computers attached to a keyboard's MIDI jacks. When a computer is part of a MIDI setup, its main function is usually to run the software sequencer. (Most computers don't have built-in MIDI jacks the way keyboards do, so you must buy a *MIDI interface* that brings the computer up to speed with the MIDI realm, and gives it MIDI jacks.) Software sequencers are, by far, the most powerful type of sequencer, and used by MIDI enthusiasts who are serious about composing and recording with keyboards.

Music Speak

A **sequencer** digitally records sequences of MIDI information for playback and editing. There are built-in, stand-alone, and software sequencers available.

What do I mean when I refer to a sequencer as being "powerful"? A sequencer's power depends on two sets of features:

1. How many tracks it lets you record

2. How many ways it lets you edit your recordings

It is the multitrack capability that makes MIDI a virtual orchestra (or jazz ensemble, or rock band). The more tracks you have to work with, the better—assuming you have enough instrument sounds in your keyboard(s) to fill up all those tracks. Sequencers built into home keyboards sometimes only have one or two tracks, while the sequencers built into professional keyboard workstations have eight or sixteen tracks. (As with professional multitrack tape decks found in live recording studios, tracks tend to be added in increments of eight, for some reason.) By contrast, software sequencers offer at least sixty-four tracks in most cases, and sometimes hundreds.

Grace Notes

Many musicians already use their home computers to make their own digital recordings. With recordable CDs now available, you can make and distribute your own albums from your own home studio all by using your computer!

When it comes to editing music, sequencers are like word processors for music. After playing into a sequencer you can change individual notes; assign an entire track to a different instrument sound; transpose the performance to a different key, and alter the tempo without altering the pitch of the notes. (If you speed up a tape recording, everything gets high-pitched and comically squealy.) Software sequencers have very advanced editing features, plus the big computer screen for displaying the recording's MIDI data in various ways.

Tone Modules

One peculiar aspect of MIDI is that you can hook two keyboards together, and use each keyboard to play the other keyboard's sounds. In other words, you can access the sounds inside of a keyboard through the MIDI cable connecting the two instruments. Since that is the case, you may be asking, why have the second set of keys? Why not just put the second keyboard's sounds in a box, played by the first keyboard? It's a good question, asked by instrument designers several years ago, and that's exactly the solution they chose.

Boxes filled with preset sounds, lacking keyboards, are called *tone modules*. They are modules (hardware boxes) with tones (instrument sounds) inside them, sporting MIDI jacks on the back panel.

Many MIDI setups contain just one keyboard attached to multiple tone modules. Tone modules take less space than a keyboard, although they usually cost about the same as the keyboard model of the same instrument.

Drum Machines

One specialized MIDI device worthy of mention is the time-honored *drum machine*. The drum machine isn't honored by too much time, come to think of it, but there were drum machines being used in hotel lounge gigs as early as the late 1970s, predating the MIDI revolution. Drum machines do what you would expect; they make drum sounds. Featuring little pads on their top surface, you can play them with your fingers. Drum machines are traditionally used as nifty accompanists that have infallible rhythm, are never late to the gig, weigh less than a single real drum, and don't get upset when you ask them to play softly.

The heart of the drum machine is its built-in sequencer that allows you to prerecord drum patterns in various tempos and styles. Drum machines fulfill the same basic function as auto-accompaniment features on home keyboards, but they generally have better drum sounds. (These days, almost all drum machines use digitally sampled—recorded—drums.)

A related MIDI component to the drum machine is the *percussion module*. Percussion modules are the tone module versions of drum machines, just as tone modules are alternate versions of keyboards. Percussion modules lack the built-in sequencer, and are meant to be used with a hardware or (ideally) software sequencer. Percussion modules are connected with MIDI cables to the keyboard, which accesses its sounds. Accordingly, the pads that drum machines have are missing from percussion modules.

Music Speak

Tone modules are like keyboards without the keyboard. What's left? The brain of the keyboard, including all the sounds the keyboard can make. Tone modules are used in MIDI studios with one master keyboard that controls various tone modules and drum machines.

Music Speak

Drum machines provide drum sounds for people using the MIDI capabilities of digital keyboards. You can hook up a drum machine to a keyboard, and automatically have access to many realistic drum and percussion sounds.

Grace Notes

Most MIDI professional-level instrument manufacturers create tone module versions of their keyboards, so you have a choice. In most cases all the features are the same in the keyboard and module, except, of course, that the module doesn't have a set of keys, and can be played only with another keyboard. You can get tone module versions of both synthesizers and samplers, but usually not of home keyboards.

Hooking It All Up

Now that you've bought two keyboards, three tone modules, a sampler, a drum machine, a computer, and sequencing software—well, if you've bought all that, you can't even afford MIDI cables to connect it together.

It's beyond the scope of this book to provide a complete tutorial on connecting all the many types of MIDI studio. But I don't want you to put down this chapter before getting a basic understanding of what the MIDI jacks are for and how to use them. Armed with that understanding and fortified by the literary excellence of the owner's manual that no doubt complements whatever new MIDI gadget you buy, you should be able to hook up a component or two without problems.

Keeping this book in your hand, walk around to the back of your keyboard to find the MIDI jacks. Are you there? Good. Look for the black, circular jacks with six holes in each jack. There should be at least two (possibly three) jacks, labeled MIDI. Once you see them, look more closely at the labeling, and notice that one jack is MIDI IN, and the other is MIDI OUT. Here's what they mean:

➤ MIDI IN jacks are for *receiving* MIDI data.

➤ MIDI OUT jacks are for *transmitting* MIDI data.

Use the MIDI OUT jack when you want to send MIDI data from the keyboard to another device, such as a tone module or sequencer. Just plug one end of a MIDI cable into the MIDI OUT jack of the keyboard, and plug the other end into the MIDI IN jack of the second device. Then, when you play the keyboard, all your keystrokes are automatically sent through the MIDI OUT jack.

> **Grace Notes**
>
> Early synthesized drums were the heart-and-soul of '70s-era disco music. Without the ability to reproduce mechanically a steady beat, this music wouldn't have had its characteristic thump-thump-thump accompaniment.

Listen to the Music

When you begin to play the piano, it opens a whole new sense of appreciation for piano music—its beauties and difficulties. Perhaps you've been listening to piano music for years, and need no help from me sorting through the piano repertoire. Or, maybe you like jazz but don't know much about classical, or you appreciate New Age piano albums but would like to broaden your music collection.

As a budding pianist, it's important to not only listen to yourself play, but to listen to others. Hearing how other pianists approach a work can be quite inspirational and give you new ideas of how to improve your playing. Plus, listening to different pianists can give you a taste of a variety of different styles, so you can better focus your study in areas where you have the greatest interest.

Jazz Pianists

Jazz piano is a subject worthy of several books by itself. For now, I just want to point you to a few jazz piano artists from different points along the jazz spectrum who represent a broad range of listening experience.

➤ **Bill Evans.** The quiet, thoughtful, introspective jazz stylings of Bill Evans are often considered the birth of modern jazz piano. A great innovator, even with his modest playing style, Evans developed the jazz harmonies and chords all jazz players now take for granted. Evans was a great melodist whose improvisations never became abstract or confusing. When playing a jazz standard, he takes you on a melodic journey at the end of which you may not remember how you got there, but you sure enjoyed the ride. Bill Evans recordings make great background music, because they are so unassuming and undemanding. But don't forget to listen carefully from time to time, and appreciate his subtle harmonies and reverant melodic sense.

➤ **Oscar Peterson.** Sheer virtuosity isn't restricted to the classical field, and Oscar Peterson proves it. One of the great technicians of jazz piano, Peterson will stun you with his speed and power, while reaching your soul with a masterful grasp of the blues and traditional jazz. Not much of a composer, Oscar Peterson has built a legendary career playing both solo and in small jazz ensembles. His style and touch are so distinctive that when you've heard him once, you'll probably recognize his playing in the future. He represents a perfect marriage of virtuosity and musicianship.

➤ **Chick Corea.** Chick is what musicians call a "monster." Bringing a stupendous musicianship to the service of both acoustic and electronic jazz, Chick Corea is a legend in his own time who easily crosses from one genre to another. He has even composed several classical works—before Paul McCartney and Billy Joel made it vogue to do so. To hear him as a keyboardist you can get his Return to Forever albums from the 1970s, or, more recently, the Chick Corea Electric Band CDs. As a pianist, check out the Chick Corea Acoustic Band albums.

➤ **Keith Jarrett.** Master of free-form, pure piano *improvisation*, Keith Jarrett made a big splash in the 1970s with voluminous live recordings of his spontaneous playing. The so-called Koeln Album, recorded live in the city of the same name, created the same sort of stir in jazz circles that the Beatles' *White Album* did in the pop world. Jarrett is known for his idiosyncratic performance style, replete with wild swayings on the bench and unself-conscious singing along to his own music. These quirks can be heard on many of his recordings.

Naturally, this list barely scratches the surface. One way to acquaint yourself with jazz pianists is to listen to a jazz radio station, if one broadcasts in your area. If you have Internet access, try one of the many jazz-programmed netcasts.

Classical Pianists

Since the invention of the gramophone (thanks, Thomas), it has been easy to hear all the great pianists of the current era. What a shame we'll never know what Chopin and Liszt sounded like as pianists! This section points out a few of the legendary modern pianists, and their musical specialities.

➤ **Rubinstein.** Artur Rubinstein was one of the great Romantic pianists of the mid-twentieth century. Well, for most of the century, actually, considering what a long life he lived. Not considered one of the knuckle-crunching virtuosos, Rubinstein specialized in bringing a clear and sweet presentation of the Romantic repertoire. He was one of the great Chopin interpreters of all time. Rubinstein's playing was never encumbered by excess emotion or drippy sentimentality, but was tasteful, to the point, and clear.

➤ **Horowitz.** Vladimir Horowitz is the recording era's preeminent piano virtuoso—so far. He brought unheard-of power and an almost unbelievable technique to bear, and would routinely shatter modern piano strings as if they were flimsy nineteenth-century models. Horowitz loved to play Liszt, Scriabin, Rachmaninoff, and other Romantic composers of the big, flashy romantic repertoire. He also performed Chopin, but less convincingly. Surprisingly, his concerts usually featured the small, late Baroque sonatas of Scarlatti, and sometimes Mozart pieces. Although Horowitz retired early in his career (only to emerge again later), his recorded output is substantial. Get anything you can find, especially the incredible live performances.

➤ **Ashkenazy.** Another Vladimir, Ashkenazy is now conducting orchestras more than he is playing piano in concert, but his early career was primarily as a pianist. For my money, Ashkenazy's blend of virtuosity and elegance is unbeatable. He has taken a stab at recording across all the music periods, but stick to his playing of Romantic pieces like Chopin and Rachmaninoff.

➤ **Gould.** Glenn Gould is one of the strangest, most idiosyncratic, and genius-laden figures in the annals of classical pianism. His uniquely precise, almost mathematical playing style made him a natural for the music of Bach, and that's primarily what he is known for, though he recorded other composers as well. Stay away from his rare Romantic releases, and stick to Bach with Gould. When I first heard Gould's Bach playing as a teenager, I became permanently spoiled, and have never been satisfied with any other pianist's interpretations since. A compulsive musical personality who was most comfortable in the recording studio, Gould's Bach recordings are fastidious, technically brilliant, marvels of clarity, and thrilling in their boldness. He somehow brings a completely modern quality to the music, without sacrificing the antique ornateness of Baroque composition.

Grace Notes

Stories of Glenn Gould's eccentricities abound. Once he sued the Steinway piano company for a large amount when one of its representatives shook his hand too vigorously. He conducted his own chamber orchestra but refused to allow an audience to attend its performances. He always had a glass of distilled water within his reach while playing, and placed a rug under his special, 14-inch-high chair. In 1964, he abruptly quit public performing because he felt the only "perfect" performance could be caught on record. In his recordings, he spliced together several performances in order to achieve this perfection.

➤ **Ohlsson.** Garrick Ohlsson emerged on the scene in the early 1970s after winning the prestigious International Chopin Competition in Warsaw. Not since Van Cliburn won the Tchaikowski Competition in the 1950s has a piano prize-winner received such acclaim. Ohlsson didn't attain the rock-star status of Cliburn, but he has continued with a solid career. His playing is breathtaking, featuring a prodigious technical command of the keyboard and an extroverted, devil-may-care style that has left me on the edge of my seat more than once. His personal repertoire is wide-ranging, covering centuries of piano composition. Still known for his Chopin interpretations, he recently embarked on a two-year project to record and perform every one of Chopin's pieces.

As with the jazz pianists earlier in this chapter, the list above is a tiny tip of the iceberg. Listen to classical radio and netcasts to become familiar with other names in the pantheon of classical piano artistry.

The Least You Need to Know

➤ Practice makes perfect, but taking a break can keep it interesting. And sometimes the rest improves your playing.

➤ Make sure you're on the same page with a prospective teacher before starting lessons.

➤ MIDI is the digital interface that connects keyboards to each other and to computers. It's a heck of a lot of fun.

➤ Broaden your horizons by taking time to listen to jazz and classical piano music.

Part 5

Bringing It Home: Buying an Instrument

This final part is a buyer's guide for pianos and all kinds of electronic instruments. I do not provide a brand-name tour of available instruments, a topic deserving of a separate book. However, I do bring to light all the general considerations you should keep in mind when shopping for a new or used piano, and a new or used keyboard.

Chapter 21 addresses issues in buying a new or used piano, while Chapter 23 does the same for electronic keyboards. In between, Chapter 22 covers everything you need to know about maintaining a piano in your home, including what kind of climate pianos thrive in, where to avoid placing them in your home, and how to find a tuner.

Buying a Piano

In This Chapter

➤ The reasons for buying a piano instead of an electronic keyboard

➤ Whether to shop for an upright or grand piano

➤ How to shop for a used piano, and whether to in the first place

➤ How to maintain a piano in your home

There was a time—not too long ago—when almost every American home had a piano in the parlour. Maybe no one could play it very well, but still it was a fixture in American life. Young people—especially young ladies—would be expected to entertain guests by playing the popular songs of the day, and families would gather round the piano to sing their old favorites.

The day may come when you consider the ultimate keyboard purchase: a piano. This chapter walks you through the general steps of buying a piano, from the "why" to the "how" of it, and from the "which" to the "how much."

Why Buy a Piano?

There are some obvious disadvantages to buying and owning a piano. Pianos are big, heavy, and difficult to move. Pianos are far more expensive than electronic keyboards. To top it off, a piano is a finicky resident in your home, requiring tunings and other maintenance. On the surface, it seems that electronic keyboards and digital pianos are such a convenient alternative that there would be no reason to buy a piano. Yet, pianos have not become the dinosaurs of the musical instrument kingdom. In fact, their popularity has grown during the time that digital keyboards have also become popular. This section describes a few of the reasons why pianos are still the keyboard of choice for many people.

The Real Piano Sound

The most compelling reason for buying a piano belongs to your ears. Technology has come a long way in imitating the sound of acoustic instruments through the use of digital sampling, and digital pianos are startlingly similar to real pianos when you first hear them. (Other types of electronic keyboards don't even come close enough for comparisons.) After playing a digital piano for a while, though, it becomes apparent to pianists that a lot is missing from the sound and feel of a piano. There are a couple of reasons why pianos have a superior sound to their digital cousins:

Musical Mouthful

"Music with dinner is an insult both to the cook and the violinist."

—G. K. Chesterton

➤ **Real strings and dampers.** The difference between real vibrating strings and samples stored on memory chips is more than just a difference in materials and space. The sound waves bouncing around inside a piano create an acoustically complex sound that cannot, at least at this stage of the technology game, be replicated with circuitry.

The dampers—the felt pads that rest on the strings, and are lifted by the sustain pedal—play a part in the piano's unique sound. When you press the sustain pedal of a piano, all the strings are free to vibrate in response to those rampant soundwaves inside the instrument, creating a sonority that you may not be able to identify while playing, but certainly notice when it's missing. That extra sonority is definitely missing in digital instruments.

➤ **The inner machinery.** The piano mechanism that starts with the keys and ends with the hammers hitting strings is called the piano's action.

Grace Notes

Pedaling on a piano can be a subtle *skill* involving half-pedals and other tricks that control how the strings vibrate. Digital pedaling, by contrast, is a simple on/off experience that applies *only* to whatever notes are being played. I should also mention the piano's soft pedal (see Chapter 15, "Pedals: Where's the Clutch?") which exerts control over the instrument's tone and sonority. Digital pianos often include soft pedals, but they make a simple change to the instrument's volume, not the tonal characteristics.

You, as the player, control this complex mechanism through its interface, which is the keyboard. It may seem surprising, but a good player actually can wield a fair degree of control over a piano's tone depending on how the keyboard is played.

Advanced piano study focuses to a large degree on coaxing the best tone out of the piano by refining the player's "touch" on the keyboard. All of these subtleties of touch are lost on digital keyboards, whose keys trigger on/off switches attached to tone-generating circuitry. Digital keyboards can register changes in volume according to the force with which you press the key, but that's the limit of their responsiveness.

The Mechanical Piano Action

Every piano keyboard has an individual feel to it, reflecting the construction and sheer weight of all the action's parts. When you press a key, you set in quick motion a whole series of mechanical events. Some pianos have a light feel while other are heavy; some actions feel fluid and fast, while others are stiff and demand slower, more deliberate playing.

Digital pianos try to emulate the weight and feel of piano actions, and some of them even replace the plastic keys normally used by electronic keyboards with wood keys. But there is no replacing the complex feel of a real piano action, with its solid "thunk" when the hammer hits the strings, and the tiny recoil of the hammer that you can feel in the key.

These all may sound like tiny details, but they add up to an entirely different experience when playing a piece on a real piano, compared to a digital.

Appearance

There's no denying that pianos are beautiful. Even a lover of technology and gadgets would have to admit that a gleaming ebony grand piano makes a more striking impression in a room than a dial-encrusted keyboard housed in plastic. The choice of a piano instead of a keyboard can legitimately be made strictly on its furniture value, aside from all musical considerations. Upright pianos may not have the dramatic appearance of grands, but are still dignified additions to a room.

Educational Value

If you are buying a keyboard instrument primarily for the kids in your household, the piano's tradition may appeal to you for their sake. Pianos have an entirely different educational value than keyboards—and both are worth considering for their respective merits. If you're buying an instrument for your kids, you really must choose between tradition and modernism.

MIDI Pianos

With all this talk about choosing between a digital piano and an acoustic piano, I'd be remiss if I didn't mention a compromise: MIDI pianos. Yes, MIDI pianos actually exist, though they may seem like a contradiction. MIDI pianos are real pianos, with strings, dampers, and everything, but with MIDI functionality built in. It's quite a feat, but some ingenious piano manufacturers have figured out how to turn an acoustic piano into a digital instrument, complete with a disk drive.

A lot of extra hardware is built into the piano, including a system of sensors near the keyboard that register every time a key is played, and turn the keystrokes into MIDI data, just like an electronic keyboard. That data can be sent to a computer or other MIDI device through a MIDI cable, again just like a digital keyboard. MIDI pianos also receive MIDI data, and play back MIDI sequences with a real piano sound—which is bound to be better than any sampled piano.

But MIDI pianos present a couple of problems. First of all, they are very expensive. Enough said on that topic. Second, they are finicky, sometimes needing a lot of regulation and adjustment of the electronic components built into the instrument, as well as the natural piano parts like hammers and dampers. Making it all work together

Key Thought

The action is like a Rube Goldberg device: a long succession of levers and springs that culminates in a felt-tipped little hammer shooting forward (or upward, in the case of grand pianos) and smacking the strings of a note (see Chapter 2, "Hammers and Strings" for a description of the piano's inner workings).

Grace Notes

One of the most popular piano-variants of the turn-of-the-century was the player piano. Using a punched paper roll, it could reproduce performances at home. There was something magical about watching the keys move up and down by themselves. On more sophisticated instruments, the original pianist's touch could be accurately rendered, as if a ghost were playing the instrument! Today, there are digital player pianos which play automatically off prerecorded discs.

227

is quite a feat, and though the manufacturers have ironed out the main problems, you still can count on hiring a trained technician more than you'd have to for a simple non-MIDI piano.

Key Thought

Although pianos and electronic keyboards each have individual learning challenges, it is much easier for a pianist to play a keyboard than for a keyboardist to play the piano. The difference is due primarily to the heavier action of a piano, which is hard to cope with if you have only played the light actions of keyboards. Of course, piano players are clueless about the auto-accompaniment features of a keyboard, not to mention sequencing and other MIDI learning curves discussed in MIDI and Home Music Studios.

The Big Questions

If the day comes that you decide to buy a piano, you are immediately faced with two whopping-big questions: Should you buy an upright or a grand? Ideally, you can resolve these questions before beginning the shopping experience, as it's best to know what you're looking for before placing yourself under the influence of persuasive salespeople. Practically speaking, though, you may find your priorities changing as you see what's available. Even so, following are the main questions to keep in mind at the outset.

Musical Mouthful

"There is no such thing as new music; there are only new musicians."
—Paul Dukas

Upright or Grand?

Pianos come in two basic design types, and there are big differences in cost, quality and practicality between them. Here are the considerations upon which your decision should be based:

Space

They're not called *grand* pianos for nothing. Grand pianos are big! If you live in a small apartment, squeezing in a grand may be out of the question right from the start. If you have a larger living space, but are targeting a medium-sized room for the piano, you may or may not want the instrument dominating your decor. Fortunately, grand pianos come in many sizes. The term "baby grand" refers generically to small grands, but is not defined by a particular size range.

The following table gives you examples of typical grand piano sizes in four size ranges. The largest range, concert grand, is listed for information only—concert grands are usually not appropriate for home use (unless you want the whole neighborhood to hear you practice).

Grand Piano Sizes

Range	Piano size
Baby grand	4' 9"–5' 5"
Mid-size grand	5' 5"–6' 2"
Large grand	6' 2"–7' 5"
Concert grand	7' 5"–9' 0"

This table should be taken as a very general reference. Some piano brands may advertise sizes larger than 5' 5", and call them "baby grands."

All grand pianos are measured from the front edge of the keyboard (the part of the piano closest to your lap when you're sitting at the keyboard) to the very end of the instrument, at the point farthest away from you. The width is another measurement to keep in mind: most grand pianos are no wider than sixty inches (five feet) at their widest point, which is the keyboard plus the wood surrounding it. Keeping all these facts in mind, you can do a rough measurement in your room to see how large a piano you can fit. (My experience is that grand pianos tend to look bigger when delivered than you think they will when measuring.)

Upright pianos vary quite a bit in height, and very little in width or depth. Like grand pianos, uprights are about sixty inches wide. The height can range from about forty inches from floor to top, to about fifty-two inches. Uprights are usually pushed up against a wall, with the keyboard facing out, making them very space-efficient. Upright pianos are really grand pianos stood on end, with the strings running up and down instead of parallel to the floor. Accordingly, increasing the height of an upright piano affects the sound by providing longer strings, but doesn't have much effect on whether you can fit it into your room (unless your home has surprisingly low ceilings).

Sound Quality

Sure, grand pianos are beautiful pieces of furniture, and sure, they represent an excellently indulgent way to spend a large chunk of money. But is there a musical reason to choose a grand over an upright? Yes, there certainly is. For my money, the musical persuasiveness of grand pianos is their strongest selling point.

There are two essential features of a grand piano, compared to an upright. One is that the strings are longer. The other main difference is that grands have lids that lift up, exposing the full length of the strings to the room. Both these crucial differences have a dynamic result: a much louder instrument.

Of course, the loudness of grand pianos may be a reason *not* to get one, if you live with close neighbors or in a small house or apartment. But there are tonal differences that come into play with the

Key Thought

Some people think that there's something downscale about a "Baby Grand" as opposed to a "Grand" (and they certainly wouldn't even consider an upright!). Actually, some uprights are better built than grands, and may be more suited to your needs. Don't get too distracted with categories—just find the right piano for your space.

Grace Notes

A special, very small type of upright is called a **spinet**. Spinets are extremely short, but are technically distinguished by a different type of action—the mechanism that makes a hammer hit the strings when you press a key. Despite the technicalities of action construction, which are far too boring to spell out, most people rightly consider spinets quite simply as very small uprights.

longer strings, too. Grands have greater sonority than uprights, even when played softly. Greater sonority means a richer, fuller, long-lasting tone. The larger the grand, the greater the sonority (generally speaking, though different piano brands have different characteristics), especially in the bass notes.

In a piano store, play an octave toward the left end of the keyboard on a grand, then try a bass octave on an upright. The difference, in most cases, is startling.

Tall uprights have longer strings than short uprights, and are usually correspondingly louder and more sonorous. However, most uprights can only let the sound out through a small lid on the top, limiting the kind of full-throated volume you get by opening the lid of a grand. (Some uprights also let you remove the lower panel beneath the keyboard. Doing so lets out a lot of volume, but exposes the unsightly innards of the piano to the world. For some reason, upright innards are an eyesore, while grand innards are glamorous. Go figure.)

Grace Notes

There are certain sizes at which the musical differences between uprights and grands converge. In other words, very tall uprights can produce the volume and tonal richness of very small grands. If considering a large upright and a baby grand, assuming you like the sound of both, the decision should be made on the basis of appearance, interior design, and cost.

Cost

It should come as no surprise that grand pianos are more expensive than the upright pianos. You may find some very tall, high-end uprights that cost more than very small baby grands, but the two price ranges converge only at the extremes. Cutting right to the chase, here's a rough idea of price ranges from the smallest upright to a large grand.

Piano Price Ranges

Piano Type	Price
Small upright	$2,000 – 3,500
Medium upright	$2,800 – 4,500
Tall upright	$3,800 – 6,000
Baby grand	$3,500 – 5,500
Medium grand	$4,800 – 10,000
Large grand	$7,500 – 20,000

Please note that the dollar amounts are very general. You should not take that table into a piano store and use it as a negotiating tool! There is a huge divergence in pricing among the various piano builders, not to mention the uneven markups you're liable to see in piano stores. These prices demonstrate, if anything, how difficult it is to estimate the cost of a new piano outside of a store. Although the prices in the table represent extremes, I wouldn't be surprised if you occasionally found prices for the different piano types that fall outside those extremes.

New or Used?

The second big question facing prospective piano shoppers is whether to look at new or used pianos. The considerations are similar to deciding whether to buy a used or new car, except that pianos last much longer than most cars, so your choices represent a greater range of age.

What about damage to a used piano? What happens to pianos as they age, and is it safe to buy an instrument that's five, ten, twenty or more years old? The answers to these questions vary with each individual situation. But generally, shopping for a used piano is worth the effort if you're willing to put in the time and effort to find the right instrument. If a piano is built well, it can last for many decades.

Here are some considerations and tips when shopping for a used piano.

➤ When shopping around, or after having narrowed your choices down to a few pianos, take somebody with you who knows pianos inside and out. It's worth paying a tuner for a few hours of time to check out instruments you're seriously considering. As with buying a used car, it's advisable not to close the deal until the piano is checked by a technician. (Most tuners have a good technical awareness of all aspects of the instrument.)

➤ If buying a used piano from a store, check on the warranty provided by the store. If the piano is younger than about ten years, the original manufacturer's warranty might be transferrable. Older instruments are usually covered by the store in a limited way—a typical store warranty might extend for six months, which is long enough to detect and fix small problems that escaped your notice before buying. Also, try to get a free tuning (or three) worked into the deal.

➤ When looking at used pianos, whether in a store or in a private home, you can do a basic tire-kicking check by yourself. First of all, look at the instrument as a piece of furniture. Spot any scratches in the wood? You probably want to bring them up when discussing price.

Key Thought

The basic advantage in buying a used piano, as with a used car, is that you can get more for your money as a tradeoff for owning something with some wear and tear built in. The cost savings could result in the opportunity to purchase a used grand for the cost of a new upright.

Key Thought

The technician doesn't need to take the piano anywhere—he or she can give it a once-over right in the store, and there is no piano salesman who should object to this. If you're looking at a private purchase of a piano in someone's home, arrange an appointment to bring a tuner to the piano.

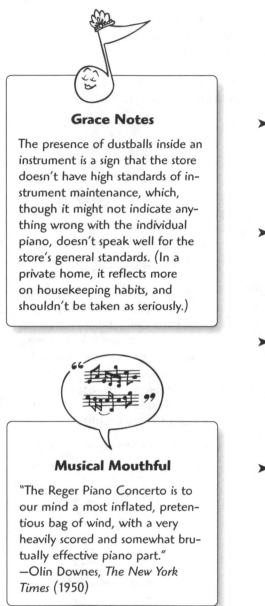

Open the piano lid (upright or grand) and look inside. You may not understand the mechanisms, but you can look for rust on the metal parts and strings. Look at the hammers (the felt-tipped things that hit the strings when you play the keys) and see if they are all aligned evenly. Check for any woodworking anomalies like warping or cracks anywhere inside.

➤ Cracked soundboards are a famous drawback of used pianos. But, the truth is, many soundboard cracks don't hurt the instrument or change its sound. However, a crack is a sign that you need to maintain careful control over the climate around the piano in order to protect the soundboard, and other wood parts, from further damage.

➤ Play every note of the keyboard. Playing all the keys is probably the best basic test you can do on a piano, and it's easy enough to tell when a note doesn't work. Common problems with old pianos are notes that don't play at all; keys that stay down after you release them; and keys that play the note twice (the hammer double-strikes the note).

➤ Don't be concerned with used pianos in private homes that are drastically out of tune. The seller is perhaps foolish not to present the piano in its best light by tuning it before showing it, but bad tuning doesn't necessarily indicate any problem with the instrument. However, ask when it was last tuned. If the date is more recent than two months ago, then you know there's a problem.

➤ If you are visiting a store to which you intend to bring a technician at a later date to check some instruments, you might want to ask some questions during the first visit, then check the veracity of the answers when the technician is present. Ask whether the piano still holds its tune well, then have your tuner check the health of the pin block. Ask if the action needs regulation, then have your tuner check that. If the store's answers and reassurances differ too widely from your tuner's verifications, consider shopping elsewhere.

The Asian Connection

Earlier in this century, there were more local piano builders than there are now. Nevertheless, there has been a renaissance of sorts in modern piano building, especially in Asian countries. This brings up the question of what piano brands are worth considering. Although I don't make specific recommendations of piano companies, I can tell you the general differences among some of the most well-known piano builders of our day.

Asian pianos have proliferated in the United States and other countries, giving consumers a choice of such brands as Yamaha, Kawai, Hyundai, Young Chang, and others. Asian pianos have built a reputation of competitive prices and reliable, assembly-line craftmanship. Some Asian companies have leveraged high-tech automation procedures to create pianos that are essentially built by machines, defying the European tradition of hand-crafting pianos.

No company represents the emergence of Asian piano-building technology more than Yamaha, which is probably the highest-profile piano brand after Steinway. Yamaha concert grands are the choice of some internationally respected pianists, though Steinway still has a more glamorous roster of affiliated artists. Yamaha pianos, on both the concert and home level, have a reputation for consistency, internal precision, and smooth actions. Steinways are renowned for beauty of tone and hand-crafted excellence.

Key Thought

You should never buy a piano on name reputation alone. Although they probably wouldn't admit it, all pianists know that even Steinway has turned out some dreadful instruments from time to time. Any manufacturer can't avoid turning out a clinker now and then.

The two major brands have plenty of competition. Baldwin pianos have a long history of quality on the concert stage and in homes, with a reputation for clear, bright tones. Kawai is a Japanese company that has made quite a splash in the United States and elsewhere for reasonably-priced pianos with rich tonal characteristics. Kimball is a company that builds a wide range of piano sizes, and sells them at very tempting prices.

I've spoken with many people who do not consider buying Asian pianos for political reasons. That of course is a personal decision of the same sort that you might make about a car. But there is no reason to discount Asian pianos for musical reasons. Pianos from Japan and other Asian countries are ready for prime time.

The Least You Need to Know

➤ Pianos are less portable than digital keyboards and generally more expensive, but sound and feel far better than electronic instruments.

➤ Upright pianos are less expensive and space-saving compared to grands, but have less sonority. Grand pianos are glorious pieces of furniture.

➤ Take a piano technician with you before deciding to buy a used piano.

➤ There are many fine makers of pianos, including European and Asian brands, from Steinways to Yamahas.

Chapter 22

Piano Maintenance and Repair

In This Chapter

➤ Why maintaining your piano is important

➤ Placing a new piano in the safest place

➤ Finding a good piano tuner

➤ Understanding types of piano regulation

➤ Knowing what the warranty means

Now that you've plunked down a couple thousand dollars on the piano of your dreams, you will want to be able to keep it in A-one, tip-top condition. Small problems—such as placing your new instrument to close to a heater duct—can lead to big headaches, and may even render your instrument useless.

Pianos are a bit finicky, both as musical instruments and pieces of furniture. Their wood cabinetry requires the same care as any other fine furniture, if it is to look its best and endure the ravages of spillage and dust. (Geez, I sound like a commercial for a household cleaning item.) The instrument components within the piano are made of materials that are affected by climate and temperature, so they need frequent attention to keep operating properly.

All in all, the piano is one of the high-maintenance instruments around, thanks to its zillions (approximately) of parts which must fit together perfectly. This chapter will tell you how.

Why Upkeep Is Important

You wouldn't buy a new Mercedes and then park it in a high crime area. Or, you wouldn't take your brand new stereo and leave it outside without any protection in the rain. Yet, many folks spend a life's savings on a new (or used) piano and then fail to keep it up properly.

Here are the main reasons the piano maintenance is so important:

Musical Mouthful

"If music be the breakfast food of love, kindly do not disturb until lunch time."
—James Agee

Key Thought

Pianos generally last a good long time, and good ones can be considered lifetime investments. Keeping a piano well-adjusted is part of protecting your investment.

➤ **Health of the instrument.** The piano is really a complex and finely constructed machine, whose interacting parts need adjustment from time to time to continue interacting perfectly. Even the wear and tear of simply playing the piano causes changes in the tight-fitting interconnections of parts. The climate further stresses the many types of wood that go into the delicate construction of the inner mechanism. Maintenance is always required to keep pianos operating at their best.

➤ **Musical satisfaction.** If your instrument isn't healthy, it won't give you the musical satisfaction you bought it for. Some of the unhappy results of a piano going out of adjustment are stuck keys that won't stop playing when you push them down; broken keys that don't play at all; buzzing notes; rattling sounds when you play; and, of course, the ever-popular going out of tune. Believe it or not, none of these problems contributes to the beauty of music.

➤ **Durability.** I'm talking about the piano's durability, not yours. When a piano isn't regulated and adjusted properly, its inner parts don't last as long. When some of the inner parts go bad, they usually affect the life of other inner parts. The ultimate result is that the instrument as a whole may not deliver good performance for as long as you want it to.

➤ **Resale value.** Speaking of protecting your investment, one of the foresightful reasons for maintaining your piano regularly is that if you ever want to sell it, you'll be glad if it's in good shape. In this way pianos are like cars, except they last much longer.

For all these reasons, taking good care of your piano should be a lifestyle habit. Read on to understand your piano's needs and how to service them.

Where Should We Put This Thing?

Amazingly, piano maintenance begins from the moment your bring a new (or used, for that matter) instrument into your home. In fact, it really begins during the shopping process.

Once it reaches your home, you will be faced with a key question: where to place the piano. Of course, interior decorating is part of your concern, especially with grand pianos which are striking pieces of furniture. But whether you are getting an upright or a grand, you want to consider piano-friendly placements in addition to good room decoration.

Pianos are sensitive to climate. Oh, they don't shiver in cold or sweat during heat waves, but they silently undergo changes when the climate takes a sharp turn. You can minimize undesirable alterations inside the piano by placing the piano in a location whose climate can be controlled.

Here are a couple of specific tips:

➤ Don't place the piano near a window that would allow sunlight to strike the piano.

➤ Don't place the piano next to a heating duct. (Imagine how you'd feel if you had hot air blowing in your face!)

Pampering Your Piano

Pianos are more sensitive to humidity changes than temperature changes. Wet air causes the instrument's wood parts to expand, and dry air generally causes contraction. The most obvious way you can tell that a piano is responding to humidity change is when it goes out of tune. The piano's strings are wound around metal tuning pins, and those pins are driven into a block of wood. It is the wood that responds (with expansion or contraction) when the room's humidity changes, which causes the tuning pins to slip, which makes the piano's strings go out of tune.

Slipping out of tune is not a problem for pianos, as long as the tuning is corrected fairly regularly. Two tunings per year is recommended for pianos in most temperate climates. Not only is such maintenance good for your ears, but the piano benefits from keeping the strings at their proper tension.

Some people take piano maintenance seriously enough to install humidifiers in the dry season and dehumidifiers in the wet season, controlling the humidity artificially around the piano. If you go this route you needn't control the climate of your entire home—it is easier and less expensive to focus on the single room that houses the piano. Piano dealers can tempt you with climate-control devices that attach directly to the piano and direct their beneficial influence directly to where it's needed: the inside of the piano. Alternatively, you can make your piano happy simply by using standard humidity control appliances found in department stores.

The All-Important Tuner

Never try to tune a piano yourself! Promise? OK. It's not like tuning a guitar or a fiddle. Pianos have over 150 strings in them, and it takes years of practice and training to manipulate the tuning pins with the delicacy and skill to bring the whole thing into tune. Professional players, especially classical virtuosos, consider piano tuning an art, and some artists have developed lifelong artistic collaborations with favorite tuners.

Key Thought

Extremes in hot and cold will hurt any musical instrument. Wood expands and contracts, and if it's forced to do so too frequently, it may also crack, warp, and in general deteriorate.

Grace Notes

The effect of humidity on pianos is especially evident in climates that have drastic seasonal humidity changes. In the northeastern United States, for example— the New York, New Jersey, Pennsylvania area—the summers are damp and the winters are dry. Every piano in those three states that doesn't live in a humidity-controlled room goes out of tune in the late spring and late fall, as the air quality changes. It's not a subtle difference, either—it's an ear-wrenching change.

How do you find your special tuner? I wish there were an easy answer. Fortunately, tuning a home piano is a fairly basic task for a trained tuner, and you're not too likely to go wrong by just picking a name out of the phone book. Still, if you have friends with pianos, ask around for recommendations.

You're looking for someone with the following qualities:

➤ **Not too expensive.** A piano tuning should cost $50 to $65

➤ **Not too slow.** Tuning a piano can take up to an hour, but shouldn't require much longer than that. If the piano hasn't been tuned for over a year, some additional time to wrestle with the strings may be needed.

➤ **Not too incompetent.** I haven't had bad experiences with piano tuners, and I hope you don't either. But if your piano doesn't sound right when the tuner is done, don't call him or her again. If you are a beginning player (most likely if you're reading this book, and if I'm not mistaken you *are* reading this book), have the tuner play some chords and scales up and down the keyboard. Ask the tuner if there are any problems.

➤ **Not too limited.** The best piano tuners are all-purpose piano technicians. They are competent at basic repairs and adjustments beyond simple tuning. Other experts specialize in rebuilding piano actions (the entire internal key mechanism), and sometimes a tuner will recommend someone else to handle a serious repair job. But you want your basic tuner to recognize any problems developing in your instrument, and be able to correct them before they get worse.

➤ **Not too disorganized.** Some piano tuners remind you with a mailed card or phone call when your instrument is due to be tuned—usually about six months after the previous tuning. While they obviously stay in touch for the benefit of their own businesses, it's also a convenience to you not to have to remember the tuning schedule. You are never obligated to receive a tuning—the schedule is always up to you.

If you let your piano go too long without being tuned, and it slips drastically away from its optimal tuning, it may need two or three tunings in quick succession to bring it back "up to pitch." Good piano tuners inform their customers when a single tuning isn't sufficient, but they never insist on multiple tunings. It's always up to you.

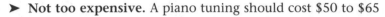

Musical Mouthful

"Can't you listen to chords without knowing their names?"
—Claude Debussy (1926)

Key Thought

When strings are tightened after slipping for more than a year, they don't hold their new positions well at first, and you can usually hear the piano go out of tune again within a month. A second tuning at that point solves the problem and gets you back on the every-six-month track.

Regulating, Adjusting, and Tinkering

Good piano tuners perform a variety of minor adjustments that improve the piano's playability and musicality. Here are some of the symptoms you may notice over time as you break in your piano, and what a tuner can do about them.

➤ **Uneven keys.** At some point it may become apparent that some keys are harder to press down than other. Ideally, the keyboard should be completely even up and down its entire length. The tuner can work on the keys or the internal action to correct such discrepencies.

➤ **Double striking.** Occasionally notes play twice when you press a key. The double strike usually isn't obvious, and the second strike isn't usually loud. In many cases, you can only hear the faint second strike when pressing a key very softly—it doesn't happen at all during loud playing. Or if it happens all the time on a certain note, the second strike is very soft. Still, it's annoying, and you shouldn't have to put up with it. In most cases, it's an easy problem for a competent tuner to fix.

➤ **Stuck keys.** Piano keys can be stuck in two ways. First, the key may not return all the way to its natural position when you release it. This is very disconcerting, not least because it makes it hard to play a second time. Another stuck key problem is when a note refuses to stop playing even after you release the key. The two stuck key problems are quite different, but neither is difficult to correct.

➤ **Bad sustain pedal.** A number of problems can plague the sustain pedal, and some of them are strictly a matter of taste. Accomplished piano players are very particular about how the sustain pedal "feels," and the abruptness with which it dampens the strings when the pedal is released. Likewise, it is important that the pedal take effect at just the right point when you depress it—not forcing you to push down too far, nor taking effect too soon. All these conditions can be adjusted by a tuner.

Understanding New and Used Warranties

When you buy a new piano, you receive a warranty for its good repair and flawless operation. You may never use the piano warranty, even though some of them extend for as long as twenty years. (New warranties can also be as short as five years.) The warranty is generally provided by the manufacturer, not the piano store. However, you should get a couple of perks from the store, too. Specifically, the store should warranty a safe delivery of the instrument, and perhaps provide one or two free tunings. (Piano tunings are often thrown out of kilter by moving. Whatever a kilter is.)

New instrument warranties are meant to cover drastic problems like cracked soundboards, broken strings, ineffective pin blocks that are incapable of holding a tune, broken pedal assemblies, and other structural defects. These problems may not mean anything to you, and let's hope they never do. As to other inevitable adjustments that are necessary during the warranty period: when in doubt, ask your tuner.

Grace Notes

Occasionally, on very old pianos, part of the ivory or plastic covering of the key can break loose and fall off. This makes it very difficult to play and should be fixed as soon as possible.

Key Thought

It's important to understand that tuning is not included in piano warranties, just as normal car maintenance isn't part of an automobile warranty. Normal tuning and regulation is up to you. However, if the piano requires excessive regulation or adjustment when it is brand new, it's a warranty problem. Your tuner can advise you whether to appeal for warranty reimbursement. The store from which you bought the piano can also be helpful.

> ## Key Thought
>
> Except in situations of absolute calamity—like if the legs crumble (the piano's, not yours) and the instrument crashes onto the floor and explodes—used piano warranties are rarely invoked. They are meant to soothe the worries of the buyer without providing much actual protection.

Warranties for used pianos are a whole other kettle of fish. (Never put fish inside your piano, new or used.) Buying a used piano from a store should involve some kind of warranty, but they vary drastically in length and quality. Furthermore, all used instrument warranties are provided by the store, not the manufacturer.

Generally, store warranties cover the same type of major, or extraordinary, repairs and adjustments that are covered in new warranties. However, the store may specify exactly what is covered depending on the condition of the piano. For example, if the strings are a bit rusty, the store may not replace the strings within the warranty period.

> ## The Least You Need to Know
>
> ➤ Maintaining a piano keeps the instrument more musically satisfying and durable.
>
> ➤ If possible, new pianos should be placed away from windows and heating ducts.
>
> ➤ Pianos are sensitive to humidity, and go out of tune easily when the air quality changes. Using humidifiers and dehumidifiers helps keep pianos stable and healthy.
>
> ➤ In most climates, pianos should be tuned twice a year.
>
> ➤ Most piano tuners can make minor repairs and adjustments to the action when needed.
>
> ➤ Warranties for new or used pianos generally only cover major defects.

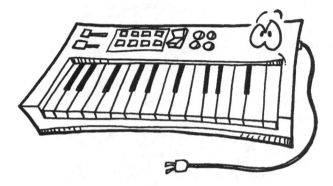

Chapter 23

Buying a Digital Keyboard

In This Chapter

➤ The three main types of digital keyboards

➤ Understanding the basic features of keyboards

➤ Exploring the pros and cons of buying a used keyboard

➤ Small and portable or big and unwieldy?

➤ Considerations when shopping for a digital piano

➤ Things to keep in mind before buying a home keyboard

Around the turn of the century, when someone mentioned a "home keyboard," they probably meant the good old reliable upright piano that could fit in the parlor of just about every American house. Today, the piano is just one of many choices for the parlor, crowded by a wide variety of electronic keyboards, from kiddie-sized toys to sophisticated musical *synthesizers*. Still, the point-of-entry to playing any keyboard instrument is ... well ... the keyboard: the collection of black and white keys you probably first saw on a piano.

One question I often receive is, "Are digital keyboards replacing the piano?" The worry is understandable. Digital pianos and other keyboards do a decent job of emulating the sound and feel of an acoustic piano, and they often cost much less. In addition, there are important conveniences to digital keyboards missing from pianos. However, I'm glad to report the answer to the troubling question is "No." People are still buying real pianos, and pianists are still performing on them. Digital keyboards are an alternative to the piano, but hardly a replacement.

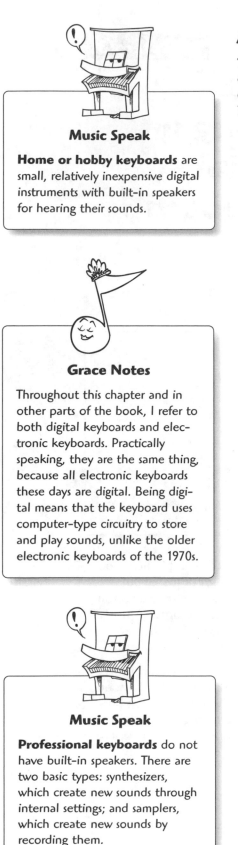

A Trio of Keyboards

There are so many models of keyboard that distinguishing among them can drive you back to the relative simplicity of pianos. To make matters easier, you can categorize all electronic keyboards as three basic types. Why yes, I'd be delighted to describe them; thanks for asking.

➤ **Home keyboards.** Also known as *hobby keyboards*, this category consists of small, lightweight keyboards with built-in speakers. Home keyboards are popular as first keyboards. Although not as advanced in some ways as professional keyboards, home keyboards have become quite sophisticated in recent years, providing a mix of good sound quality and plenty of technical features. Home keyboards are usually very button-intensive, with every technical function given its own dedicated button.

➤ **Professional keyboards.** *Professional keyboards* differ from hobby keyboards in one crucial aspect; they don't contain built-in speakers, and must be connected to an amplifier to make any sound. Aside from the speaker difference, pro models generally have excellent sound quality, are heavier, and are more expensive. Their technical features focus on internal memory, disk drives, and sound creation settings that improve the instrument's performance in a studio or stage environment. They are like musical computers. Usually, you need to have more skill to operate these machines; there aren't as many easy-to-use buttons as are found on the home keyboards.

The two main types of pro keyboards are *synthesizers*, which create new sounds using internal settings, and samplers, which create new sounds by recording them.

Samplers are the most acoustically realistic of all digital instruments, because they reproduce actual recordings of real instruments when you play the keyboard. With enough real instrument recordings stored in its memory chips, a sampler can sound just like a piano one minute, and a flute the next. Furthermore, you can record any sound into a sampler, and suddenly the keyboard mimics that sound perfectly.

➤ **Digital pianos.** Pianos are wonderful instruments, but require lots of maintenance (tuning, dusting, and admiring), and are too heavy to carry around the house (unless you have recently come to this planet from Jupiter, where the gravity is much stronger). Enter the modern solution: the *digital piano*. Digital pianos are not replacements for real pianos, but they are effective alternatives for a few reasons. They don't require tuning, can be moved more easily, and sound remarkably like the real thing. They usually don't contain as many technical gadgets and buttons as home keyboards, and they don't carry as many different sounds. Nor are digital pianos as sophisticated in certain ways as professional keyboards. They are fairly expensive, and you are mostly paying for high-quality digital reproductions of piano sound.

When electronic keyboards were first becoming popular, the difference between a home keyboard and a professional keyboard was like a chasm separating two cliffs. Home keyboards were cheap-sounding and amateurish; pro keyboards were state-of-the-art machines. Furthermore, you paid a big price premium for the extra quality of a professional instrument.

Now things are different, and the line between hobby and professional has blurred significantly. The bridge across that once-wide chasm has been built by high-quality home keyboards on one end, and lower-cost professional models on the other. The one feature you can count on to distinguish home keyboards from pro models is the built-in set of speakers.

Music Speak

Synthesizers are a specialized type of digital keyboard, able to mimic acoustic instruments as well as produce unearthly sounds that don't sound like any known instrument.

Basic Keyboard Features

Electronic keyboards are strange instruments, both simpler (in some ways) and more complex (in other ways) than pianos are. At first glance they can be a bit intimidating, bristling as they are with controls, dials, message screens, buttons, and even disk drives. On close examination, some of today's music keyboards look like odd computers—and, in fact, that's not far from the truth. Contemporary music keyboards have more processing power than anyone would have dreamed possible not too long ago. In this book, I'm concerned more with musical power than the number-crunching capacity of keyboards, which is mostly hidden from the user.

What Does This Button Do?—Oops!

Actually, there is absolutely nothing you can do "wrong" by pressing a keyboard's buttons or controls. Oh, you can make bad music, no question about that, and doing so is fun in its own way. But you shouldn't feel afraid to press all the buttons and see what results. The worst that can happen is that an electronic genie pops out of the back panel and pinches your nose, but that is very rare.

Music Speak

Digital pianos are computer-age alternatives to real pianos. By storing sampled (recorded) notes from acoustic pianos in their memory chips, digital pianos can sound reasonably like concert grand pianos. The verisimilitude only goes so far, though, and experienced pianists agree that digital pianos are no replacement for the real thing.

Grace Notes

All the basic keyboard features are covered in these pages, though I cannot deal with particular models and controls found on individual keyboards. Most keyboards are basically the same in function, even if the specific dials and controls differ. Read on to get the gist of whatever keyboard you may be facing.

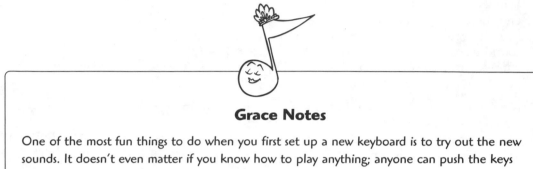

Grace Notes

One of the most fun things to do when you first set up a new keyboard is to try out the new sounds. It doesn't even matter if you know how to play anything; anyone can push the keys down. As soon as you plug the keyboard in and turn it on, try playing a few notes. Usually, the sound that keyboards are set to play when you first turn them on (called the *default* sound) is a piano-like tone. Find the sound buttons on the front panel, and start pressing them like crazy. For each button, play a few notes. Before long you'll have a good idea what sounds your keyboard can produce.

A Sound Is a Sound by Any Other Name

Keyboards come with lots of different sounds. It's a miracle of the digital age that one instrument can sound like many other instruments. Maybe it's not a miracle on a par with healing the sick, but it's pretty nifty. The sounds that come preinstalled in a keyboard are referred to as *sounds* (how radically original), *sound programs* (for when you want to sound like a nerd), or *patches* (ooh—that's a keeper). Actually, the owner's manual of your keyboard may assign a name for its sounds, and instrument makers sometimes go to extremes to invent vocabularies that apply only to their instruments—as if what we all need is to learn nonessential new vocabularies in our spare time. Forget the pretensions of your owner's manual and just call your keyboard's sounds *patches* or simply *sounds*.

Music Speak

The instrument sounds that are built into digital keyboards are alternately called **patches**, **sounds**, and **sound programs**. Professional keyboards (and musicians) usually refer to sounds as patches. Home keyboards generally label them just as sounds.

Keyboard patches are usually assigned buttons, and each button is labeled with the patch's name. The exception is on professional keyboards, where the patches are stored in internal banks, and the keyboard's screen tells you what patch is currently dialed up; you can flip through the patches using a single dial or button. On home keyboards it's much more intuitive: just press the *piano* button, for example, or the *flute* button, and the keyboard's sound changes instantly. Whether the result sounds exactly like a piano or flute depends on the keyboard, but the important advantage is variety.

Tiny People Inside the Keyboard

Home keyboards have *auto-accompaniment* features that provide rhythms and harmonies at the flick of a switch. Want to play some disco? How about a fancy bossa nova? These things are really amazing and fun, and even the new musician can enjoy improvising a simple melody over these preset grooves. While some ascribe these miracles to the ability to prerecord rhythm and harmonic patterns on tiny computer chips, I figure the only real explanation is that there are tiny musicians hidden inside the keyboard. While this interpretation may be too scientific for the average person, we must acknowledge that we live in a wondrous age, and many technical marvels are possible.

Auto-accompaniment is one of the most important features of home keyboards, and I refer to it often in this book. You don't ever have to use auto-accompaniment, and if you aspire to learn how to play keyboards with a piano-style technique, it's best to disregard it. But for those interested in making the most of the keyboard's technical features, understanding auto-accompaniment is crucial to making good music. The purpose of auto-accompaniment is to simplify playing to the point where, at the extreme, all you need to do is pick out a melody with one finger. A less-radical use of auto-accompaniment lets you play with more fingers of both hands while filling in some harmonies and the rhythms. Unfortunately, auto-accompaniment doesn't do the dishes.

Following are the basic functions of *auto-accompaniment*. They are included to varying degrees on different keyboards.

➤ **Musical style accompaniments.** Automatic styles provide complete accompaniments in a variety of rhythms and "grooves," from waltzes to hip-hop, sambas to rock 'n' roll, swing jazz to new age.

➤ **Auto-harmonies.** The musical style accompaniments described above don't necessarily give you any harmonies along with the rhythms. The lack of harmonies makes sense, because the keyboard doesn't know what song or piece you want to play against the musical style, so it doesn't know which chords to put in. (I define and describe chords in Chapter 8.) The auto-harmony feature (which may be called something different on your keyboard) lets you play simple chords with your left hand while picking the melody out with your right hand. The keyboard supplies a harmonic background that matches the chords you're playing, along with the rhythms. (I describe chords and how to use them in Part 2 of this book.)

➤ **Auto-bass.** A simpler version of auto-harmonies, auto-bass lets you play one-note bass lines with your left hand, underneath the melody of your right hand. This feature is commonly called *fingered bass* or *single-finger mode*. The keyboard supplies a moving bass line related to your left-hand notes. In some keyboards, a full harmony is inserted based on the left-hand notes.

Immortal Music Deserves to Be Recorded

I don't mean to put the pressure on you to fulfill your latent musical genius—at least, not right away. It's fun to record even mortal music, and many keyboards let you do just that. We're not talking

Grace Notes

Most keyboards have the same basic features. In reading my descriptions of these common features, don't be distressed if your particular model doesn't seem to match up in one way or another. If your keyboard is lacking in one department, it probably makes up for it with other features. Some keyboards have great sound, and don't go in much for fancy controls and zillions of buttons. Other keyboards take the opposite tack, offering a cheesy–sounding tone but lots of snazzy control features that make it a gadget–lover's dream instrument.

Music Speak

Auto-accompaniment is a feature of home keyboards that provides continuous rhythms and harmonies in preset musical styles. You can play the keyboard while the auto accompaniment is pounding out a rock 'n' roll groove, or swinging to a jazz beat. Most auto–accompaniments let you determine the harmonies with your left hand while playing a melody with your right hand.

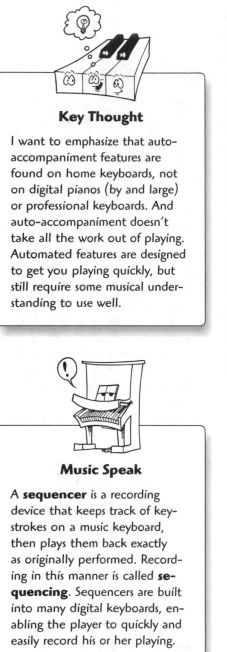

Key Thought

I want to emphasize that auto-accompaniment features are found on home keyboards, not on digital pianos (by and large) or professional keyboards. And auto-accompaniment doesn't take all the work out of playing. Automated features are designed to get you playing quickly, but still require some musical understanding to use well.

Music Speak

A **sequencer** is a recording device that keeps track of keystrokes on a music keyboard, then plays them back exactly as originally performed. Recording in this manner is called **sequencing**. Sequencers are built into many digital keyboards, enabling the player to quickly and easily record his or her playing.

about tape recording here, but *digital recording* that's built right into the keyboard. Not every keyboard can do this, but most modern home keyboards have some kind of recording feature, called *sequencing*. The recorder portion of the keyboard is called a *sequencer*.

Why the esoteric tech-head names for simple recording? It's called sequencing because you're not recording actual sounds, you're recording sequences of keystrokes as you play. Then the keyboard plays back the keystroke sequence and you hear your performance replicated, for better or worse. Along with the simple keystrokes, most keyboards record how hard you hit the keys, which translates into the loudness and softness of each note, plus the depressions of the sustain pedal (keep reading a little further down to learn about keyboard pedals).

Sequencing systems in keyboards vary from simple to complex. The main complexity involves recording on more than one track, which is intelligently called multitrack sequencing. It's not important to know much about sequencing at this point—or ever, if composing and recording aren't your interests. Sequencing has nothing to do with playing well. But recording yourself can be fun, and multitrack sequencers, which let you build musical pieces with several different parts, are great tools for making up music.

Sequencing brings into play some of the most advanced technical features of modern keyboards:

➤ Some home keyboard models contain rudimentary sequencers that don't hold much music and only record on one track; other models pull out the stops with fairly sophisticated recording systems featuring multiple tracks and a floppy disk for storing your creations.

➤ Professional model keyboards called *workstations* contain more advanced sequencers with editing tools that make the keyboards resemble word processors for music. You can record a music track (remember, you're only recording the keystrokes and pedalings, not the sound) and change it around by correcting wrong notes, placing notes on different rhythmic beats, and other very fancy maneuvers. Non-workstation pro-keyboards don't contain sequencers at all, but can be hooked up to computers that do an even more sophisticated job.

➤ Digital pianos often, but not always, have built-in sequencing. Sometimes they sport disk drives, like computers, for storing recorded pieces. The sequencers in digital pianos tend to have fewer tracks, or just one track.

Oh Joy! A Stick!

I admit it, I'm easily pleased. The stick in question is a joystick, which is found on some keyboard models. What does the joystick do? It varies from keyboard to keyboard, but one common function is to bend the pitch of notes being played, upward or downward. The joystick is one of several accoutrements that come with electronic keyboards and are sometimes inexplicable at first glance.

Here is a rundown of what you can expect to find:

➤ **Joystick or pitch-bend wheel.** Most keyboards give you some way of bending the pitch of notes. When musicians take a keyboard solo, especially in electronic jazz and rock, they generally play single notes with the right hand, using the left hand to manipulate the pitch bend wheel (or joystick). Used discreetly, swooping the pitch of certain notes up and down lends a more fluid style to the solo than the keyboard alone would deliver.

➤ **The pedal.** Almost every keyboard comes with a plug-in foot pedal that mimics the right-hand pedal of a piano. Called a *sustain pedal*, pressing it causes any played notes to continue sounding (sustaining) even if you take your hands off the keys. The sound continues until you lift your foot off the pedal, or until the sound naturally fades away, whichever comes first. The sustain pedal is essential to many playing styles, because it helps you connect the notes of a piece smoothly with each other without your fingers doing all the work. (It's harder than you may think!)

Home keyboards usually include a single pedal that you must plug into a jack on the back panel insightfully labeled *PEDAL*. Professional keyboards sometimes contain an extra pedal jack, which, together with a special pedal connected to it, let you change the keyboard's sound (patch) with your foot. Digital pianos are more sturdy, often carrying complete pedal assemblies hanging down from the bottom of their keyboards, with two or three pedals attached—just like a piano.

➤ **Sheet music holder.** A metal gizmo is sometimes included in keyboard boxes that is used to hold up sheet music so you can read and play easily at the same time. It gets attached to the top of the keyboard's front panel. Crack open that owner's manual to see exactly how your sheet music holder gets attached, if indeed you have one.

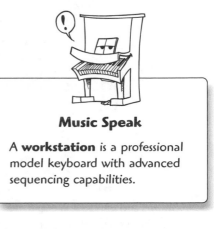

Music Speak

A **workstation** is a professional model keyboard with advanced sequencing capabilities.

Grace Notes

The term "track" comes from the old-fashioned days of tape recording. You can think of a track as a single line of information, such as a melody part or a rhythm line. Multitracking allows you to add additional "tracks" on top of your initial recording without erasing it. In this way, complex compositions can be created out of individual parts.

Where to Shop

Unlike pianos, which are generally sold only at music stores, electronic keyboards are sold at a variety of outlets. Simple home keyboards are available at such consumer palaces as K-Mart, Wal-Mart, and Whatever-Mart. When buying at one of these places, the most help you can expect from the sales folks is vague directions toward the correct aisle.

On the other hand, professional keyboards and certainly digital pianos are generally available at larger music retailers or specialty dealers that specialize in musical merchandise. This means (I hope) you will be given the same attention and help that you'd expect from a reputable piano dealer.

There are also mail-order and Web-based specialty dealers who offer a wide variety of equipment, sometimes at discounted prices. However, unlike a walk-in store, you won't be able to "try before you buy," and the information provided by phone clerks will probably be fairly minimal.

Grace Notes

If you are fairly knowledgeable about what you want, buying mail order or from discount dealers is not a bad thing. You'll save money and probably don't need the TLC that a music store can provide. If you don't know the first thing about what you want or need, then spending the extra bucks in return for some knowledgeable advice may be the route to take.

Key Thought

Essentially, a digital music instrument consists of a keyboard attached to a circuit board, controlled by dials and buttons. Keyboards can be damaged if they are dropped, but if you find a used instrument that has been treated well, and is in good working order, it is probably almost as good as new.

New or Used?

It's not surprising that a large and dynamic used marketplace has developed for keyboards. Consider how popular music keyboards have become since the late 1970s, and how hobbyists and professionals alike tend to shed last year's model for the newest high-tech instrument, and it's obvious that all those older keyboards must exist somewhere. That "somewhere" is classified ads in newspapers all over the world, as well as music stores that stock pre-owned instruments.

Is it safe to buy a used keyboard? As pre-owned purchases go, music keyboards are one of the safest items. Whenever you're buying used electronic equipment, the main risk lies with devices that have delicate moving parts. Accordingly, tape recorders are more risky, say, than computer monitors, because tape recorders have motors with moving parts and delicate recording heads. Just about the only moving parts in a music keyboard are the keys themselves, and they are hardly delicate. You could hit most keyboards with a hammer and the keys would still work fine. (I'm not recommending that you treat your instrument in such a brutal fashion, mind you. Keyboards have feelings, too.)

If you are dabbling with the idea of buying a used keyboard, here are some important considerations to keep in mind:

➤ **The warranty, or lack thereof.** Although used keyboards are relatively safe purchases, things can definitely go wrong with keyboards sometimes. These instruments are reliably built, but when one stops working, you may want to have warranty protection.

Buying a used keyboard from a store generally gives you some kind of limited warranty, with an accent on the word *limited*. In most cases you can count on (and should request) a warranty period within which the store makes good on defects with either store credit or returned cash. The warranty period on a used keyboard may be between one and six months (usually quite a bit closer to one month).

Buying a used keyboard privately, from someone's home, guarantees the lack of any guarantee. By contrast, purchasing a new instrument from a major manufacturer, through a reputable store, makes it easy to get a replacement instrument if your original is a lemon.

➤ **The shininess, or lack thereof.** You don't have to be a compulsive consumer to appreciate the new-product shine on a factory-fresh keyboard. Used instruments sometimes show signs of wear on the keys and dials.

➤ **The newness, or lack thereof.** Music keyboard technology is constantly evolving. So are the designs in which that technology is packaged. Buying a model that's one, two, or three years old may save you some bucks, but it deprives you of whatever new features have become standard in the interim.

Let's be honest. What are these new features worth? The truth is, there haven't been many ground-breaking advances in home keyboards in the last few years. For one thing, a keyboard is still a keyboard, with the same arrangement of black and white keys that has held forth for centuries. If your goal is to learn basic keyboard technique, it really doesn't matter what fancy gizmos surround the basic keyboard.

Portable or Not-So-Portable

Another shopping consideration, whether you are buying a new or used keyboard, is how big and heavy you want your instrument to be. One of the great advantages to electronic keyboards compared to real pianos is that you can tuck one under your arm and go to another room. Or put one in a carrying case, sling it over your shoulder, and haul it to a friend's house. (Slinging a grand piano over your shoulder is likely to result in a slight strain of the tricep muscle, plus a wrinkled shirt.)

The most significant factors in determining the weight and portability of a keyboard are the keys themselves. Take these two aspects into consideration:

➤ **The size of the keyboard.** Most home keyboards have a five-octave range (sixty keys), but some professional keyboards, like synthesizers and keyboard workstations, have an extra octave and a half (seventy-six keys in all). The larger range makes for a heavier instrument. Naturally, a piano-sized keyboard of eighty-eight keys weighs even more.

➤ **The weight of the keys.** It's not necessary to get out a scale or otherwise try to weigh the keys. Simply find out if the keyboard is weighted or unweighted. Weighted keyboards are heavier—you don't say!—than unweighted keyboards.

Of course, the true test of a keyboard's portability is to simply lift the darn thing up, and listen for ominous crackling sounds emanating from your vertabrae. The more cracks, the less portable.

Shopping for a Digital Piano

If you want the closest thing to a real piano that the electronic realm offers, a digital piano is the instrument for you. A good digital piano approximates the sound and feel of the real item at a fraction of the cost, with greater convenience.

Key Thought

Not all electronic keyboards are equally portable. Home keyboards that have five-octave, unweighted keyboards are a breeze for most people to pick up. Professional synthesizers tend to be heavier, thanks to the additional circuitry, larger control panel, and heavier materials. Digital pianos are the weightiest members of the electronic keyboard family, and usually require two people to move from one room to another.

Grace Notes

Portability doesn't mean that you can treat your electronic keyboard like a paperback book that you sling carelessly into your backpack. Getting your keyboard wet, cold, or otherwise exposing it to the elements; spilling drinks on it; leaving it out all night for the squirrels, bears, and beasts to trample; all are likely to damage your instrument.

There is considerable variety in the features of different digital piano models. Here's a summary of what you can expect to find as you shop:

➤ **Keyboard.** It goes without saying that every digital piano is equipped with a keyboard, but I feel like saying it anyway. Every digital piano is equipped with a keyboard. You almost never see a digital piano with only a five-octave keyboard range, which is a typically small keyboard on home keyboards. Five octaves (sixty keys) really isn't enough to play intermediate or advanced piano pieces, and since digital pianos are piano alternatives, they usually forego the small keyboards for larger, seventy-six-key or eighty-eight-key arrangements.

Furthermore, in a continuing effort to mimic real pianos, most digital instruments weight the keys to some degree. Shop around enough, and you will end up playing a range of weights, from keys that are barely heavier than home keyboards to key actions that feel as meaty as concert grand pianos.

Key Thought

How much weight is enough weight? Well, if you're used to a real piano, a truly weighted keyboard will be extremely important. But, just like power steering on cars, you'll want to try a number of models to find one that fits your own particular playing needs.

➤ **Sounds.** Every digital piano has at least one sound built in: that of a piano, of course. Most digital pianos feature multiple piano sounds for variety. Related instruments—like electric piano, organs, and vibraphones—may be built into the instrument's memory, available by pushing buttons. In some cases a whole range of orchestral instruments is represented on the button panel, but only in the most expensive models.

➤ **Miscellaneous features.** The playing experience of some digital pianos is enhanced through sound-altering features like reverb. Reverb adds an echoing quality to the notes, as if you were playing in an auditorium or concert hall. Other tone controls may be at your disposal, such as an equalizer, or treble and bass sliders. Advanced features such as MIDI recording and disk drive storage polish off fancy digital pianos.

Surveying the range of digital piano products, it's useful to separate all the instruments into three general categories:

Key Thought

Before being overly enticed by all the bells and whistles available on high-end digital keyboards, ask yourself (realistically) how many of these features do you really need? If you just plan to play "Chopsticks" with your friends, you probably don't need fancy built-in recording capabilities!

➤ **Entry-level digital pianos.** The smallest, lightest, least-expensive digital pianos offer a good basic piano sound or two, a decent keyboard, and little else. A scant choice of other instrument sounds may be available. The keyboard may be slightly weighted, but probably has a less substantial feel than most pianos. The price range of entry-level digital pianos is about $1,200 to $2,500.

➤ **Middle-of-the-road digital pianos.** The vast middle ground in the digital piano kingdom contains mid-priced instruments with an assortment of features. Keyboards are either seventy-six-key or eighty-eight-key models, and are weighted to appeal to pianists and professional keyboardists. A good instrument selection is sure to include at least a few different pianos, electric pianos, organs, and a smattering of others—you can expect to find eight to twenty instrument settings, enhanced by reverb. Some mid-priced models include a rudimentary sequencer and a disk drive for storing recordings. Instruments in this category range in price from $2,000 to $3,500.

➤ **Advanced digital pianos.** When manufacturers pull out the stops, the result is an impressive modern instrument that sounds and feels great, and is bristling with miscellaneous features. Some of these digital wonders sport a hundred instrument settings, and extensive tone controls and reverb settings. On-board sequencers let you record your own playing, and disk drives both record your performances and play back prerecorded pieces from an available library of disks. Advanced digital pianos are almost like computer workstations, and are rewarding instruments for technically inclined players. The price range for such sophisticated digital pianos is $3,000 to $6,000.

As you shop for the right digital piano, there are several questions to keep in your mind. Here are the crucial considerations:

➤ **Does it sound right?** Regardless of your playing expertise or level of experience, you must be pleased with the sound of the instrument you buy. Contrary to what you might think, digital pianos do not all sound alike. In fact, there is almost as much variety in the sonority of digital pianos as there is among acoustic pianos. Each model features digital samples of different grand pianos, so they sound almost as different from each other as the original grand pianos would.

➤ **Does it feel right?** If you are upgrading from a home keyboard, digital pianos will universally feel stiff to the touch, and perhaps hard to play. The difference in touch is due to the weighted actions of digital pianos compared to the unweighted feel of home keyboards. If you prefer the light action, select a digital piano with a slightly weighted keyboard, as opposed to the heavier actions of digital instrument that emulate real pianos. If, on the other hand, your playing background includes real pianos, and you prefer a more substantial-feeling to the keyboard, find a digital piano with the heaviest action possible.

➤ **Does it look right?** In this category, you don't have much choice. Most digital pianos look pretty much the same. Still, you may prefer a clean button panel that doesn't have lots of dials and flashing lights—or you may go for the high-tech look.

➤ **Does it cost the right amount?** This consideration goes without saying, perhaps. You need to find the instrument that meets your personal needs in the best way, while sticking to your budget. Refer to the earlier paragraphs in this section for general price guidelines.

Key Thought

Most digital pianos offer a choice of pianos sounds, so look (and listen) for the model that gives you the best choices, or even just one choice that you can really fall in love with.

Grace Notes

Some manufacturers offer big, well-marked controls, with each button, joystick, or knob performing a single function. Others offer little, chicklet–sized buttons, row upon row, with no clear indication of their functions. (Yes, a single button can be used to control multiple functions.) What you choose will depend on how comfortable you are with the controls.

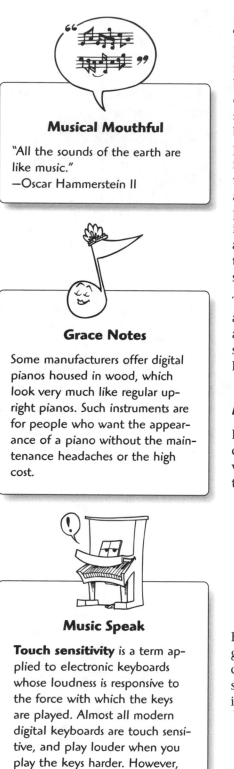

Shopping for a Home Keyboard

Home keyboards are popular because of their potent combination of features and cost-efficiency. Simply put, you get a lot of bang for your buck. The "bang" consists of a five-octave keyboard, which is large enough to learn on and to play simple keyboard arrangements; several sound selections; auto-accompaniment features that make the keyboard sound like a one-person band; built-in speakers and battery power; and a light, portable package that you can pick up and carry into the next room or put in an airplane luggage compartment. All these basic features come to you at a price that shames most digital pianos, and doesn't even appear on the radar screen of somebody shopping for a real piano. The downside to the home keyboard marketplace is sound quality: Home keyboards just don't sound as rich or sonorous as professional keyboards or digital pianos. Still, they are good enough to learn on, and you can always upgrade later if you (or your kids) get serious about playing.

The main problem when shopping for a home keyboard is that there are so darn many of them. Each manufacturer has several new models at all times, and there is a bustling used-instrument marketplace at the same time. The following sections outline the main considerations to keep in mind as you browse.

Making Sense of the Bells and Whistles

First and foremost when shopping for a home keyboard, you must feel comfortable with the controls. If you're new to electronic keyboards, viewing all the buttons and dials coherently may seem like too much to ask for. Here's how to handle the techno-intimidation:

➤ The first key is to *take your time* when shopping. Don't be rushed into any purchase.

➤ Find salespeople who can explain what all the buttons do.

➤ Ask the salesperson to get the owner's manual for the display unit, so you can simulate the learning experience you'll have at home if you buy that instrument.

By spending some time with a possible purchase in the store, you can get familiar (and possibly comfortable) enough with all the controls to determine if the keyboard is configured in a friendly fashion. Here are some questions to ask yourself as you fiddle with any home keyboard in a store:

➤ Is the keyboard *touch sensitive*? Touch sensitivity means that if you play a key softly, it makes a soft note, and striking a key hard results in a loud note. Keyboards that lack touch sensitivity make the same volume no matter how you play the keyboard, though even they are equipped with a volume control that affects all the notes equally. You can learn the basics of music and music notation on a non-sensitive keyboard, but it's impossible to play musically when the notes don't get louder and softer according to your playing touch.

➤ Is the screen easy to read, and large enough to spell out clearly what functions you're accessing? Small screens often use cryptic abbreviations for various functions and features—if you can decipher them, you earn an honored place in the Secret Service's cryptography division. The larger screens inform you clearly what sound you're playing, what auto-accompaniment style is currently in use, and which sequencer track is recording or playing.

➤ Do you like the keyboard's sounds? In most cases, you have plenty of sounds to choose from—possibly a hundred or more. Don't expect the quality of a symphony orchestra, but you should at least feel that the keyboard's basic tonal quality won't drive you crazy during extended use.

Also, check out the auto-accompaniment styles for an indication of the on-board sounds. The single sound that probably gets the most use is the built-in piano sound, which may not sound the slightest bit like a piano.

➤ Does the auto-accompaniment provide the kinds of styles you like? If you're a rock 'n' roll type, and the on-board styles feature waltzes and military marches, you're likely to suffer a pang or two of disappointment. Most keyboards have a broad range of styles, aiming to please everyone a little bit. Pick out the styles you figure using most heavily, and see if you like the way they sound.

➤ Does the auto-accompaniment provide enough flexibility? One specific question you should ask about the auto-accompaniment is whether you can change the tempo easily. Making the styles faster and slower is crucial to their useful-ness. Then, find out whether you can change the key of the style. Check out whether you can add and subtract instru-ments from the style while it's playing—it's handy and fun to reduce the style to drums alone while it's playing, then add bass, chords, and other musical elements as the style continues playing.

Finally, make sure there are left-hand style controls. The left hand is used to determine the chords played by the style arrangement, and better keyboards give you three ways of doing so: full-chord play-ing; two-finger chords; and one-finger bass lines. Full-chord playing is for people who know chords well and can play them on the fly. Two-finger playing is a kind of chord shorthand that's easier to play, but still requires a knowledge of chords. One-finger playing re-duces the auto-accompaniment to either a bass line or all major chords, and is the least useful way of controlling a style's harmony.

Grace Notes

Not all home keyboards have such screens at all. Less-expensive models indicate sound and style selections with simple lights illu-minating the selection buttons, which works fine. My point is, if you're going for a model with a screen, make it a good screen.

Musical Mouthful

"It's only rock 'n' roll (but I like it)."
—Mick Jagger

Key Thought

One good way to test the key-board's overall sound is to play any demo songs that are built in. The songs use keyboard sounds in a more complex manner than the keyboard may allow you to, but you can get an idea of the instru-ment's capability nonetheless.

Many home keyboards feature built-in demonstration songs that salespeople use to show off the instrument in its best light. In addition to the demos, other songs may be included for playing at your leisure. These songs are different from the auto-accompaniment styles, which are meant to be used as an accompaniment to your playing.

Key Thought

What purpose do the built-in songs have? Very, very little. It's important not to be too impressed by demo and built-in songs, or to—heaven forbid!—buy a keyboard on the basis of them. Have fun with the demos, be briefly impressed by them if you must, then move on to the business of getting to know the useful features of the keyboard.

Key Thought

For a complete rundown of pedal functions and playing styles, as well as exercises for learning to use the sustain pedal well, see Chapter 15, "Pedals: Where's the Clutch?" For now, all you need to know is that the pedal that came in your keyboard box is a sustain pedal, and needs to be plugged into the back panel of the keyboard to work.

Taking It Home and Turning It On

If you're new to the world of electronic instruments, the first big lesson is that the darn thing must be turned on to make any sound. That basic fact may seem a little elementary (as Holmes commented to Watson), but you'd be surprised how easy it is to forget the basics when working with modern musical devices. (Of course, I'm not speaking from personal experience; I've never forgotten anything basic, no sir.)

So the first thing to look for is the power button. It's harder to find than you may think on some of the button and dial–laden models sold today! If you have trouble turning your instrument on, don't panic—just take a look in your owner's manual for a diagram of all the controls.

If you have an electronic keyboard (assuming you got it from a store, not from a frustrated cousin), you have an owner's manual. That's not saying much, considering the quality of many such manuals. Many people consider them sophisticated, information-age torture devices designed to erode the foundations of modern civilization. Why the enmity? Owner's manuals have a well-earned reputation for being more of a hindrance than a help, thanks to confusing writing, failure to define new words the user needs to know, and basic carelessness in presentation.

To be fair, instrument builders make an honest attempt to include a book that really helps you learn the keyboard for which you've just shelled out big bucks. However, one thing no owner's manual attempts is to teach you music. They are designed only to teach you the function of the instrument's technical features—all the buttons and dials. No problem. I'll teach you the basics of how to play, plus the generic technical features common to all keyboards. Then you can fill in specific knowledge with the manual—and I wish you good luck!

Once your keyboard is turned on, it should begin to speak (with notes, that is). Try playing a key. If you don't hear anything, and you're sure the keyboard's power is on (don't forget to plug it in!), something is definitely amiss. You know the instrument is turned on if you see any lights on the front panel. There is usually a small light right next to the power button, and many models sparkle with other lights next to dials and buttons.

If there is a message screen in the center of the panel, you should be able to read something at this point (though it may not be immortal prose or any other soul-edifying content). If everything is working properly (which it almost always is), you can now play the keyboard and hear sounds. Great! Please play *The Flight of the Bumblebee* at this point. Oh, sorry, I'm getting ahead of myself.

Grace Notes

When electronic keyboards first came on the scene, many of the best and most popular manufacturers were (and still are) Japanese, and the manuals sounded as if they had been written by grammar-school students of English. Phrases like "When desiring to make selecting of new sound, pressing button of calling program change initiating desirable new tone" resulted in equal measures of hilarity and frustration.

If you've turned your keyboard on and still don't hear anything, these are the most likely explanations and solutions:

➤ You have a model of keyboard that doesn't contain built-in speakers. All *home keyboards*, also known as *hobby keyboards*, have speakers in them, as do most digital pianos. But professional keyboards almost never come with speakers, and if you have one of these instruments you must plug it into a keyboard amplifier to hear it. Alternatively, you may be able to attach headphones to the keyboard and listen through them, as long as the keyboard has a headphone jack.

➤ You have turned the keyboard on, but failed to plug it in. Don't worry, I won't tell anyone. It's not as big a downfall as, say, neglecting to get dressed before stepping outside, or failing to breathe. However, I understand and sympathize with the humiliation you must be feeling at this moment. The solution, of course, is to plug the darn thing in before your mortification deepens further.

➤ You are the unfortunate recipient of a Transylvanian curse that causes you to disable electronic devices in close proximity. Have you noticed street lights blinking out as you pass them? That confirms it, then. The solution, unfortunately, has something to do with drinking vinegar while sitting on a castle turret under a full moon. Best of luck to you.

Remember that keyboards, even digital pianos, are not replacements of real pianos. They are alternatives, with their own peculiar advantages and disadvantages. Think of digital keyboards as distinct instruments—cousins of the piano.

Key Thought

The headphone jack is often located on the front edge of the instrument, near a corner, but is sometimes placed awkwardly on the back panel. Search around and look in the dreaded owner's manual.

The Least You Need to Know

➤ Home keyboards are small, relatively inexpensive digital instruments with built-in speakers. Professional keyboards have more advanced features, lack the built-in speakers, and cost more money.

➤ Digital pianos are alternatives to acoustic pianos, and do a fairly good job of imitating the sound and feel of a real piano.

➤ Auto-accompaniment, found on almost all home keyboards, provides preset rhythms and chords that you can play along to.

➤ Home keyboards are sometimes equipped with sequencers, built-in devices that let you record your own playing.

➤ Used keyboard are relatively safe, as used purchases go, because of their lack of delicate moving parts.

➤ When shopping for home keyboards, check out the function of all the buttons and dials, and try to see an owner's manual of the model you're considering. The keyboard must sound pleasing, too.

Glossary

Accidentals   Another name for the notation symbols that indicate sharps and flats in sheet music. Nobody knows how accidentals got their name, so it should just be considered, well, an accident.

Accompaniment   The musical part (or parts) that is played underneath, and supports, the main melody. In piano music, the left hand usually plays the accompaniment, though in classical music the accompaniment switches between the two hands.

Acoustic instruments   A fancy way of referring to musical instruments that don't get plugged in. Every instrument in the orchestra is an acoustic instrument. Electronic guitars and keyboards, by contrast, require electrical power to make a sound.

Action   The action of a piano is the entire mechanism that starts with pressing a **key** and ends with a hammer hitting the strings. Included in the piano action are many finely crafted wood, plastic, metal, and leather parts that work together, giving the piano its characteristic "feel" and sound. Piano technicians can remove the entire action from the piano case to adjust its parts.

Arpeggios   Chords played by rippling the notes quickly from bottom to top.

Auto-accompaniment   A feature of home keyboards that provides continuous rhythms and harmonies in preset musical styles. You can play the keyboard while the auto-accompaniment is pounding out a rock 'n' roll groove, or swinging to a jazz beat. Most auto-accompaniments let you determine the harmonies with your left hand while playing a melody with your right hand.

Bar lines   Divide the music staff into **measures**, and every measure of a piece contains the same number of beats. All the note values in any measure add up to the same number of beats.

Baroque   A period of music that ran through the seventeenth and early eighteenth centuries, and featured complex, ornate music. Typically, composers fashioned multiple melodies to play at the same time, fitting them together with mathematical accuracy in pleasing harmonies. Bach is the most famous Baroque composer.

Broken chord   Chords whose notes are played one at a time. A left-hand accompaniment style popular in classical music from the eighteenth and nineteenth centuries, Mozart and Beethoven used broken chords extensively.

Chart   Also called **lead sheets**, a chart notates the melody of a song, with chord symbols above the notes to indicate the accompaniment harmonies for the left hand. Charts (lead sheets) are compiled in **fake books**.

Chord Clusters of notes played simultaneously. Most chords create a pleasing harmonic effect, but strictly speaking, a chord can be any group of notes, regardless of how awful it sounds.

Clef Signs used at the beginning of staffs to indicate which hand should play that staff. The **treble clef** is for the right hand, and the **bass clef** is for the left hand. Actually, in intermediate and advanced piano music, the right hand sometimes plays bass clef notes, and the left hand sometimes strays into treble clef territory. But mostly, each hand stays in its own clef.

Counterpoint **Contrapuntal** music features separate melodies that sound good when played against each other. (Contra means against.) One of the most mathematical styles of music composition, it has many rules that the composer must follow. (Otherwise the contrapuntal police get you.) Bach was a master of counterpoint music.

Digital keyboard Throughout this book, I refer to both **digital keyboards** and **electronic keyboards**. Practically speaking, they are the same thing, since all electronic keyboards these days are digital. Being digital means that the keyboard uses computer-type circuitry to store and play sounds, unlike the older electronic keyboards of the 1970s.

Digital piano Computer-age alternatives to real pianos. By storing sampled (recorded) notes from acoustic pianos in their memory chips, digital pianos can sound reasonably like concert grand pianos. The verisimilitude only goes so far, though, and experienced pianists agree that digital pianos are no replacement for the real thing.

Dotted notes The dot extends the time value of the note by one half its original value. For example, a dotted half note equals three beats, and a dotted quarter note equals one and a half beats.

Drum machines Electronic instruments that provide drum sounds for people using the MIDI capabilities of digital keyboards. You can hook up a drum machine to a keyboard, and automatically have access to many realistic drum and percussion sounds.

Dynamics The loudness of sound and music. Pianists talk about the dynamics of a piece, meaning that some passages are played loudly, and others softly. **Dynamic range** indicates the limits of loudness and softness contained in a piece, or capable of being played by an instrument. The piano has one of the largest dynamic ranges of any instrument.

Electronic keyboard Throughout this book, I refer to both **digital keyboards** and **electronic keyboards**. Practically speaking, they are the same thing, since all electronic keyboards these days are digital. Being digital means that the keyboard uses computer-type circuitry to store and play sounds, unlike the older electronic keyboards of the 1970s.

Fake book Each song in a fake book consists of the melody, written in music notation, and chord symbols above the notes. Taking cues from the chord symbols, the player must improvise (fake) an arrangement for the song.

Fingerings Music notation sometimes labels notes with numbers that indicate which finger should play which note.

Flat Accidentals that lower any note by one half step.

Hammers Piano hammers are the last parts of the piano action, and perform the impactful assignment of striking the strings. When a hammer hits the piano strings, it immediately and automatically rebounds, letting the strings vibrate, which causes the piano to sound. Hammers are covered with felt—the perfect material for producing the sound of piano notes.

Harmony   The musical underpinning of a piece. Harmony is usually created by clusters of notes played together, called chords, that provide a context for the melody. You may not notice the harmony when you hear a song, or sing it in your mind. But without the tune's harmony, the melody would be harder to learn and remember.

Harpsichord   One of the predecessors of the piano. Harpsichords had a metallic, unvarying sound. They could not be played loudly and softly as a piano can, and their strings were plucked by mechanical quills, not struck with small felt hammers as a piano's strings are.

Home keyboards   Small, relatively inexpensive digital instruments with built-in speakers for hearing their sounds.

Improvisation   Creating the music as you play. It is an essential skill in playing jazz piano.

Intervals   The distances between notes on a keyboard. Play any two notes, and you're playing an interval. Intervals are named with ordinal numerals: thirds, sevenths, twelfths, fifteenths, and so on. The size of the interval is determined by how many keys lie between the two notes.

Inversions   Different varieties of the same chord, with the notes stacked in different orders.

Key signature   A symbol showing the key of a piece by indicating which sharps of flats are necessary to play a scale in that key. Key signatures make their appearance at the beginning of every staff in a piece, and look like a cluster of sharp or flat symbols.

Keyboard   Refers to a traditional arrangement of black and white keys that play musical notes. The keyboard may be attached to an acoustic piano or an electronic instrument. Electronic keyboard instruments are usually referred to simply as "keyboards," confusing things somewhat. A keyboard (an electronic keyboard instrument) contains a keyboard (an arrangement of keys), just as a piano does.

Key   In music, the key indicates the main note of the piece, and which sharps or flats are needed to play the piece around that central note. Every key has a scale, which is a sequence of notes starting with the main key note.

Lead sheet   Music *charts*, also called lead sheets, notate the melody of a song, with chord symbols above the notes to indicate the accompaniment harmonies for the left hand. Charts (lead sheets) are compiled in fake books.

Legato   Means smooth playing, without undue breaks between notes.

Leger lines   Lines used to extend the five-line staff upward and downward. Leger lines (and the spaces between them) are used to hold notes that are above or below the notes of the five-line staff.

Measure   One measure is the space between two bar lines, and the notes in that space. Each measure of a piece contains notes that add up to the same number of beats.

Melody   A sequence of notes strung together into a tune. Melodies are often the most important part of a musical piece, certainly in popular music.

Metronome   A mechanical instrument that keeps you "on tempo" by clicking audible beats while you play a piece. By setting the metronome to a faster or slower tempo, you can keep up the pace or stop yourself from rushing the pace. Metronomes come in mechanical and electronic models.

MIDI An acronym for Musical Instrument Digital Interface—a fancy way of saying that MIDI connects keyboards to other keyboards, and keyboards to computers. There are other types of MIDI devices as well, including drum machines, tone modules, and sequencers.

Modes Scales based on ancient music systems, which can be played on the white keys of the piano, beginning on any note. They have seven notes, just like major and minor scales.

Music notation The written form of music. Notation is what music looks like on the printed page, in sheet music and music books. For the most part, notation consists of round notes placed on the lines and spaces of a music staff, but even guitar chord symbols are music notation. In short, notation is anything written down that tells you what to play on an instrument.

Natural A sign that neutralizes previously established sharps and flats. The natural sign is an accidental just like a sharp sign or flat sign. Naturals lower sharped notes by a half step, and raise flatted notes by a half step.

Octave The keyboard distance between any note and the next (higher or lower) same note. The two notes that form an octave are said to be an octave apart from each other.

Patch The instrument sounds that are built into digital keyboards are alternately called *patches*, *sounds*, and *sound programs*. Professional keyboards (and musicians) usually refer to sounds as patches. Home keyboards generally call them just sounds.

Pianoforte The first pianos were called *pianofortes*, which in Italian means "softloud." Pianofortes were the first keyboard instrument whose volume (loudness) could be altered by playing the keys more or less forcefully.

Pins Metal pins hold the piano strings at one end of their length. Piano tuners turn the pins with a special tool when tuning the strings. Pins are driven into a block of wood called the **pin block**.

Pitch Refers to the highness or lowness of a note. Women can sing higher pitches than men. (Except for men who don't mind sounding ridiculous.) **Pitch range** is defined by the highest and lowest possible note of an instrument, a human voice, or a piece of music. Tubas have a lower pitch range than piccolos. Pianos have a larger pitch range than any nonkeyboard instrument.

Ragtime One of the first forms of jazz piano, developed early in the century in southern urban centers like New Orleans. Featuring a *stride* left hand, bouncing back and forth between bass notes and mid-range chords, set against jaunty melodies in the right hand, ragtime is joyful and playful music.

Relative major and minor Keys that share the same key signature. The major key with a key signature of two sharps (D major) is the relative major of the minor key with a key signature of two sharps (B minor). By the same token, B minor is called the relative minor of D major.

Repeat sign Symbols that bracket portions of a piece to indicate that it should be repeated. Repeat signs make music notation more compact, especially in pop music, since the repeated portion doesn't have to be written out a second or third time.

Repertoire The collected works for any instrument. The piano repertoire includes great music from most of the composers in classical and jazz traditions, as well as the work of modern composers who are not so easily categorized.

Rests Symbols that indicate when you should not play. Rests are the opposite of notes, which tell you when to play. Rests have the same time value as notes, and they make measures add up to the right amount of beats when there aren't enough notes.

Rhythm A term that refers to the beat of music, and its movement through time. Quick rhythms create music that makes you tap your foot quickly, and slow rhythms are more langorous, used in ballads and torch songs.

Sampler The most acoustically realistic of all digital instruments, samplers reproduce actual recordings of real instruments when you play the keyboard. With enough real instrument recordings stored in its memory chips, a sampler can sound just like a piano one minute, and a flute the next. Furthermore, you can record any sound into a sampler, and suddenly the keyboard mimics that sound perfectly.

Scale A sequence of notes starting with the tonic note of a key, and going up or down to the next tonic note. Every key has its own scale.

Sequencer A recording device that keeps track of keystrokes on a music keyboard, then plays them back exactly as originally performed. Recording in this manner is called **sequencing**. Sequencers are built into many digital keyboards, enabling the player to quickly and easily record his or her playing.

Sharp Alterations to music notes that raise any individual note upward by one half step.

Slur Phrase marks, or slurs, indicate when groups of notes should be played without any breaks between the notes. The effect of a slurred phrase is smooth and seamless.

Soft pedal The left-most pedal of the piano, the soft pedal makes the whole instrument softer by affecting how the hammers hit the strings.

Sonata A piano piece written in three connected parts. Each part is called a *movement*. The movements may sound like entirely separate pieces, and in a sense they are. Ideally, the entire sonata hangs together as a satisfying musical experience. Handel, Haydn, Mozart, and Beethoven wrote famous sonatas.

Sostenuto pedal The least-used of the piano's three pedals, it sustains any notes being played as the pedal is being pushed down. While holding down the sostenuto pedal, other notes are *not* sustained after being played. On some smaller pianos, the sostenuto pedal is missing.

Soundboard A large piece of wood placed just a couple of inches away from the strings inside a piano. When the strings are struck by hammers and caused to vibrate, the soundboard picks up the vibration and amplifies it to a volume that is easily heard.

Spinet A special, very small type of upright. Spinets are extremely short, but are technically distinguished by a different type of action — the mechanism that makes a hammer hit the strings when you press a key. Despite the technicalities of action construction, which are far too boring to spell out, most people rightly consider spinets quite simply as very small uprights.

Staccato Sharp, detached playing, with breaks between the notes.

Staff A group of five parallel lines stretching across the width of a page. Notes representing the keys of the keyboard are placed on the lines and the spaces between lines, indicating which keys to play. In piano music, each hand gets its own staff.

Stem The stick-like line that extends upward or downward from the circle of the note. Whole notes are the only type of note that doesn't have a stem.

Stride   A style of piano playing in which the left hand bounces between bass notes and chords. Stride is used in various types of jazz playing, but was made popular by ragtime.

Strings   Piano strings are thin metal cords stretched tautly around a frame called a harp. When struck by piano hammers, the strings vibrate, and it is the vibrating strings that create a piano's sound.

Sustain pedal   The right-most pedal of the piano, and the pedal used most. The sustain pedal holds notes even after you release the keys.

Synthesizer   A specialized type of digital keyboard, able to mimic acoustic instruments as well as produce unearthly sounds that don't sound like any known instrument.

Tempo   The speed of music. It's mostly classical music that refers to fast tempos and slow tempos, but it's also a general term for all kinds of music, and the speed with which it's played.

Ties   Tied notes are connected by a curved line, indicating that the time value of the two notes is added together. You only play the first note, but hold it for the duration of both notes.

Time signature   A symbol placed at the beginning (far left end) of the music staff that tells you how many beats are in every measure, and what note value is assigned one beat. For example, 4/4 time has 4 beats per measure, and a quarter note receives one beat.

Tone module   The brain of the electronic keyboard, including all the sounds the keyboard can make. Tone modules are used in MIDI studios with one master keyboard that controls various tone modules and drum machines.

Touch sensitive   Touch sensitivity is a term applied to electronic keyboards whose loudness is responsive to the force with which the keys are played. Almost all modern digital keyboards are touch sensitive, and play louder when you play the keys harder. However, some inexpensive home keyboards can be found with nonsensitive keys that play at the same volume all the time.

Transpose   Changing a piece from one key to another is called *transposing* the piece. Transposing a piece from C to D, for example, moves it up one whole step. Transposing a piece from G to F moves it down one whole step. You can transpose any piece to any key, and the process moves every note of the piece up or down the same number of whole or half steps.

Triplet   A triplet is a group of three notes grouped into a certain rhythm. Quarter-note triplets are played in the time value of a single half note, and eighth-note triplets are played in the same number of beats as a quarter note.

Tuning hammer   The primary tool of piano tuners, the tuning hammer fits around the pins, letting the tuner turn them to adjust the tension of the strings, changing their pitch.

Una corda   In classical piano music, very occasionally, you see a notation marking indicating use of the soft pedal. That marking is the phrase *una corda* written into the music. By and large, though, players use the soft pedal whenever they desire the softest touch possible in a delicate musical passage.

Unison   When two parts are playing the exact same note, that also is considered an interval, even though there is *no* distance whatsoever between the two notes. The interval is called unison, and when two singers or two instrumentalists are singing or playing the same notes, they are said to be singing or playing *in unison*.

Resources for the Beginning Pianist

Unfathomable though it may seem, there are other books about how to play the piano. Needless to say, none of them combine such depth of information with poetry of expression as this one does. Nor do they have such modest authors. Nonetheless, you may want to broaden your learning approach by checking some of these out.

I've included three categories of resources in this appendix. First, a large number of so-called method books. Some of the method books are general, and others concentrate on a type of playing, like jazz or blues. Second, I've listed a few books by great pianists of the past—in some cases, the long-ago past. These are for interest more than useful instruction, as they deal with learning how to play older versions of the piano, or pianoforte. The third and final section of this appendix points you toward instructional videos that might be helpful.

Not all the books may be easy to find. I've included the ISBN number in all cases, so you can order any book that strikes your interest. If you have access to the Internet, you may search for any of these titles at the Amazon bookstore, located at the following URL: http://www.amazon.com.

Modern Method Books

How to Play Piano
Roger Evans
St. Martin's Press
ISBN: 0312396015

How to Play Popular Piano in 10 Easy Lessons
Norman Monath
Simon & Schuster
ISBN: 0671530674

Instant Keyboard: Quick and Easy Instruction for the Impatient Student
Gary Meisner
Hal Leonard Publishing
ISBN: 0881886246

Mastering Piano Technique: A Guide for Students, Teachers, and Performers
Seymour Fink
Amadeus Press
ISBN: 0931340462

The Piano
King Palmer
Teach Yourself Books
ISBN: 0844239364

Piano Technique: Tone, Touch, Phrasing, and Dynamics
Lilly H. Philipp
Dover Publications
ISBN: 0486242722

The Osborne Piano Course
Katie Elliot
EDC Publications
ISBN: 0746020007

You Can Play Piano
Amy Appleby
Music Sales Corp.
ISBN: 082561516X

12-Bar Blues Bible for Piano/Keyboards (book and CD)
Andrew D. Gordon
A.D.G. Productions
ISBN: 1882146581

24 Karat Piano Skills
Billie Ray Erlings
Kendall/Hunt Publishing
ISBN: 0787234680

60 of the Funkiest Keyboard Riffs Known to Mankind
Andrew D. Gordon
A.D.G Productions
ISBN: 1882146484

Encyclopedia of Picture Chords for All Keyboards
Leonard Vogler
Music Sales Corp.
ISBN: 0825615038

Contemporary Keyboard Styles for the Absolute Beginner (book and cassette)
Andrew D. Gordon
A.D.G. Productions
ISBN: 1882146166

David Bennett Cohen Teaches Blues Piano: A Hands-On Course in Traditional Blues Piano
David Cohen
Hal Leonard Publishing
ISBN: 0793562570

The John Brimhall Piano Method
John Brimhall
Hansen House
ISBN: 0849427681

Precious Lord! How to Play Black Gospel
Robert L. Jefferson
Pensacola Publications
ISBN: 1880549042

A Whole Approach to Jazz
Marc Sabatella
A.D.G. Productions
ISBN: 1882146557

Great Pianists as Teachers

Basic Principles of Pianoforte Playing
Joseph Lhevinne
Dover Publications
ISBN: 0486228207

Essay on the True Art of Playing Keyboard Instruments
C.P.E. Bach (translated by William J. Mitchell)
W.W. Norton & Co.
ISBN: 0393097161

On Piano Playing: Motion, Sound and Expression
Gyorgy Sandor
Schirmer Books
ISBN: 0028722809

Piano Playing With Piano Questions Answered
Josef Hofmann
Dover Publications
ISBN: 0486233626

Letter to a Young Lady: On the Art of Playing the Pianoforte
Carl Czerny
Da Capo Press
ISBN: 0306761238

Video Instruction

Learn the Essentials of Piano (4 graded tapes, available separately)
Talc Tolchin
Kaleidospace
http://kspace.com/tolchin

Piano-by-Ear (adult and kid video courses)
David Wayne Lawrence
1-800-44-BY-EAR
http://www.piano-by-ear.com/

Easy Piano; Country & Rock Piano; Blues Piano; Jazz Piano (4 separate video courses)
Homespun Tapes
1-800-338-2737
http://www.homespuntapes.com/

Web Resources

The Piano Page

An ambitious resource to piano links around the Web.
www.ptg.org

Piano on the Net
This remarkable site provides thirty-four piano-playing tutorials.
www.artdsm.com/music.html

PianoSpot
An e-commerce site dedicate to piano sheet music.
www.pianospot.com

Steinway
There's something incongruous about the tradition-soaked Steinway & Sons putting up a Web site, but it's an irresistible browse.
www.steinway.com

The Official Glenn Gould Web Site
One of the most professional and extensive sites devoted to a classical pianist
www.glenngould.com/gg/index.html

Jump! Music
An online catalog of over five-million pages of sheet music, most of it for piano.
www.jumpmusic.com

Patti Music Company
Originally an offline sheet music retailer, Patti Music has put its entire music catalog online.
www.pattimusic.com

Allexperts Piano and Keyboard
Part of the wide-ranging Allexperts site, this piano Q&A page is staffed by fifteen volunteer experts in piano playing, maintenance, tuning, teaching, and music appreciation.
www.allexperts.com/getExpert.asp?Category=650

Classical Piano Page
A generous and heartfelt online listening station.
pianoland.cjb.net

Chord House
Remarkable interactive chord and scale finder.
www.looknohands.com/chordhouse/piano

Piano World
A deep resource about all kinds of piano-related issues.
www.pianoworld.com

Question and Answer Page
Type a question; get a response via e-mail.
home.netcom.com/~quikscor/paragonquestions.html

Music Magic: A Piano Exploration
From a reference encyclopedia to a virtual concert hall to online piano lessons.
library.thinkquest.org/15060/index.html

Piano Education Page
Advice about finding a teacher and buying an instrument. No online lessons.
www.unm.edu/~loritaf/pnoedmn.html

Index

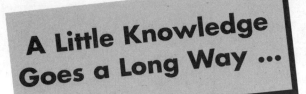
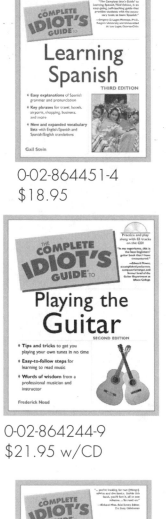

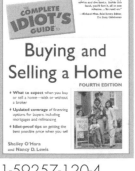
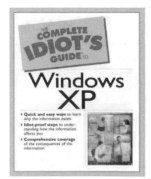